EMBODYING

PRESENCE

A Developmental Guide for Therapists, Coaches and
Those Dedicated to Self-Actualization & Awakening

JOHNNY BLACKBURN

MEDICAL DISCLAIMER: the following information is intended for general information only. While any reader may find the knowledge, understanding, practices or takeaways in this book to be useful, it is written with the understanding that neither the author nor the publisher are presenting specific psychological, emotional, spiritual or medical advice. Additionally, nothing in this book is intended to diagnose, treat, prescribe or cure any specific type of psychological, emotional, spiritual or medical problem. Each person should consult and engage in a program only with a qualified and licensed therapist, physician or other trained professional before administering any suggestion made in the book. Any application of the material in the following pages is at the readers discretion and is his or her sole responsibility.

Originally published as *Presence: A Practical Guide to Awakening Greater Potential in Work, Love & Life (2017)*

Printed in the United States of America

First Printing, 2017

ISBN 978-0-578-52403-0

Presence Academy, Inc.
San Diego, California
www.presence.academy

TABLE OF CONTENTS

PART 1   INTRODUCTION & INTENTION

"The privilege of a lifetime is being (and becoming) who you are."

— Joseph Campbell —

author, professor & cartographer of comparative mythology & world religion
(1904-1987)

QUESTIONS TO GUIDE YOUR READING

DEVELOPERS: SELF-ACTUALIZERS, WAYSHOWERS, & AWAKENERS

What does Presence feel like?

How do we access the immediacy of Presence & the power of Now?

Which presence skills do you need to cultivate so that your embodied nervous system can relax, open, receive & transmit greater Presence?

PRACTIONERS: THERAPISTS, COACHES, FACILITATORS & TEACHERS

How does your own groundedness, relaxation, openness, integration & depth of presence allow you to be a more skillful instrument of healing, transformation & awareness?

How does understanding how each of these aspects of Presence develops & gets distorted, enhance your capacity to support clients in healing, restoration of healthy function & thriving?

How does your capacity for embodiment, connection & awareness enhance your ability to impact the shared relational presence in a one-on-one interaction or the group space?

DEDICATION

This guide is dedicated to the Wayshowers,
the explorers, the cultivators and the groove wearers of
human potential throughout the millennia, now and in the future
To those human torchbearers who have devoted their precious
human lives to our evolution of greater potential for our world.

To those who have brightened and elucidated the way,
the mystics who have opened to the aliveness of Presence
living through us all, pointing to and transmitting It
illuminating our essential nature, that has been here all along.

To those who have healed and evolved what has been,
the therapists and healers devoted to cleaning the past,
the social change agents who fought for equality and justice,
all the teachers, guides and torchbearers who showed possibility,
to all those who were tortured, killed or lost their lives in service,
and especially those dedicated to practice and embodiment in the world,

To all those courageous voyagers, mapmakers and instruments of service,
who have contributed to this collective evolutionary intelligence,
to who went ahead and agreed to come before, preparing the way
for a time in the future when it would be safer and have greater critical mass
to accelerate the healing, development and awakening of humanity.

May this work, be a contribution, in its own way
to the great evolutionary process living through us all.
And through our deeper embodiment, connection and awareness
may we be more fully human AND live wide Open as Love Itself.

THE 21ST CENTURY CALL FOR PRESENCE

We are overloaded with information and stimulation, yet we long to embody a greater range of our potential to feel deeper connection, inspiration and openness in our bodies, with others and all of Life.

We live in unprecedented times in this 21st Century post-modern digital age. Technological advancements have radically enhanced the efficiency of the digitalized lifestyle, yet have equally increased the level of complexity, amount of sensory stimuli and pace of life. Humanity clearly appears to be evolving and in many regards we are adapting and integrating new ways of being, while other qualities and skills are being neglected or under emphasized.

Many of these advancements are compromising our presence in life, real felt-sense of heart connection with others, as well of more expanded Awareness beyond our phones or personal sense of self. We have the opportunity to harness these technological innovations AND live with greater presence and connection in work, love and life. This is the essential thread that weaves together our personal uniqueness with the collective We of humanity and the radical aliveness of Life itself. Presence is the real key to awakening our greater human potential and thriving for us all.

Presence can seem nebulous & elusive to define.

Presence is not just for executives, performers & spiritual teachers.

Presence is not just for big interviews, conversations & important situations.

Presence is both extraordinary & ordinary; in peak states or here & now.

Presence is for all of us.

HOW TO READ AND INTEGRATE THIS MATERIAL

When reading the Dedication, sense into how you are a part of the evolutionary process living through humanity? How do you honor all those who have come before you and dedicated their lives to the healing, development and awakening of humanity? How actively will you participate in and positively contribute to this process?

With the Essential Questions section, whether progressive or practitioner or both, how will these skills influence your own developmental process and your work?

When viewing a comparison graphic in the degrees of presence section, compare that with your own experience. How is your current presence in these areas of life & how could more presence enhance your work, love & life?

When exploring the heart of this guide in the Presence Skills section, really explore the graphic depictions & the definition, reflect on the benefits of why that skill matters to you in your life, check if any of the barriers limit your access to that skill, allow the success stories to inspire you & compare how the developmental process of the way each skill tends to develop matches your experience.

Visit Presence Academy online (www.presence.academy) to check out the online video training program if your really want to learn some of these presence skills in a highly engaging, gamified way for awakening greater potential in work, love & life.

PART 2 DEFINITION & THESIS

WHAT IS THIS "PRESENCE" WE CAN ALL EMBODY, CONNECT TO AND BE AWARE OF?

the presence of a loving mother deeply attuned and connected to her child,

the presence of the authentic executive leader inspiring their team,

the presence of an athlete in the zone and the captivated spectators,

the presence of the powerful speaker on stage and the engaged audience,

the presence of the inspiring yoga instructor and the opening students,

the presence of the visionary artist expressing beauty in creative flow,

the presence of the entrepreneur in focused engagement at work,

the presence of friends connected in rapport and depth of real conversation,

the presence of an emotionally intelligent father listening to his son,

the presence of romantics deeply connected, making ecstatic love,

the presence of Joe living his "ordinary" life with extraordinary openness.

PRESENCE DEFINITION

PRESENCE is:

(1) your felt sense of embodiment

(2) intimate connection with and

(3) open Awareness as the totality of the present moment.

THESIS OF THIS GUIDE

Presence has 3 aspects Embodiment, Connection & Awareness. Presence can be directly accessed NOW & increasingly cultivated with practice.

This is the definitive and developmental guide to Presence
and it's essential components: embodiment, connection and awareness
by directly accessing the immediacy of Presence each moment AND
by progressively cultivating more relative presence through practice.

DIRECT WAYS TO ACCESS PRESENCE

Presence, in the absolute sense, is ever-present and can always be accessed NOW

The following are some common direct access points into immediacy:

Breath & Body Sensing	Listening	focusing **Attention & Flow**
feeling **Emotion**	Emotional Vulnerability	**Silence & Stillness**
Heart opening	Transparent Communication	**Awareness** Spaciousness, Witness, Non-Dual

Absolute & Relative Presence Paradox

While we can, in any moment access the absolute Presence—the ever-present power of Now—the paradox is that we also simultaneous experience the relativity of life through our human bodies as social beings wired to connect and relate with others. From this relative human view, we can practice cultivating greater relative presence by training our nervous system in learning various presence skills in work, love and life.

Another way to think of this relative presence and absolute Presence paradox is conceptualizing a temporary state and baseline stage-view (vantage). The qualities of our state of being can change dramatically from moment to moment including emotions, quality of thoughts, as well as sensations spanning from tension to relaxation and from numbness to aliveness. In one moment, we may feel anxiety, rapid thoughts, muscle tension and narrow self-absorbed focus, then by shifting our attention to our breath, grounding more into our feet and legs, sensing our whole body, our whole system begins to relax, the breath deepens, the muscles relax, the mental chatter quiets, awareness expands. In another moment while listening in conversation, we can be anxiously waiting for our turn to talk unaware of our own body or even the other person, or we can feel more relaxed, connected and open-heartedly listening to the precious human sitting across from us. Or we can be in a state of contracted self-absorption lost in our own thoughts, versus seamlessly unified with the emergent aliveness of this ever-present moment. Each of these examples can shift in a moment, either through Grace or practicing presence skills. If we consider absolute Presence as the totality of the present moment, then this state shift also opens us to a greater view or vantage of absolute Presence. The intersection of relative presence and absolute Presence is a dynamic dance between Grace and intentional practice.

Imagine what it would feel like if suddenly, as if the sky opened up such that your personal, individual view relaxed and a vast window opened up with an infinite vantage, unified with everything, even the sense of "you" subjective viewer and the objects being viewed dissolved into a seamless unfolding. In the stages of vantage and worldview sections of the presence skills in this guidebook, we will learn about how our baseline center of gravity tends to develop through sequential stages and although it tends to be rather consistent over the short-term, it can be progressively developed, expanded and deepened over our lifetime through practice, supportive surrounding culture, inhibiting environmental conditions of living, and Grace.

While some people can win the Power of Now Presence Lottery and be blasted into a permanently expanded vantage of Awareness like Eckhart Tolle, Byron Katie, and a few very blessed others, the vast majority of the rest of us can really benefit from practicing presence skills. Furthermore, just because someone has a lot of business prowess, is a star on stage, has a lot of friends on Facebook, or are a great athlete doesn't mean he or she has developed the presence and connection skills to be an attuned, listening, communicative, emotionally available, open-hearted loving human being in relationship. So, even if someone has spent years meditating, doesn't necessarily mean he or she has developed relational presence, feels safe and grounded the world, can open his or her heart and connect with others. Or someone might have developed presence skills in some areas but may still be sexually manipulative and developing his or her moral impact awareness in consideration of others. Similarly, we might be a really good at relational presence and intimacy as a devoted caring mother, wife and friend, but if we are neglecting our own needs, self-care and connectedness with something greater than ourselves, then we have only developed a small portion of potential presence skills.

Thus, we need to be careful not to overlook, hide from, avoid, deny or "spiritually bypass" the totality of life by only focusing on the things we are good at, that come easily to us, getting lost in relationships, or escaping into hyper-mental intellectualization or escapist spirituality to the neglect of being practically grounded, emotionally intelligent, connected with others, morally considerate of our impact, as well as living from a greater vantage of open Awareness. The Way of Practicing Presence helps us develop our presence skills and cultivate greater human potential in work, love and life through mastering the essentials of Embodiment, Connection and Awareness. As Ken Wilber, at Integral Institute, one of the greatest living philosophers, emphasizes that as we continue to develop individually, relationally and collectively, that we maintain awareness of Waking Up (spiritually), Growing Up (developmentally), Showing Up (professionally & morally) and Lightening Up (psychologically).

PRESENCE SPECTRUM: Degrees of Presence

There is one important concept to be aware of before we look at some examples in daily life. Presence is not an all or nothing phenomenon. Some people misuse the term "being fully present" as if they thought "okay, sorry I wasn't paying attention but now let me now become fully 100% present as the most Olympically spiritual dude ever."

Personal presence exists on a relative spectrum of degrees and a unique individual can inhabit more or less presence at any given moment. Even from a non-dual Vantage, which we will learn about later, it is still possible to disown certain body, emotional, interpersonal, sexual, moral or life aspects. The essence of this book is to offer both a practical guide to progressively cultivating greater relative presence over time while also pointing out the absolute, always available, ever-present Presence that contains All. Therefore, since we are now focusing more on greater or lesser presence than the misused phrase "fully present", the following presence skills offer us a map to greater presence throughout our daily lives.

Each of us have certain areas of life that come easily to us—areas in which we have a natural presence, skill and potency. And it is likely that there are also areas in which we don't feel as confident or competent—areas that scare us, frustrate us, confuse us, that we avoid or are totally unaware of in this vein, we each have stronger and weaker areas of embodied, intimate & aware presence skills. As we are continuing to explore presence more deeply, let us pay attention to which presence skills already come more naturally as well as others those that we are still learning.

LESS PRESENCE ← → MORE PRESENCE

PRACTICING PRESENCE: WAYS TO CULTIVATE

Presence, in the relative sense, can be increasingly developed over time with practice.
In other words, each person's unique nervous system, can relax and open to be able to embody, connect to and transmit greater relative Presence.

If the 3 aspects of PRESENCE are embodiment, connection and awareness, let's take a closer look at how presence shows up, to greater or lesser degrees, in our daily activities and roles at work, while relating and throughout our lives.

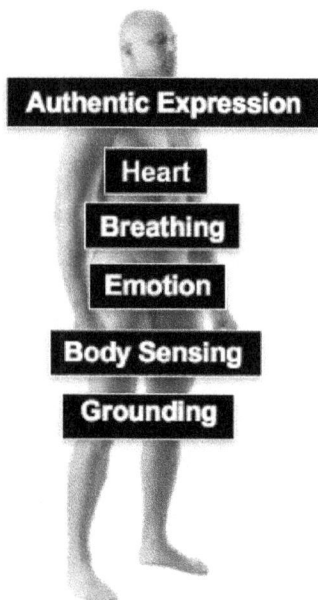

Embodiment

Authentic Expression

Heart

Breathing

Emotion

Body Sensing

Grounding

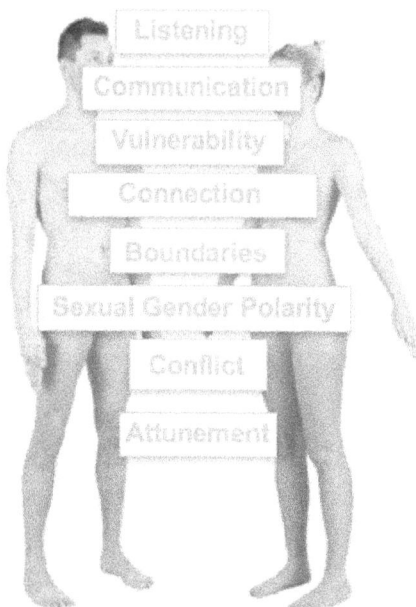

Connection

Listening

Communication

Vulnerability

Connection

Boundaries

Sexual Gender Polarity

Conflict

Attunement

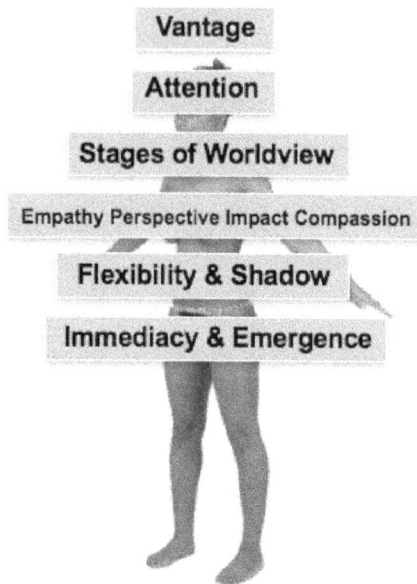

Awareness

Vantage

Attention

Stages of Worldview

Empathy Perspective Impact Compassion

Flexibility & Shadow

Immediacy & Emergence

Now let us once again take another look at this page before we move into exploring each of these 20 presence skills in the heart of this guidebook Again, we will be exploring each skill by way of:

Throughout the remainder of this guidebook, we will be learning more about each of these skills for mastering presence and awakening our greatest potential in work, love and life. Specifically, we will be exploring each quality via:

DIAGRAMS: detailed visual depictions of lesser and greater presence

DEFINITIONS: clarifying explanation of each presence skill or quality

BENEFITS: why each skill matters to us in our life

BARRIERS: ways we limit ourselves from embodying each skill

SUCCESS STORIES: of men and women who have cultivated a quality of greater presence and how it has improved various aspects of their lives

DEVELOPMENT: how each skill tends to develop

TAKEAWAYS: a summary of the most important concepts for each skill section

PRACTICES: the best practices to learn, embody & apply each skill in your life

PART 3   MY STORY

MY STORY

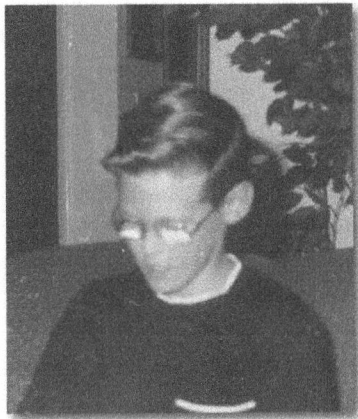

"What a shame, he wasn't paying attention" my Mom used to say with a combination of humor and caution—insinuating that if I wasn't more present when crossing the street, I was going to get hit by a car and on my gravestone that is the statement they would write to summarize my life. In my younger years, I wasn't the most present kid on the block. Actually, growing up, we didn't really have a block, as our neighbors were more like fields and open space in the southern-most basin of Central California.

Other than wearing very thick glasses and zoning out too much, I was a pretty typical kid who liked sports, French fries and playing outside. But at 16 years old, a single experience began to dramatically shift the trajectory of my life. It seems as though we can have life altering tragedies or synchronistic blessings such as a flash insight, a "chance" meeting or a single profound sentence that can serve as powerful pivots in our life direction. Or, in other cases, incrementally actions engaged in consistently over-time can alter our course just slightly like a ship on a long journey that shifts 2 degrees can end on a radically different destination.

**Have you ever experienced anything that shifted the course
of your life either drastically in an instant or slightly, yet incrementally over time?**

For me, a profound experience graced my path, while driving to high school one day on a dusty, backcountry open road. Suddenly, the entire moment relaxed open profoundly, like a vast seamless unity, in what seemed like a silent eternity beyond time. Then in a clear deep unwavering voice, similar to the beginning scene in the movie Meet Joe Black, a sound that was not localized in any place, *"Have no fear of death, the body is just a vessel, you have a mission."* And then just as quickly as it opened to infinity, the scene collapsed back into the high school boy driving down the road in his grandfather's pickup truck—although the afterglow endured in his young body circulating with subtle tingles of aliveness, magnitudes greater than he had ever felt before. Partially elated, and also very shocked, I pulled over to the dirt shoulder and wandered into the natural landscape nearby, falling to my knees in humility and profound curiosity about what had just transpired. In the mind's search for meaning, I began reading a variety of religious, spiritual and philosophical books from various cultures and traditions, which ever so slightly with newfound depth, curiosity and widening perspectives, progressively steered the life trajectory beyond typical teenage boy concerns.

After high school, I studied Business Management Consulting at a university in Los Angeles, an hour and a half from home, but it felt like I was **living a dual life**, unable to integrate what seemed like polar opposites: on one hand being a conventional teenager studying, socializing, partying and dating, and on the other end, a secret depth seeker and explorer of possibility. Working in Management Consulting in downtown Los Angeles on the conventional "road to success", I noticed many middle-aged people were not happy. And I was asking the deeper questions of *"Why are we here?" "How are we to best live?" "What does happiness feel like?"*

Have you ever asked some of these questions?

I started observing life and noticing more nuances, increasingly examining societal constructions and questioning my own inner assumptions. After work one clear summer evening in my early 20's, while sitting on my balcony after work in downtown Los Angeles, watching the sunset to the west, I curiously acknowledged in the ethers *"There has got to be more to life than this...",* just as Neo had been doing right before he discovered the deeper reality in the movie, *The Matrix*.

Just a few months later, after this deeper inquiring, an unexpected back injury occurred. As a result, I was unable to sit for more than a short period and basically had to stand all day long as I tried to continue a normal life. After more than a year of semi-functional living with continuous low-level pain by standing all the time that was not improving with diligent, but ineffective physical therapy; I opted for an experimental surgery that failed horribly. (It is worth noting that the "experimental" procedure had a short-lived trial period, because it was not only unproductive, but made many patients, like myself, who tried it much worse. Prior to the surgery, I had difficulty sitting for more than 30 minutes, but I worked within the limitation, doing the best I could and was still relatively functional in my life. In fact, with a combination of ingenuity and necessity, I became an early adopter of the stand-up desk at work.

But after the botched surgery — able to stand for barely 5 minutes at a time — I became floor-ridden for the next 2 years and for the worst 5 months of which, I laid down on the floor for 22 hours a day. I was in so much pain that I didn't want to feel my body or emotions. Very humbled and unable to take care of myself, I moved back home with my parents. **At first, I resisted,** *"Woe is me...why is this happening...what did I do to deserve this..."* But after a few days I realized that a negative attitude only made things worse, toxifying my inner state and being a downer for others around me. Also, in the midst of the initial shock and pain, I had forgotten that I had been asking the Universe to take the red pill *"There has got to be more to life than this..."* So, I decided to shift my perspective and make the best of the situation.

How would it feel for you to spend 22 hours a day flat on the ground in pain?
Would you wallow in sorrow or try to heal and rise up?
What would you do with your time?

Though I was certainly physically limited and geographically confined — what some would have considered imprisoned

— leaving my parents' home maybe 10 times in an entire year, mostly to go to the doctor—in some ways I became freer internally in realizing that no matter what my external circumstances, I had power over my attention and perspective. Secondly, I now had an abundance of time. I remembered all of the moments in the past when I wished I had had more time. I started learning to meditate, read books most of the day, began learning a foreign language, and watched a classic movie each night—as a reward! I was most inspired by *The Count of Monte Cristo*, in which the lead character, who is wrongfully imprisoned, trains, learns and makes the best of his limited circumstances.

Initially only able to walk short distances, I begin taking walking breaks on the dirt road by my parents' home, gradually increasing the frequency and duration, as my body was becoming stronger and able to stand longer. After one year, I went from being able to stand for 5 minutes and walk a hundred yards, to being able to stand for 30 minutes and walk half a mile at a time—up to a total of 5 miles per day. Yet I was still in too much pain, unable to sit and not fully recovered. Though I had been making the best of the situation and had physically improved, progress was still too slow, and amidst frustration, confusion and doubt I wondered if I would ever get better. As I had been continuing to seek the advice of two of the leading spinal doctors in Southern California, both recommended that I have a disc fusion surgery. In their worldview, the surgical knife is the most common choice. However, part of me wondered if this was the best solution. I asked for guidance and greater clarity through prayer.

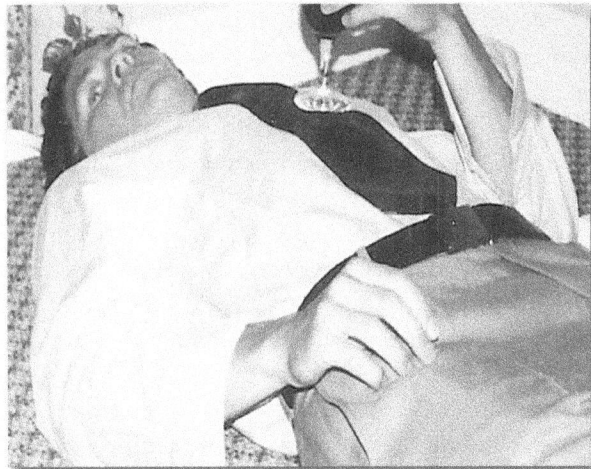

Have you ever been in a situation like this? What did you do or what would you do?

On the very same trip to a second opinion spinal specialist doctor had also suggested a second fusion surgery, I synchronistically was connected with an eccentric older man, who became **a wise ally**. This man inspired me to take full responsibility for my situation and that it was possible to heal my body, instead of passively relying on drugs and surgery to fix me. I was a little skeptical at first, but his knowledge, wisdom and intuition inspired enough trust to get me to commit to giving it a try.

In truth, the first day I vomited up green bile as the journey to purify my past had begun. For the next 10 days, a strong, kind, wise man named Steve helped me strengthen and stretch my body for hours a day, morning until night. I felt like a combination of Luke Skywalker in the swamp with Master Yoda in Star Wars, soaking up new information like a sponge mixed with the training of an Olympic athlete. In this hyper-speed transformation of my mind and body, I made so much progress that I canceled the surgery and moved up to the Bay Area in Northern California to continue with newfound hope. Though I would be **entering an unfamiliar world**, I had **crossed the threshold** and never looked back.

The next 18 months proved to be an intense **period of training**, healing, learning and development. Determined to fully recover, I was open to learning to become more aware of my body and breath, food quality and how my body responded to different foods, etc. I engaged in many different embodiment practices (stretching, weight-training, healthy eating, breath awareness training, progressive relaxation, biofeedback, qi gong, tai chi, yoga, somatic experiencing, trauma desensitization, etc.) and awareness practices (meditation, mindfulness, journaling, reading, and developmental coaching).

This healing phase ended up being not just about my back and physical capacities, as I was opening to healing on all levels. Indeed, one day while wandering into a new health food store for the first time, I magnetically gravitated toward the back into a small room that seemed to be holding a lecture that had participants captivated. As I curiously sat down, I realized the topic was natural vision improvement and yours truly had been severely near-sighted and wore thick glasses not only in grade school, but all the way back since the age of 8 months old after pneumonia, 105* fever and seizures disturbed my vision. I sat with rapt attention as the confident, inspiring speaker described his own personal step-by-step vision improvement process, as well as the successful documented cases of numerous others. Beaming with inspiration and excitement, all I needed was to know it was possible; that others had done it before; that we stood on the shoulders of giants who had worn the groves of possibility. I returned home, and struck with a lightning bolt of inspiration, that very night I made a vow to naturally improve my vision so that I would no longer need contacts or thick glasses.

There were plenty of naysayers along the way: optometrists who said it was impossible and family members fearfully told me *"Don't be silly. That's not possible. Put your glasses back on, you are going to go blind"*. But I believed and used the doubt as fuel for my own determination. I did eye exercises 30 minutes a day and went to a progressive behavioral ophthalmologist for 2 hours a week where I did a training program to restore natural vision. Fifteen months later, and 24 prescriptions of glasses reduced, I passed optometrist and DMV visual exams with 20/20 vision and got the corrective lens restriction removed from my driver's license.

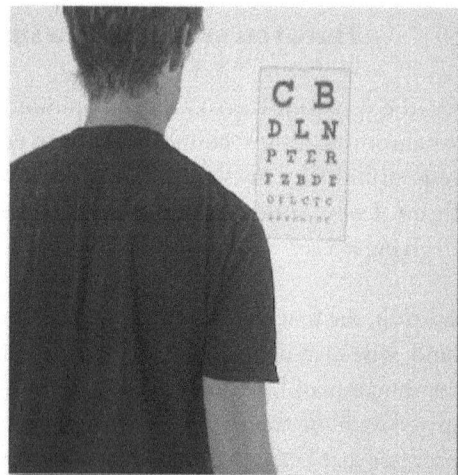

In some traditions, there are legends of a dismemberment—whether literal or symbolic—before the transformative rebuilding and after this, I had a new body and new eyes to experience the world through. Progressively, greater presence developed as I got healthier, stronger, clearer and more flexible in body and mind.

What originally began as an impetus to heal my back, sit without pain, be functional, work, and enjoy life, eventually began aligning with a **deeper motivation** to actualize my unique gifts and bring them back into the world as a contribution of service. While I had been training the physical and mental parts of myself, in order to allow that deeper motivation to fully express itself, I would be tested in a new arena, one that I had been neglecting.

Next I would be venturing into the interpersonal realm of connection and relating. A lack of relational presence and skills was now blatantly holding me back. Most of my life, I was so afraid of judgment and rejection, I barely made eye contact, let alone knowing what authenticity or transparency felt like or how to do them. Of course, from the outside I obviously interacted "normally" with friends, family and a series of girlfriends, but the greater human potentials of presence are not conventionally normal. in all honesty, my capacity for relational presence (real connection, listening, emotional vulnerability, etc.) was low for most of my previous life. Some friends occasionally commented that I always "seemed so busy", I was never available to just hang out and connect. Underneath the self-created constant busyness, truthfully I didn't know how to feel real connection with others.

What area of life do you avoid because it scares or confuses you?

Once in a one-on-one conversation with a female friend we shall call RJ, as my eyes darted to and fro unaware of my body while talking really fast, she lovingly guided my face into direct eye contact and it was if I had settled into a form-fitting space suit and shoes for the first time. My mind got quiet and time seemed to slow down as I could really feel my whole body, two feet standing on the ground, my mind chatter got so quiet I could hear my breathing and best of all through a soft openness in the center of my chest I felt connected to her. It was as if for the first time, I could actually feel what a real alive human connection felt like; so incredibly beautiful, something part of me had been searching for my whole life, yet at the same time also kind of scary. Just because RJ had gifted me with a brief glimpse of possibility, that didn't mean it was wired into my nervous system as an actualized everyday stable baseline.

Some months later, in a romantic relationship with a woman who was very loving, but wasn't feeling it reciprocated, looked at me with sweet tears streaming down her face whispered *"I want to feel your heart, Johnny"*. Even though I didn't know how to open my heart to connection, through her beautiful vulnerability it actually registered in my system how important it was. With humility and undefended self-honesty about the recurring feedback, I proceeded with a genuine willingness to learn something new. I read books, went to various workshops, learned *Authentic Relating and Getting Real*, did attachment healing work and practiced, played and experimented a lot with being real, open, transparent, emotionally vulnerable, listening, and feeling connection in relationship, friendship, community, family and strangers.

My favorite relational practice was by far Argentinian Tango—such an intimate dance—given to me by Integral coach James Baye. The practice was designed to help me deepen my ability to be embodied, initiate and lead, while also being attuned and connected to my partner, generating sexual polarity between masculine and feminine, aware of the space around, all while flowing together to the rhythm, embellishing creative moves with within the Tango form. And it was so fun and sexy!

How do you practice loving more deeply and feeling more connected while staying in your own embodied center?

Alongside all of this personal development over the past decade, there had been a parallel track of career, purpose and profession development to be of service to others. Thousands of hours of reading, daily meditation and integral life practices, watching videos and listening to audio lectures and interviews (this was before podcasts), more workshops and experiential trainings than I can probably recall, a Master's Degree in Psychology, a 2-year program with the developmental masters, Integral Coaching Canada® (ICC), thousands of hours coaching clients, hundreds of hours speaking and facilitating groups and events.

After all of this active driving development, the next phase of the journey would involve deeper relaxation, stillness and integration. Amidst a sufficient but light work schedule, the next couple years of my life were more introverted, involving hours of sitting or lying still, eyes closed or staring into walls and ceilings, which allowed for a profound internal transformation. Many inner states came and went during this unlearning and disintegration phase, some involving the relaxing of fixed identities as the personal self began fading in and out, which felt like having Velcro straps removed from thoughts, beliefs, concepts, or identities.

For some people this process can be terrifying or feel like a death of sorts. For others, it can be a blissful and ecstatic ride into the depths of infinite openness as more fixated attention is liberated from identifications leaving radical emptiness, stillness and peace underneath. Then even these distinctions between movement and stillness, integration and disintegration, subject and object, transcending and including, ecstatic fullness and spacious emptiness merge into Opening as the moment itself.

Although personal development often begins for some in order to get out of pain, overcome struggle or develop healthy connection with others (all of which were initial drivers for me), ultimately our development, self-actualization and self-transcendence are not just for our own personal gain. The more our hearts open and Awareness expands, the more of the world we are able to feel, be aware of, take perspectives on, and Open as, while increasingly realizing and ultimately feeling we are all in this together.

Life continues on, though eventually not as much as a destination, but a continuously evolving process amidst an infinite changeless perfection. Some say this is all Love, others Presence, it has been called many names over the millennia, although all our human minds can really do is point to the Unspeakable.

Ultimately our healing, development, secure attachment, embodiment, and awakening is not just for our own ego, but so that we may be increasingly used as liberated and loving instruments of service, as transmitters of greater potential which includes the full, dynamic range or our humanity from our humility, unconsciousness and continuous learning to our ninja skillfulness, glorious greatness, and the astounding Grace that can shine through All.

This book Presence: a practical guide to awakening greater potential in work, love & life is dedicated to this mission.

PART 4   PRESENCE SKILLS

BREATHING

How relaxed & open is your breath right now?

Can you feel your breath while working, talking, & making love?

When feeling stressed or tense can you use your breath to relax your embodied system?

"The importance of breathing... provides the oxygen for the metabolic processes; literally it supports the fires of life. But breath as "pneuma" is also the spirit or soul. We live in an ocean of air like fish in a body of water. By our breathing we are attuned to our atmosphere. If we inhibit our breathing we isolate ourselves from the medium in which we exist. In all mystic philosophies, the breath holds the secret to the highest bliss."

— Alexander Lowen —

WHAT IS **BREATHING**

the capacity to witness effortless breathing or direct attention to your breathing to intentionally alter your state of being including relaxing or energizing

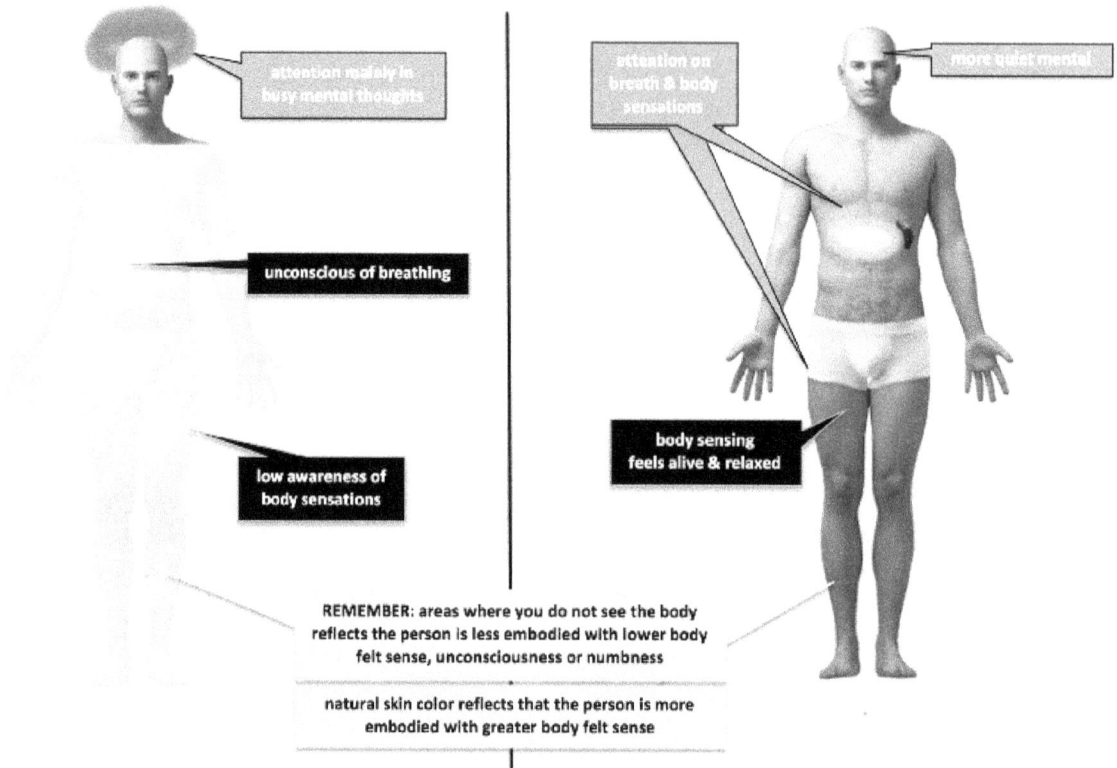

attention mainly in
busy mental thoughts

attention on
breath & body
sensations

more quiet mental

unconscious of breathing

low awareness of
body sensations

body sensing
feels alive & relaxed

REMEMBER: areas where you do not see the body
reflects the person is less embodied with lower body
felt sense, unconsciousness or numbness

natural skin color reflects that the person is more
embodied with greater body felt sense

WHY **BREATHING** MATTERS

Base: Awareness of breath & body is the foundation for every other quality of presence

More Relaxation / Less Anxiety: anxiety & relaxation are polar opposites; breath is the fastest way to induce the relaxation response

Quieting Mental Chatter: mindfulness starts in the body; the more relaxed your breath & body, the quieter the mental activity

Mood: deeper breathing releases endorphins & other brain chemicals that elevate mood & reduce pain

Oxygenation, Energy & Vitality: more oxygen = more blood flow, relaxed muscles, energy & stamina

Detoxification: deeper breathing stimulates the lymphatic system which is designed to release carbon dioxide & metabolic toxins through exhalation

Altered States: breath is one of the most effective natural ways to induce a change of state such as relaxing or energizing the nervous system

BARRIERS TO **BREATHING**

Dissociation: not feeling & inhabiting your body due to trauma, defense or hyper-mental

Stress: stress increases breathing rate & muscle tension while decreasing body sensing

Hyper-Mental: excessive mental activity that is overly theoretical, living in a fantasy, lost in the past or future

Emotional Suppression: unfelt past emotion can be stored as body tension and/or inhibit natural
      breathing rhythm

Food Sensitives: immune/inflammatory food reaction can increase inflammation, lowers body sensitivity & speeds breathing rate

Excess Caffeine or Stimulants: too much caffeine can increase nervous system activity, breathing rate & speed of speech

Emotional Overwhelm: inability to feel & release emotions, result in strategies like numbing & dissociation to
      reduce overwhelm

Self-Referencing: part of healthy boundaries; the ability to be grounded & self-reference from central axis rather than from others

DEVELOPING **BREATHING** SUCCESS STORY

Like most people, I was often unconscious of my breathing, although on the rare occasions I did notice it, my breath was tense & shallow. I started to notice that during peak states of joy, sexual pleasure or peace that my breath was deeply open or effortless. So I realized that my baseline breathing was unconscious shallow & tense, but that there was always a correlation in the extraordinary states that my breath was open, relaxed & deep. With new intention, I embarked upon a twofold process that my new baseline breathing be open, relaxed & deep. On the one hand, I used trauma desensitization methods to release past emotions related to emotionally charged trauma experiences that were constructing my breathing, which progressively yet dramatically begin to open my baseline breathing throughout the day. Another component involved learning to retrain some activities, in which I had a negative habit of breathing shallowly. At a biofeedback conference in 2007, I came across *Respirate*—a simple breath monitor using a strap with a sensor that could be belted around my diaphragm & measure rate of breathing per minute. For a few months, I used this breath monitor most waking hours, while working on the computer, reading, watching movies & driving as I continually trained my attention to be aware of & breathe with more depth & relaxation. Although, I still sometimes use *Respirate* while working on the computer, including in the typing of this sentence, eventually as breathing increasingly became the anchor of attention throughout the day, baseline breathing became deeper, more open & relaxed. Breath is one of the primary doorways to deeper presence.

BREATHING HOW IT DEVELOPS

NATURAL BREATHING

If we have ever watched a healthy infant breathe, we might have noticed the seemingly effortless belly or diaphragmatic breathing that occurs. When our embodied system is integrated in its experience of the world and is authentically expressing itself, our breath, body sensations, emotions, energy, thoughts and words are all connected. Because our bodily systems are designed to be integrated—although this requires a healthy development process—our breath is a great gauge of the quality of our overall inner state and an indicator of contraction somewhere in our overall system; whether physical, emotional, mental or energetic. Recall the last time we felt stressed and physically tense, or emotionally anxious, or mentally preoccupied in the past or future—if we were even aware of it, I bet our breathing was also shallow or tense. Many of us go about our day with more of our attention in the mental world of thoughts and conceptual representations—layers removed from the more direct experience of presence and life through our embodied experience, animated by the aliveness of our breathing.

Being more attuned to our breath includes being more aware of qualities such as shallowness, depth, constriction, openness, tension or even an effortless subtle ripple. Most of us are not usually aware of our breathing throughout the day and the average adult takes 16–20 breaths per minute. However, biofeedback research indicates that an optimal range for relaxed breathing is 5-6 breaths per minute (technically called "resonant frequency of heart rate variability"). The average adult, who is most often completely unaware of their breathing, inhales in less oxygen, breaths more shallowly in their upper lungs and lives in a baseline state of low-level stress. By contrast, an infant and natural breathing adult organically breathes more deeply using their diaphragm—a horizontal muscle above the abdomen and below the chest. This diaphragmatic breathing is also referred to as abdominal or belly breathing, and when this diaphragm muscle relaxes, the lungs fill with more air, which allows the body to take in more oxygen. Our breath is our main feedback system of relaxation—when we feel safe and relaxed we are able to breathe more deeply and absorb more oxygen, and when we breathe more deeply it signals our body's nervous and hormonal systems to go into a state of greater relaxation. In fact, all mammals in nature breathe in a deeper diaphragmatic way when safe in their environments. Again this feedback loop works in both directions, deeper breathing is the body's natural relaxation response and using attention to breathe more deeply during stress interrupts the fight or flight reactivity and begins to restore relaxation. Some people can store past emotion or trauma in their diaphragm and belly region, which can inhibit natural deeper breathing functionality.

BREATHING SELF-EXPERIMENTATION

After attending a biofeedback conference in 2007, I began using a breathing device called Resperate while working to maintain continual breath and body awareness as well as training my system to relax, be productive, and maintain presence and vitality throughout my workday. (As I look over at the readout on the breath monitor, is indicating 5.4 breaths per minute right now, which corresponds to flow state of deep relaxed, focused engagement while writing.) Recently, I have been experimenting with a high tech breathing biofeedback device called Spire that is the size of a stone that clips onto the waist of your pants or bra, synchronizing with your phone and offering a mobile breathing monitoring system.

TEST: inhale right now, without any preparation, exactly as you are and count how many seconds you inhale and how many seconds it takes to exhale?

Also notice if your belly expands as it fills up with air or if you lift your chest to try to inhale. If you used the lifting of your chest muscles or you were unable to inhale for at least 5 seconds, then chances are your natural baseline belly breathing and healthy relaxation levels are inhibited.

Breathing techniques and practices can be used:
- for restoring natural breathing function in daily life
- as consciousness state changers

In general, the more relaxed and open our breathing, the more relaxed and calm our body, emotions and mental world. And so too, for all of us, greater breath awareness is the first place to start, or return to, in the process of embodying deeper presence each moment.

ADVANCED BREATHING PRACTICES

In many meditation traditions, the first stage of meditation involves concentration training and the breathing is often used as the object of attentional focus. The early stages of meditation training is essentially training the mental attention to focus and stay, and in doing so, common by-products include quieting the mental activity, increasing relaxation of the nervous system and muscles, which are foundational steps before relaxing the sense of self and unlocking greater awareness. It is no coincidence then that martial artists, yoga practitioners, singers, motivational speakers and many athletes train their breath to be more relaxed and open, because they have found that more relaxed breathing can help to unlock their greater human potential including a more relaxed and powerful body, a quieter mind, greater emotional freedom, expanded awareness—all of which are foundational ingredients for peak performance in sport, work and life.

Some may be familiar with Wim Hof, a Holland native who is nicknamed "The Iceman" for his ability to withstand extreme cold by using breathing exercises to turn up the heat on his own "inner thermostat." As a Westerner, Hof has helped to scientifically support and increasingly popularize the power of breathing, which Eastern practitioners of yoga, meditation and martial arts have been refining for thousands of years. He allows scientists to study him to validate what he considers to be untapped human potentials, which he unlocks with the power of breath and meditative techniques (particularly *Tibetan Tummo breathing*). Wim also passionately teaches others to do the same in his live workshop training as well as online videos and courses (https://www.wimhofmethod.com). A friend of mine who attended a U.S. based workshop led by Wim Hof early in his teaching career describes him as both a warrior and a playful, loving ball of joy. Recounting a story in which, as my friend was submerged in ice cold water, Wim came over, leaning in intimately close to him and with the biggest smile, whispered, "Relax and embrace the cold to turn on your inner fire. Love it. Open your heart. Relax into it. Love the cold..."

Growing up in a very hot & dry climate where it has only snowed 3 times in my life, I previously avoided the cold, but after hearing my friend's love inspired experience with Wim's transmission, now instead of tensing and resisting the cold, I increasingly breathe deeply, while relaxing and embracing the cold more and more. Learning to consciously open, deepen and relax our breathing is not only a foundational pillar of physical health and mental well-being but it is also essential for helping to regulate our emotional state and is the most essential doorway to deeper states of presence.

BREATHING KEY SUMMARY & KEY TAKEAWAYS

- ➢ Many adults baseline breathing is too fast & too shallow reflecting heightened baseline stress.
- ➢ All mammals in nature breathe in a deeper diaphragmatic way when feeling safe in their environment.
- ➢ As we breathe diaphragmatically more deeply & slowly, it increases oxygen & relaxation.
- ➢ Past suppressed emotion & unintegrated trauma can inhibit deeper, relaxed baseline breathing.
- ➢ Food sensitivities & eating excess glycemic load foods can decrease energy & depth of breathing.
- ➢ Deeper breathing, body sensing & grounding are essentials for enhancing emotional presence.
- ➢ Breathing techniques in Yoga, Qi Gong, Tantra & the Wim Hoff Method can be profound state changers.
- ➢ Breathing is one of the most foundational access points to deeper presence.

BREATHING DEEPENING PRACTICES

- ➢ An updated list of the Best Practices for all skill sections can be found by visiting www.presence academy/practices

BODY SENSING

How alive & pleasure-filled
does your body feel right now?

How would you choose to work in intervals &
take breaks during your workday to maintain vitality, power & relaxation your body throughout the day?

How relaxed, fluid & open can your body
be as you move through the world?

When we have emotionally charged experiences from our past that have not been integrated & released, it can make our nervous system hyper-active with either muscle tension or collapse, which makes it difficult to be present in our bodies. It can either result in busy, looping thoughts or we might find pain when we sense our bodies. So the tendency is for us to either emotionally numb or be hyper-mental in order to manage these. The purpose of body-based presence practices such as grounding, orienting, relaxing, and releasing are often the doorway into deeper presence, joy, expansion, ease in our bodies and lives.

— adapted from a quote by Lawrence Heller PhD —

WHAT IS **BODY SENSING**

the capacity to inhabit your body while being still, moving & relating in the world including consciously feeling body sensations including relaxation, aliveness, energetics, numbness, deadzones, tension, or collapse

attention mainly in busy mental thoughts

more quiet mental

muscle tension

attention on breath & body sensations

low awareness of body sensations

body sensing feels alive & relaxed

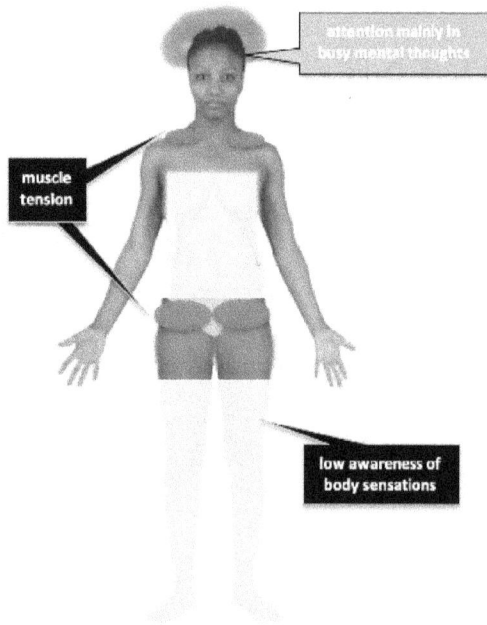

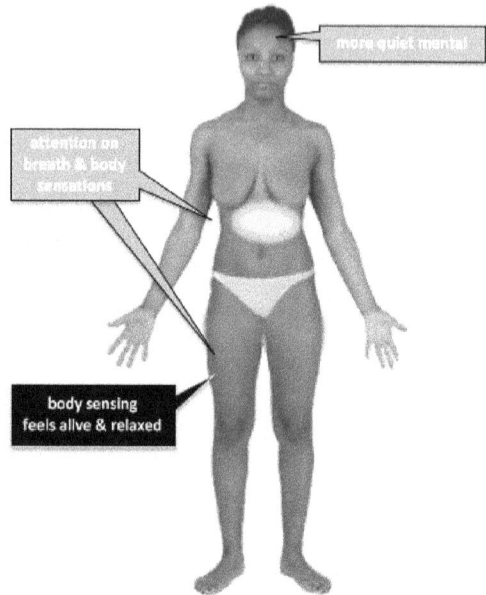

WHY **BODY SENSING** MATTERS

Comfortable in your Skin: moving in the body with ease, rhythm & coordination

Base: awareness of body & breath is the foundation for every other quality of presence

More Relaxation / Less Anxiety: anxiety & relaxation are polar opposites; the deeper your breath & body sensing, the more relaxation

Quieting Mental Chatter: mindfulness starts in the body; the more relaxed your breath & body, the quieter the mental activity

Coordination & Sports Performance: body sensing & proprioception are foundational to enhancing athletic performance & movement

Physicality & Flow: ability to know when to engage with power & when to move with relaxed flow

Vitality: increased energy & circulation; prevents low energy stagnation & muscle tension from inactivity

Body Composition: regular movement maintains health, weight, energy & vitality

Pleasure: greater pleasure throughout your day happens though greater body sensing & relaxation

Sex: more body sensing & relaxation = better, more attuned, connected, sensitized sexual relating

Intuition & Instincts: heart has 40,000 neurons & gut has 100,000,000 neurons, providing added intelligence, intuition & decision-making

Self-Actualization: your body vehicle is an experiencing & expressing instrument & your doorway to greater human potential & beyond

BARRIERS TO **BODY SENSING**

Dissociation: not feeling & inhabiting your body due to trauma, defense or hyper-mental
Hyper-Mental: excessive mental activity that is overly theoretical; living in a fantasy, lost in the past or future
Distraction: using thought, devices, addictions, substances, or activities to avoid feeling body sensations
Pain: avoiding the feeling of physical or emotional pain in your body
Food Sensitives: reaction to food for some people increases inflammation & lowers body sensitivity
Emotional Numbness: numbing your emotional sensing due to past trauma or emotional overwhelm to avoid feeling pain
Emotion & Trauma: dead zones, suppressed emotions or body-stored trauma that keeps attention stuck in the body or dissociated
Fear / Terror: believing "the world is not safe", "it is not safe to be me", "it is not safe to be in my body"
Self-Referencing: part of healthy boundaries; the ability to self-reference from central axis rather than from others
Spiritual Bypassing: using spiritual practices & beliefs to avoid your emotions, body, life & participation in the world

BODY SENSING DEVELOPMENT SUCCESS STORY

Devin was a financial controller in a privately-held investment company, a husband and a father of two young children. From a conventional viewpoint he had a great life, but he came complaining of not feeling happy. His high mental intelligence and preference for working within the rules of accounting had him over-emphasizing his mental world of words, numbers and concepts while neglecting his body, emotions and connection. Increasing body sensing awareness was the doorway for him. He did various practices to help him be more aware of his body, which allowed him to become more aware of his emotional world, then the defenses in his chest softened and his heart increasingly opened. Less overly intellectual, tense and condescending, as he relaxed and opened, those around him began relating to him differently. His coworker relations improved, his connection with his son and especially with his wife improved with increased touch, affection, openness and mutual kindness. He realized "I used to mentally think I would be 'happy' at some point in the future but I realized I feel happy when my body is relaxed and my heart is open."

"Mindfulness starts with the body"

- Catherine Kerr -

DEVELOPMENT OF BODY SENSING

Our first opportunity to begin to activate our body sensing via our skin—the external interface of our sensory nervous system—can happen during the birthing process. In a natural vaginal birth, most of our physical body is touched as it is squeezed through the mother's birthing canal—a process naturally designed to initially activate our body sensing function by stimulating the sense receptors in our skin.[1] Even if a baby is birthed via Cesarean section, or vaginally with high levels of stress hormones, close connected skin to skin holding and being massaging for the first few days after birth can also begin to activate this body sensing process and reduce baseline stress levels.[2] The opposite is also true though, that babies born via C-section delivery and separated from their mother instead of being continuously connected skin to skin and held by the mother, begin their human life with less body sensing responsiveness.

As infants, we are unable to verbally communicate, so we rely on body sensing through touch, as well as frequent eye contact, and emotional resonance to ensure we feel connected to our caregivers. Before our more mature verbal and mental capacities have come online, we are more aware of our emotional and body sensory experience—initially beginning to explore this world through touch, sights, sounds, smells, and taste. Even as adults, our brains register a felt-sense of connection through our body sensing instruments.

Our natural growing up process helps our bodies to develop through a range of movement patterns: reaching, grabbing, rolling, crawling, standing, falling, balancing, walking, running, etc. Ideally, this process can continue to develop with regular dynamic movement throughout the rest of our lives, if we continue to use our physical bodies. Our hunter-gather ancestors are thought to have walked an average of 8-10 miles per day and engaged in a variety of primal movement patterns.[3] Movement and corrective exercise genius, Paul Chek, suggests these movement patterns included pushing, pulling, twisting, bending, squatting, lunging, etc.[4] Yet, many information age cultures have become increasingly sedentary. The average American walks just 300 yards a day —again compared to the 8-10 miles per day of our nomadic ancestors![5] Granted we are lucky not to have to spend 4-6 hours hunting, gathering, creating temporary domestication, etc.[6] yet, sadly many of us have a natural tendency to take things for granted until we lose them. In this case, with the increased sedentary lifestyle, decreased physical movement activity and more limited range of movements, some first world humans are losing body awareness and movement skills.

As we continue through life, ideally we naturally utilize body sensing as an important information source and sense of orientation to the world. However, because we humans experience emotions in our bodies and our human body sensing and emotional functions are intimately related, we can also begin to turn off our body sensing function if our emotional presence is not effectively supported in its development. Some of our strategies to turn down or turn off our body sensing include using emotional suppression, numbing or dissociation to help us manage emotional overwhelm, in which case the price is that we become less aware of our body sensing intelligence unprocessed emotions can be stored in our body.[7] Also for some children, lack of physical activity can be another source of stagnation in the development of healthy body sensing function. As we continue into adulthood, the two most important factors for the body sensing of human embodiment are as follows: engaging in natural body movements with regular physical activity rather than in sedentary lifestyles feeling and secondly expressing or releasing emotions through our bodies rather than numbing or dissociating.

REGULAR MOVEMENT: PROPRIOCEPTION & FASCIA

Movement is an essential feature of aliveness as we experience life, sense and orient ourselves in space with proprioception, and move through the world via these incredible human bodies. Proprioception is a combination of two Latin words *proprius* (one's own) and *capio/capere* (to take or grasp) or in other words to have a sense of one's own body.[8] Proprioception allows us to be aware of our bodies, to move with coordination and orient in space. This proprioceptive sense extends to include the degree, quality and rate of movement, as well as how our whole body orients with its parts and to its position in space (meaning the way we can sense, without visually looking, where all our body parts are, the way they function in relation to each other and the space around). These proprioceptors or body sensors are located in the muscles and joints throughout the body and provide feedback to the brain. It is our central nervous system's ability to communicate and coordinate in synchrony with parts of our body relative to each other and their position in space. Proprioception allows us to touch our finger to our nose (by locating and orienting our finger with our nose in space), drive a car (with hands on the wheel, foot on the pedal, and eyes on the road), and walk forward in a straight line without looking down (sensing where to step and balance). Muscles, ligaments, skin, ears, and eyes send orienting feedback to the brain every fraction of a second—sensory information which our brain requires to maintain posture, position in space, stay balanced, movement with smoothness and coordination, and respond to our immediate environment.

Movement proprioception is sometimes considered to be an additional sense that must be not only developed, but regularly engaged through movement. *"Move it or lose it, sister!"* as they say. There is an interesting scientifically documented case of a young woman who lost her proprioception due to a spinal cord viral infection.[9]   Initially, she was unable to move well at all and struggled to pick up objects or control her tone of voice. She underwent physical therapy exercises, recalibrating the modulation of her voice and relearning to move appropriately by using her sight to watch her movements. For some of us, these mere technical anatomy and kinesiology terms may sound more like the language of our physical therapist, but they illustrate the importance of our body as it relates to presence. With healthy proprioception we are able to easily walk in the dark without looking down at our feet, yet she had to redevelop her proprioceptive coordination of movements. Ultimately the woman regained normal speech and is able to function in the world relatively well, although due to some degree of proprioceptive damage, her movements seem slower and stiffer. Some evidence suggests that body sensing proprioception is diminished, or perhaps turned down due to heightened brain inflammation in autism spectrum disorders like Asperger's Syndrome.[10] Perhaps, more relevant to the typical human without spinal cord injury or autism spectrum disorder, systemic body inflammation from food sensitivities can also decrease body sensitivity by increasing a sense of overall achiness and body numbness.[11] How comfortable we feel in our skin, how inflamed our body feels, the way we move in our body and, as this case illustrated, even the way we use our voice is intimately dependent upon our body sensing. We may therefore surmise that both brain-body health and physical activity (practice) are important factors in healthy body sensing awareness.

Fascia, another essential factor in flexibility and body sensing, is the 3D web of connective tissue network of gluey, fibrous proteins that holds everything in our body together like a wetsuit. A single fascial system begins as a fibrous gel that surrounds all the cells about 2 weeks into the life of the developing embryo. This single suit is progressively folded into a complex meshwork in adulthood comprised of what seems like layers of fascia. This meshwork is the bridge between stability and movement – the interface between structure and function. Its health and flexibility are vital to everything from advanced movement performance, to injury recovery, to everyday flexibility and movement. Gil Hedley, Ph.D., a fascial expert and founder of Integral Anatomy, has dissected thousands of human cadavers. He has a famous video titled *"Fuzz Speech"* in which he compares fascia to layers of fuzz. He demonstrates how each night when we go to sleep, the interfaces between our muscles and skin grow fascial fuzz and in the morning when we wake up with that stiff body feeling, part of this is due to a fascial solidifying process, but that every time we move or stretch in a certain movement pattern then we are **melting** the newly forming fuzz.

> *"Now what happens if you get an injury...my shoulder is stiff now, I'm holding my shoulder, I go to bed and wake up in the morning I don't stretch my shoulder, I'm afraid it hurts, so last night's fuzz doesn't get melted. I go to bed I sleep some more, now I have two nights fuzz built up...what if I have a week or a month's supply now those fascial fibers start lining up and intertwining and intertwined going and all of a sudden you have thicker fibers for you have inhibition of movement potential. now there is no longer simply a matter of doing some basic stretching now you need some professional work...to break up the solidified fascia and restore the original movement that you lost.... so you have to stretch and move and use your body in order to melt that fuzz that's building up between the sliding surfaces of your musculature"* [12]

Fascia is an integrated network system and although from one view it can seem like it is made of individual layers, it is treated as a system, not just as a series of parts. One fascial train runs from our ankle all the way up to our head so instead of myopically thinking one muscle is tight, explore how it relates to our entire fascial and muscular system. Apparently these layers organize themselves–depending on our movement usage and the stretching or forces that they are exposed to. Over the course of our lifetime, the less we move with our bodies due to injury or inactivity, the more solidified our fascia becomes the more limited our normal full range of motion becomes; while conversely, regular dynamic movement and stretching keep the fascia trains healthy, hydrated, and flexible. Often, when our sedentary lifestyle lacks movement, when our body has been neglected, when we are eating inflamed foods, when our proprioceptive sensing is under-developed or atrophied or when our fascia is tight, we simply do not have the same potency of physical presence.

PHYSICALITY & POWER OF BODY SENSING
The physicality of how we inhabit our physical body is not only a powerful component of presence, but it is the intersection of our primal animal origins and our higher order humanity. It is through the presence of body sensing and movement that we can inhabit our physicality and access to our physical instincts, power and smooth coordinated movement. Many athletic and martial arts movement patterns evolved from observing movement patterns in animals and activating similar potentials through the physicality of our human bodies. In many martial arts, alert relaxation and high degree of body sensing is the ideal embodied state as it allows many more possibilities of movement. Consider that if our muscles are already tense or committed to moving a certain direction, we have to relax and then re-contract as we redirect to move in another direction. This actually reduces our reaction time as opposed allowing instinctive

response from a ready relaxed body sensing state. So, not only does chronically tense muscles slow reaction time and limit movements patterns which tend to result in negative feedback loop of even more unconscious and limited habitual movement, but our brain can turn down the pain of chronic tension through a process called *"desensitized habituation"*. Chronic body tension is the opposite of relaxed, alive, body sensing, which limits our range of potential movement and the potency of our presence. Overall as we become more sedentary, chronic body tension and desensitization make us less aware of our body and its movement potential, diminishing the power presence and body aliveness. If we are interested in accessing the confidence, power and instinct of presence, it is through the body sensing that we can increasingly inhabit the vehicle of our physicality in daily life. Unfortunately, due to sedentary lifestyles, rejection of our physical power, fear of our own wild animal nature, that many of us can disown our physicality and get stuck in the mental world, neglect our bodies and lose access to the body sensing physicality of presence.

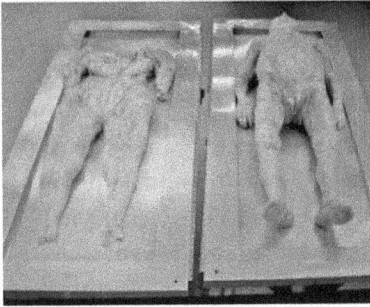

Fig 3 Superficial fascia lying beside the body from which it came. Gil Hedley, 2005. http://www.gilhedley.com

FLOW & FLEXIBILITY OF BODY SENSING

Water is most alive when it flows. Bruce Lee, martial arts and movement master has a classic quote *"Be like water my friend"* which inspires us to cultivate the ability to be fluid and dynamic with our movements in our body. Strength without flexibility is rigidity. Unflowing movements can be stiff, choppy, clumsy, or chaotic. Fluid movements require flexibility, relaxation, rhythm and coordination. Freedom of movement and fluidity in our body sensing can parallel freedom of expression, creativity, passion, sensuality, and enjoyment of life through our bodies. The opposite of flow is stagnation and if the movement aspect of presence is not allowed to flow it can also stagnate some of our important subtle dimensions like breath, emotion and life force energy. Flowing movement does not come from understanding and mentally trying; the essence of flow is allowing. It requires a level of surrender to body intelligence and instinct. Of course a certain level of nervous system integration must be activated through practice, but ultimately the natural intelligence of the body takes over and organic movement beyond thought arises and is expressed.

Flow in movement and Flow as state of awareness underlies athletes in the zone, dancers, performing artists, martial artists, fighters, musicians, stage performers, etc. Emilie Conrad created *Continuum Movement*, a flow based breath, sound and movement practice for creativity, healing and spiritual development. Moshe Feldenkrais, synthesized insights from physics, psychology, biomechanics, motor development, and martial arts, in developing *The Feldenkrais Method®*—one of the core practices of which is *Awareness thru Movement*. With the enhanced Awareness of Presence, the relaxed, novel, fluid, movements are recognized to help those with tension, restricted movement, and chronic pain as well as improving flexibility, coordination, posture, creativity and athletic ability. Another movement–related presence modality is *Alexander Technique*, a mindfulness-oriented, active exploration of how we move through life in our everyday activities, bringing enhanced awareness to unconscious habits, limited movement patterns, and body tension, to reactivate our innate ability to move with ease, fluidity, freedom of movement, coordination and effectiveness. Each of these movement methods can be a doorway into deeper presence via body sensing through greater sensory awareness and novel learning to free us from unconscious habitual patterns and allow for new ways of moving, thinking, and feeling to emerge.

SENSUALITY & PLEASURE OF BODY SENSING

Many of us we have dulled or dissociated our body sensing, numbing pain and trying to keep up with the frenzied pace of life. Some of us engage in continuous distraction from our inner experience and body sensing through constant stimulation from checking social media, email or internet on our phones or watching TV from the moment we wake up, every free moment during the day, until the moment we fall asleep. As adults, many of us in the Western industrialized world are racing through life perpetually in a hurry—tense, rushed, stressed, overcommitted, always *"trying to do one more thing"* and in constant motion. There is so much digital stimulation, so much we want to see and do, never a moment's rest, it seems, as we go from one thing to the next; barely aware of the world of pleasure buried in our bodies. For some people, a potential moment of relaxation and stillness without external stimulation might allow uncomfortable emotions to arise or that we feel how tense and uncomfortable our body truly feels, and so we subconsciously choose to distract ourselves or engage our attention externally away from body sensing. For others, an underlying feeling of "not-enoughness" or seeking perfection, propels us to continuous *"push"* and live with low to moderate levels of body tension and stress— falsely fantasizing that one day in the future we will finally find the pleasure of happiness, freedom and love. We seek these concepts as externalities when they are actually states felt through our pleasure sensing bodies.

When we are more anxious and stressed, our bodies predictably reflect this as our muscles are more tense, breathing faster and our racing thoughts have a more negative orientation. Areas of tension are like crimps in our power supply, whether we are consciously aware of an area of intensity or whether they feel like dead-zones in our body. Bodily tension equals loss of power and unlived potential. Scanning our body allows us to identify areas of tension which are indicators of stuck potential or trauma so that we can explore, release, and reclaim hidden power. By contrast, when our muscles are more relaxed, our breathing is slower, our minds are calmer, our thoughts more positive and we are more receptive to pleasure. Relaxing our nervous system and slowing down in our life allows more body sensing and pleasure. *"Relax and enjoy it"* is a common admonition in our hyper-stimulated society, because body relaxation allows enhanced experience of pleasure, enjoyment, and savoring, as well as recovery, rejuvenation, reflection and integration.

Body sensing is the doorway to sensuality and pleasure. Our body is our instrument for experience and expression; the more we can sense our body the more pleasure we get access to feeling. The opposite is true though, as we shut down our body sensing and emotional functions through numbness, then we also lose access to the highs and the lows. Joe Hudson, venture capitalist and Nondual teacher, eloquently reminds us that true authentic *"joy is the matriarch of all emotion and she won't come in our house unless all emotions are welcome."* Our body sensing is our access to emotion and pleasure, so if we can't feel our body if we can't enjoy the depths of pleasure. Some people relegate sensuality only to sexuality, but sadly many people whose body sensing is numb and hearts are closed only get to experience a fraction of the pleasure and passion possible during sexual exchange for the depth of beautiful loving heart connection. So while we can dramatically enhance our sexual connecting, the more essential point here is to bring greater awareness to the blissful sensuality possible through our body with life itself, when we have cultivated heightened body sensing. For many of us, we need to be reeducated to feel physical sensations in our body, to tolerate and breathe through discomfort, to learn how to ground ourselves, to reach for resourced connection in times of distress and increase our tolerance for well-being, touch, savoring, satisfaction, connection, intimacy, joy relaxation and pleasure. Deeply embodied, relaxed, radically open and unified with the fabric of life itself, each movement, undulation, breath, playful exchange, sensuous bite of food, or touch can be felt as a deeply pleasurable sensing through our incredible human body.

TRAUMA & DIMINISHED BODY SENSING: NUMBNESS & DISSOCIATION

Mindfulness teachings generally encourage people to take an accepting, non-judgmental noticing of everything that is arising in Awareness. While this can be a doorway into greater presence as well as helping to build greater bodily felt-sense, for many people it can be challenging due to unresolved traumas and stored emotional charge in the nervous system. This can take up a lot of bandwidth in Awareness, and be reflected as mental noise and bodily tension. It is also one of the big reasons why it is difficult for beginners to focus attention when first learning to meditate. In addition to actually learning to train the brain to focus attention, our initial sitting still attempts usually reveal body tension as well as mental tension. Conversely, the more relaxed our body feels, the quieter our mental world tends to be. Traditional mindfulness mediation is most effective when a person has experienced little trauma or engaged in healing to desensitized and integrate it. Either way access to more dynamic states of being or greater Vantages of Awareness requires that we learn to relax our body. Somatically oriented psychotherapists Laurence Heller and Aline LaPierre note:

> "Trauma, because of the associated nervous system hyper-arousal and the resulting systemic dysregulation keeps us from being present in our bodies. The tendency for traumatized individuals is to disconnect from the body by becoming overly cognitive or by numbing bodily experience or both. When there is high nervous system dysregulation, it is painful to be in our bodies...The purpose of somatic mindfulness is to progressively support nervous system reregulation by adapting techniques from Somatic experiencing such as grounding, orienting, relaxing, and discharge that are designed to address the high arousal, collapse and shock states the traumatized individuals experience" [13]

In his *New York Times Best Selling* book, *The Body Keeps Score*, Bessel van der Kolk, psychiatrist, researcher and professor *Boston University School of Medicine* is one of the world's leading experts on trauma. Since the 1970's he has successfully worked with thousands of patients as well as conducted pioneered researcher demonstrating that the spectrum of severe shock trauma to previously suppressed emotions can be stored in our body and require the emotional presence of relational connection and body sensing based approaches to desensitize and release the past so we can restore sensing and aliveness to our bodies and lives. Dr. van der Kolk writes,

> "many conventional psychologists usually try to help people use insight and understanding to manage their behavior. However, neuroscience research shows that very few psychological problems are the result of defects in understanding; most originate in pressures from deeper regions in the brain that drive our perception and attention. When the alarm bell of the

emotional brain keeps signaling that you are in danger, no amount of insight will silence it."..."for a hundred years or more, every textbook of psychology and psychotherapy has advised that some method of talking about distressing feelings can resolve them. However, as we've seen, the experience of trauma itself gets in the way of being able to do that. No matter how much insight and understanding we develop, the rational brain is basically impotent to talk the emotional brain out of its own reality... It is so much easier for them to talk about what has been done to them—to tell a story of victimization and revenge—than to notice, feel, and put into words the reality of their internal experience. Our scans have revealed how their dread persisted and could be triggered by multiple aspects of daily experience. They had not integrated their experience into the ongoing stream of their life. They continued to be "there" and did not know how to be "here"—fully alive in the present." [14]

We humans can use a variety of defenses or coping mechanism to avoid feeling emotional intensity—and two of the most significant, as they relate to losing presence and diminished body sensing are **numbness** and **dissociation**. Numbness is essentially a way in which we turn down our body sensing dial usually to avoid feeling pain. Numbing can be a very useful defense to help us get through a challenging situation, but when we repeatedly use these functions, numbing, suppressing emotion, shutting down, over and over again, we bury those unfelt emotions to be dealt with later and the price is a numbing to the aliveness of our bodies, connection and life around us.

Some people have heard the term *dissociation* in a psychology context but it's not just for psych wards. It is actually more prevalent in the general population than most of us realize. Simple everyday examples include boredom and daydreaming, which can lead to loss of awareness of one's body. Also many of us talk fast in conversation, not simultaneously sensing our own body as we speak. More extreme examples include severe detachment from physical and emotional experiences as coping strategies for stress or conflict. A fascinating research study conducted by a team of neuroscientists at the University of Geneva, Switzerland and published in the prestigious research journal *Nature*, induced dissociative out-of-body experiences with mild electric current stimulation to a specific brain region called the temporal parietal junction. One of these patients reported feeling like she was hanging from the ceiling, looking down at her body from above. [15] While these may seem like cool tricks, recurrent dissociation not only decreases functionality in the world but also usually leads to fear and the feeling of being unsafe in our bodies and the world. Furthermore, because the felt sense of connection happens through our bodies, dissociation inhibits our ability to connect with others.

While some lay people think of PTSD only in relation to war veterans or abuse, all of us humans have experienced varying degrees of traumatic incidents from low-level emotional triggering to severe trauma in which the emotional intensity was overwhelming beyond our emotional intelligence capacity to effectively feel, integrate and release the related emotional charge in the moment. These unintegrated emotional experiences keep us compulsively repeating the similar patterns or fearfully avoiding related experiences, thus restricting the fullness of our life with frozen past emotions and associated limiting beliefs. Whether we feel unsafe in our body, tense and guarded, uncomfortable in our skin, bombarded by body pains, or numb deadzones, many of us have a frozen emotional past stored in our body that is limiting the pleasure of our relaxed and energetic embodied feeling of being alive.

Dr. van der Kolk tells us that in his practice of healing and restoring body sensing:

> *"I begin the process by helping my patients to first notice and then describe the feelings in their bodies—not emotions such as anger or anxiety or fear but the physical sensations beneath the emotions: pressure, heat, muscular tension, tingling, caving in, feeling hollow, and so on. I also work on identifying the sensations associated with relaxation or pleasure. I help them become aware of their breath, their gestures and movements... All too often, however, drugs such as Abilify, Zyprexa, and Seroquel, are prescribed instead of teaching people the skills to deal with such distressing physical reactions. Of course, medications only blunt sensations and do nothing to resolve them or transform them from toxic agents into allies."* Again this is a highly respected research and psychiatrist at Boston University who has successfully changed thousands of lives over decades. As much as we may want to forget past incidents, the body never lies and any remaining negative body sensations that arise when we think about a past event is our responsibility to feel and release—paradoxically it is by getting closer to and safely feeling and releasing these past body remnants that we let them go and restore greater body aliveness and wellbeing. The first step in freeing ourselves from the past is body sensing self-awareness. van der Kolk directs us with the knowledge that neuroscience research shows that the first step in releasing our past and restoring aliveness in our bodies is *"by becoming aware of our inner experience and learning to befriend what is going inside ourselves."* [16]

MINDFULNESS: RELAXED BODY IS A RELAXED MIND

Neuroscientist Professor and Researcher Catherine Kerr gave a fascinating TED talk on this subject titled: *Mindfulness Starts With the Body: A View from the Brain.*[17] She notes that most early Mindfulness researchers were psychologists, who came from a mental perspective, yet the most recent brain imaging research demonstrates that mindfulness actually starts in the body with very close focused attention on breath and body sensations. Awareness of our body felt-sense includes areas of tension, limited range, flexibility, dead zones, sensations or other subtleties. This is especially true for people relearning to access greater presence by directing attention into sensations in the body, as opposed to dissociation or further abstraction in mental concepts. Greater somatic or bodily sensing awareness is the foundation of presence and along with breathing, is one of the essential entry points in learning to relax our bodies, regulate our emotions, quiet our minds and open Awareness. It is only from a more relaxed aware open body that we can truly feel connected with ourselves, others and life around us. This point is so important it warrants further emphasis, in order to feel deeply and intimately connected with someone else, we do so through our body and so have to be able to sense our body.

Our body is also the source of instinct and intuition. Dan Siegel, Professor of Neuroscience at UCLA and pioneer in Interpersonal Neurobiology, corroborates this using neurobiology, confirming that the middle prefrontal cortex gives us access to intuition via the wisdom of the body and offers powerful sources is of insight such as feelings in our heart, gut feelings in our belly and the rhythm of our breathing.

> *"This region (middle prefrontal cortex) receives information from throughout the interior of*

the body including the viscera heart and intestines and uses this input to give us a heartfelt sense of what to do or a gut feeling about the right choice this integrative function illuminates how reasoning once thought to be a purely logical mode of thinking is in fact dependent on the non-rational processing of our bodies such intuition helps us make wise decisions not just logical ones. A deeper sense of knowing what is true and what is really happening." [18]

Body scanning is a great way to begin increasing body sensing awareness. A body scan is like getting slowly scanned with a wand from head to toe going through airport security. It is a powerful tool we all have access to that can help us begin to distinguish sensations, emotions, and their location by scanning our body with attention and curiously exploring, sensing, and feeling. Using our attention to slowly scan our body from head to toe, we can deepen the breath in our belly we can begin to more deeply sense the experience of life in our body. When we notice an area of numbness, tension, or heightened sensation, we can allow our attention to hover there. We might feel a knot of tension in our solar plexus, fluttering anxiety in our abdomen, constriction in our chest, tightness in our upper shoulders, or a cloud of sadness hanging over our heart. But we may also feel joy in our chest, bliss in our belly, pleasure in our pelvis, or energetic aliveness throughout our entire body.

Eventually, we might be able to do this in a spilt-second or two, but when we are beginning, sometimes it might take some time and a few breaths to slow down the mental activity enough to focus our attention more fully on our bodily sensory experience. Then, eventually, as our body sensing awareness increases we can scan while moving or in the midst of conversation, but usually at first it aids in the learning process to be still. Do not worry if initially we do not feel much, feel numbness or dead-zones--this is not uncommon and remember these areas of tension or dead-zones are our hidden power and potential. There are practices we can do to progressively increase our body sensing awareness, reclaim this buried power and awaken our greater human potential through our body.

The first part of this process is scanning and increasing our body sensing awareness of what it is we're feeling, which can be learned relatively quickly. So be patient, stay with it, keep practicing being aware of breath and bodily sensation, while noticing the areas where we feel the most predominant sensations. Remember to initially not go straight into the mental story or interpret it – stay at the level of sensations while fully feeling and allowing it to be there without judgment or analysis. Then later we can extract the wisdom and understanding. If we have a tack lodged in our buttocks, we can spend time analyzing it, understanding it, identifying the origin of how it got there, etc. or we can notice and feel it, pull it out and then extract the wisdom and learning from the experience.

Sensing is the language of the body and the doorway to more fully inhabiting our powerful physicality, instinct, sensuality, pleasure and relaxation. Our bodies are instruments of experience and to feel the sensations of our bodies is to actually experience the flow of life through us. The sensations of our bodies always arise in the immediacy of the present moment. The more distant we are in thought and the more exclusively our attention is on our mental world of past memory or future fantasy, the less free attention and energy we have available for embodied presence. Mindfulness processes and the *Alexander Technique* discover these unconscious movements or areas of our physicality we are not aware of inhabiting by bringing attention to the sensations and practicing a new movement with concentration on how it feels to move in the new way. Playing things like competitive sports, aerobics classes, dance, weight-lifting, cross-fit, and certain types of functional movement can all enhance physicality while methods like *Alexander Technique, Feldenkrais Method*, martial arts, tai chi, qigong, and yoga are specifically some of the most effective movement practices to increase bodily awareness and physicality. But it is one thing to be mindfully aware of our physical sensations and another thing to profoundly inhabit our body with physicality and flow as we move through the world with access to greater power, pleasure, elegance, rhythm and the body wisdom of instinct.

We human beings experience the fullness and aliveness of life through our bodies, which are essentially sensory instruments. Our body is our instrument of experience so take care of it as the anchor of unique awareness. For many people learning greater body sensing, self-regulation through relaxation and being more embodied helps to calm the static, stress and nervous system dysregulation that takes up bandwidth in Awareness and is often the first step toward deeper more expanded presence. And from here it is a positive cycle in which the more relaxed and in touch with our body and breath, and the greater our body sensing and capacity for self-regulation.

Multitasking, distraction, avoidance, and dissociation take us farther away from the richness of life in our bodies in the present moment. Indeed, *"the body never lies"* as Martha Graham, the legendary American choreographer and dancer once said. Bodily sensations offer truthful information about the moment. We may make mental interpretations of our experience or the sensations if we are aware of them, which effectually distances ourselves from the direct experience of the sensations and the intimacy of the moment. It is also through our bodies that we experience pain as well as joy, peace, pleasure, ecstasy, passion and love. We can't have one without the other. We have to relax into deeper embodiment before we can truly relax into the peace, aliveness and expansion that lives underneath. The way out is through—the way into deeper presence is through relaxing into body sensations and feelings and then opening beyond. Our breath and body relaxation is the gateway to greater presence. The more sensing, energetically alive and activated we are in our bodily instruments, the more flexibility, skillfulness, pleasure and Awareness we have available to experience, enjoy and express in work, relationships and life.

BODY SENSING KEY SUMMARY & KEY TAKEAWAYS

- ➤ Our body is our sensing instrument for experiencing & expressing life, & our vehicle for greater human potential.
- ➤ The chronic body tension & desensitization or a sedentary lifestyle makes us less aware of our body & its movement potential.
- ➤ Dietary inflammation & food sensitivities that can also create numbness & static which decreases body sensing.
- ➤ In turning down body sensing to avoid feeling emotion by numbing or dissociating, we lose access to aliveness, pleasure & connection.
- ➤ We feel healthy individuated connection with others thru alive body sensing in our bodies, not in thought, merging or dissociation.
- ➤ Mindfulness starts in the body, the more we can sense our body, the less anxiety & mental chatter we experience.
- ➤ Body sensing helps us feel more comfortable in our skin, moving through the world with greater ease, rhythm & coordination.
- ➤ Body sensing gives us access to deeper instinct & intuition as well as sensuality & pleasure.

GROUNDING

Would your friends describe you as being **grounded**
& practically oriented in the world?

Do you feel your feet & legs **grounding** while waiting in line, standing in a conversation & even while seated?

What would **grounding** empowerment
& confidence feel like in your body?

WHAT IS **GROUNDING**

the capacity to feel safe with your feet grounded, inhabiting your body & practically oriented in the physical world

---

"Get yourself grounded and you can navigate even the stormiest roads in peace."

— Steve Goodier —

attention is dispersed & dissociated

feeling scattered & reality

can't feel legs, feet or ground

more quiet mental

attention on breath & grounding

power pose, physicality, confidence

body sensing feels alive & relaxed especially in the legs

attention is dissociated

guarded; does not feel safe in body or the world

can't feel body or sensations

can't feel legs, feet or ground

feels grounded, solid, stable base

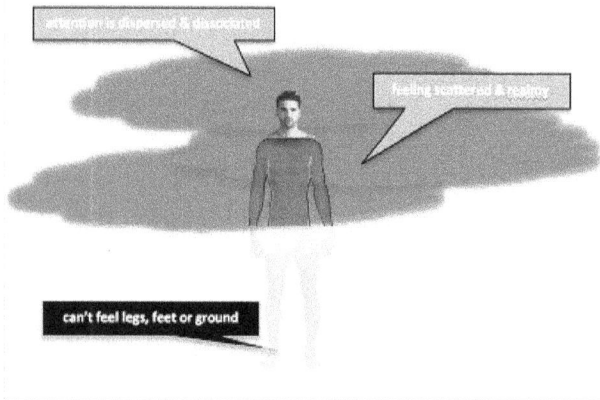

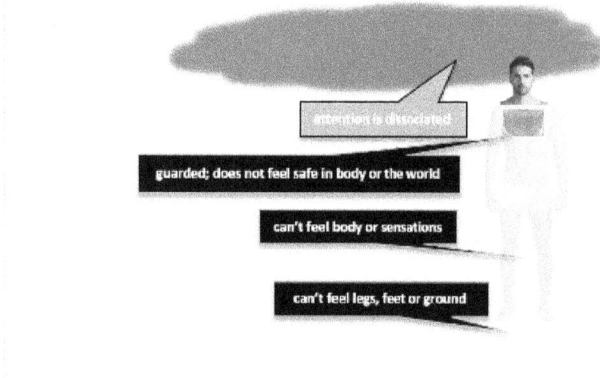

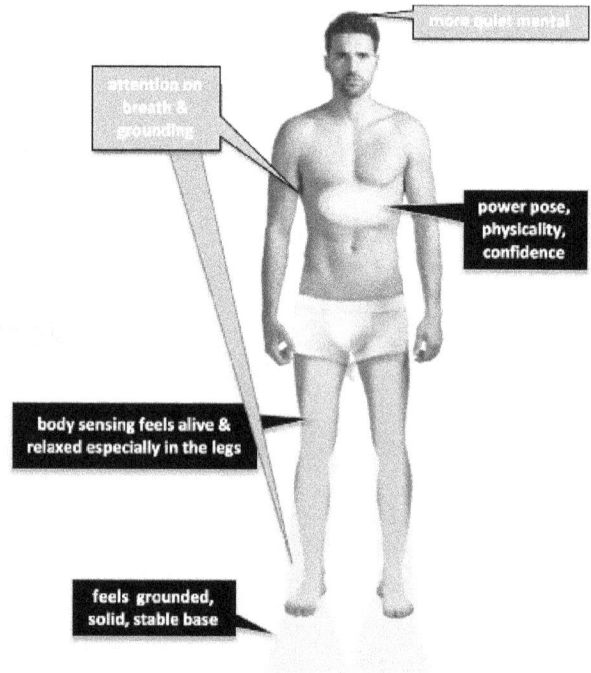

WHY **GROUNDING** MATTERS

Safe & Settled: feeling safe, settled & at home in your body & the world

Stable: feeling solid, stable, & rooted "down to earth" like a tree

Centered: feeling empowered, aligned & resourced on the ground & around your own vertical central axis

Calm: feeling more relaxed & less stressed

Confident: feeling more confident & comfortable in your skin & base

Taking Action: the foundation of taking practical action in the physical world

BARRIERS TO **GROUNDING**

Dissociation: not feeling & inhabiting your body due to trauma, defense or hyper-mental

Hyper-Mental: excessive mental activity, overly theoretical, living in fantasy, lost in the past or future

Unwelcomed: not feeling wanted or welcomed during conception or as an infant by parents or socially at school

Fear / Terror: believing "the world is not safe", "it is not safe to be me", "it is not safe to be in my body"

Emotional Overwhelm: inability to feel & release emotions, result in strategies like numbing & dissociation to reduce overwhelm

Self-Referencing: part of healthy boundaries, the ability to self-reference from the central column rather than from others

Disconnected from Nature: unfelt sense of being connected to & part of the natural world including the cycle of life & death

Spiritual Bypassing: using spiritual practices & beliefs to avoid your emotions, body, life & participation in the world

Emotion & Trauma: dead zones, suppressed emotions or body-stored trauma that keeps attention stuck in the body or dissociated

GROUNDING DEVELOPMENT SUCCESS STORY

Helen was a tall, slender Eastern European, woman who was a model in her younger years before immigrating to the US and working her way up to executive level in a US-based, global organization. While people often complimented her, inside she was terrified of being judged & did not feel comfortable in her own skin. We worked on helping her learn to ground and feel more relaxed in her body—especially in social situations—turning down her worry about what others were thinking and increasing her own internal feeling of easeful confidence. She reported, "I had a staff meeting, and a few minutes into it I noticed that I was starting to feel nervous, then I noticed I could not feel my lower body, so I put my attention on my breathing and then grounded down into feeling my feet and legs. I immediately started to feel more relaxed and confident, so then I started to make eye contact and connect with other people in the meeting, one at a time. The nervousness and rapid worrying thoughts went away with ease and I felt more and more relaxed in myself, connected and confident. Now I ground every morning before I start my day and in moments throughout the day to make sure I stay grounded so I don't get lost or spin out up in my head. Overall, I feel like I am on a new level or in a different dimension of life now." She ended up getting a promotion, a pay raise and now works from home 80% of the time. Feeling more grounded and comfortable in her own skin has not only enhanced her professional life, but she is most grateful for how much more relaxed and present she is able to be with her two young boys and husband.

"The person with a safe center doesn't fear change. We can choose change without fear before a challenge only when we are strongly centered."

— Ilchi Lee —

Our grounded inhabitation of our physical bodies is the most basic primal level of present-moment existence in our human experience. The subtly felt sense of grounding through our physical bodies both connects us to the ground of life and allows us to fully inhabit our physical bodies. Grounding is the base access point into presence, feeling empowered as well as safe in our body and the world. We refer to someone who is a practical, solid, functional human being as being *"grounded"* or *"down to Earth"*. In contrast, one of the great literary novelists of the last century, James Joyce, in his short story The Dubliners poetically articulated the ungrounded, dissociated relationship many of us have with our body in this famous line: *"Mr. Duffy lived a short distance from his body"*.[1] Dissociation and embodiment are on opposite ends of the grounding spectrum and many of us have yet to experience the empowerment, relaxation and sense of safety that comes with the presence of inhabiting our bodies through grounding.

SAFETY & BELONGING

Fear of danger and not feeling welcomed (sense of belonging) are some of the most significant, and earliest developmental culprits inhibiting us from effectively grounding in our physicality. Some perinatal, meaning pre-birth, experts suggest that our parent's reaction upon receiving the news of being pregnant and especially directly after birth are the initial most important factors in a child feeling a sense of being welcomed, wanted, and belonging in the world. In the womb and as young children it is a fundamental need to feel safe and welcomed in the world. The degree to which our conception was wanted, how we were cared for during pregnancy, received at birth, stayed in connection with versus separated from our mother directly after birthing (and some even suggest the first 40 days of infancy) are all deeply impactful for a child's and eventually our adult capacity to feel safe, welcomed, settled and "grounded" in our body and the world.

Next in developmental impact is our primary caregivers' capacity to offer protection as well as attunement and responsiveness to our survival needs and distress, which can help our nervous system to regulate and be relaxed in our bodies. The degree to which we had a masculine protective energy around our home as well as the degree to which our parents, siblings, close relatives and friends were themselves embodied and grounded as when we were an infant and child, can potentially impact our ability as adults to feel safe in our body and the world with two feet on the ground, taking action in our lives. Therapist, Ray Castellino, renowned expert in family connection during pregnancy and infancy, describes the family as a social nervous system with a potential for *"harmonic resonance"* of coherence as a more or less stable or unstable base for the child to safely grow and develop. If there is high stress, emotional overwhelm, extreme poverty, or violence in the family environment or even the local cultural environment, it can impact our sense of having a grounded safe base in the world. Of course, life is dynamic and stressful moments or days are part of the natural cycles of life, but in general it is the parent's job to ensure that their children feel an overall sense of being safe, loved and protected. The point is not that we need to live in a sheltered utopia, nor that parents or siblings stop fighting, nor that stressful incidents stop happening, but rather how our caregivers protect the overall safety of home. If something is continuously unsafe, whether environmentally, bullying, abuse, etc., it is the parent's job to intervene to the best of their ability by providing a protective parental presence to restore connection and a greater sense of safe grounding for the family unit. If not, it can subtlety affect our nervous system's sense of safety and relaxation in the world until desensitized at a later time.

Many of us have experienced varying degrees of trauma, ranging from small emotional triggers we suppressed in the moment to extreme stressors, which can subtly, yet profoundly impact our nervous system with signals of *"it is not safe"*: to be me, to express myself, to feel or express emotion, to be in my body, to be in the world, etc. Other people have a deep fear of life, even terror, at *"being in their bodies"* and really struggle to feel deeply relaxed and grounded in the body—especially the legs and feet. For some of us, the natural danger scanner in our brain (amygdala) has gotten stuck in the hypervigilant state of over aroused danger scanning as opposed to a healthy safety protection function that can turn up in the face of real threat, but turns down and allows us to relax into a grounded base when our environment is safe. The paradox of this metaphor is that leaving our doors and windows unlocked and open while going out to constantly scan for danger leaves our system ungrounded and less empowered. As Eckhart Tolle said, *"if the Master is not present in the house, all sorts of shady characters can take up residence."* Our system is much better resourced when we are inhabiting our body in a more empowered, centered and grounded way.

Though it is on the decline, many children still actually physically play outside, play in the dirt, walk barefoot on the ground without shoes. Unfortunately, many schools are cutting physical education out of the curriculum, cognitive intelligence is exclusively prioritized, and youth begin sedentary lifestyles of television, video games and digital stimuli with less and less time moving their bodies outside and standing with two feet on the ground. All of these grounding and embodied activities help to develop our bodily nervous system so we can feel safer, resourced, confident, empowered and stand with two feet on the ground. For some, this process requires developing more body sensing and breath awareness or participating in fun activities like playing sports, movement classes or martial arts or by regularly practicing Qi Gong or power posing. While for others trauma desensitization and integration modalities such as *Somatic Experiencing and EMDR (Eye Movement Desensitization & Repatterning)* can provide an effective healing process to be able to feel relaxed, safe, grounded and empowered in our bodies.

GROUNDING, POWER POSING & CONFIDENCE

Amy Cuddy, Harvard Social Psychologist best-known for her second most viewed TED-Talk of all time *"Your Body Language Shapes who you are"*, confirms the science of grounding through power-posing, which induces physiological changes in our bodies that have us look and feel more empowered. She notes that many animals do it instinctually in nature, as do congenitally blind people when they're victorious in events—even when they have never seen it or been taught to do it. Cuddy and fellow researchers found that after a mere 2-minute standing power pose, the testosterone (confidence hormone) levels of the power posers rose 20%, while the cortisol (stress hormone) levels fell sharply. So, by taking 2 minutes to do a grounding power pose, participants, as measured internally by hormone levels, were subjectively and objectively more confident and less stressed. By contrast, when the participants spent 2 minutes in more disempowered and constricted bodily poses they experienced a decrease in testosterone (less confident) and an increase in cortisol (less relaxed). Their research findings concluded that grounding power poses caused individuals to experience increased feelings of power, confidence, and risk tolerance (testosterone) as well as decreased stress (cortisol). The researchers concluded that this *"would suggest that embodiment goes beyond cognition and emotion and could have immediate and actionable effects on physiology and behavior"*.

Being more embodied, grounded and empowered is just as important for leaders, as it is for all of us. While studying the science of presence, Amy Cuddy realized how universal the yearning for presence was. She writes, *"people in every corner of the world and in all walks of life are trying to work up the nerve to speak in class, to interview for a job, to audition for a role, to confront a daily hardship, to stand up for what they believe in, or just find peace being who they are."* [6] Not only does science confirm grounding power-posing has us feel more confident, stable and relaxed, but thousands of humans across the world in a whole spectrum of professions have written Cuddy inspiring testimonials about how they did a grounding power-pose before a crucial conversation, job interview, job promotion request, negotiation, first date, conflict, etc. and how much it changed their state, increased their sense of relaxation and empowerment in an important life situation and for others helped to progressively stabilize a sense of empowered groundedness over-time.

GROUNDING IN OUR CENTRAL AXIS & BEYOND

Groundedness in our body helps us to feel safe and resourced enough in our own center axis, also called self-referencing, to be available for connection with others. It is this sense of horizontal stability and vertical centeredness that enables a sense of embodied groundedness that is a first step towards inhabiting our own center and owning our personal space that lays an essential foundation for healthy boundaries. When this sense of being grounded in our own center is activated in our embodied experience, we don't have to isolate or withdraw to manufacture space for ourselves, instead our groundedness helps to fully inhabit our energetic space, which creates a natural healthy sense of boundary. In addition, groundedness is actually the doorway into the true groundless ground pointed to by various spiritual traditions. Some try to avoid life, the body and interpersonal relating through ascension, but we can't be the unified totality if we can't feel our feet on the ground, we are trying to escape life or avoid *anything*. Include and transcend everything my friend. Our body is literally our felt sense of *"home"* and the most important base for presence—a requirement that if not met limits our sense of relaxation, safety, confidence and empowerment. May we train our nervous system to feel grounded all throughout our life at work, in conversation, in conflict, waiting in line, standing, sitting, etc. As we relax down deep into our body, deep into the ground, including it all, Awareness expands in all directions. The Groundless Ground of all being includes our body as much as the rest of the totality. Even from this vantage, if attention can't find two feet on the ground, we may have taken a detour, so relax deep come back to the grounded center and include that too.

GROUNDING KEY SUMMARY & KEY TAKEAWAYS

- Feeling grounded in our feet & legs happens when we safe, welcomed, settled & at home in our body & the world.
- Not feeling & inhabiting our body down to our feet & legs is called dissociation (due to trauma, defense, emotional overwhelm, spiritual bypass or being hyper-mental).
- Grounding in our horizontal base & centering in our vertical axis allows feeling more stable, empowered & aligned like a tree.
- Harvard research by Amy Cuddy shows that just 2 minutes of standing power posing, increases confidence & decreases stress
- "If the Master is not present in the house, all sorts of shady characters can take up residence." — Eckhart Tolle
- Some spiritual practices foster dissociation—feeling unified with all includes our body, emotions & groundless ground of Awareness

EMOTION

How literate are you at noticing & naming
emotions in yourself, others & groups?

What **emotions** do you avoid or are you afraid to feel? Sadness, anger, shame, joy, disappointment, boredom?

What is your capacity for **emotional presence**
to fully accept, allow & feel the direct feeling sensations in your body, neither avoiding nor holding onto,
until naturally expressing & releasing?

WHAT IS **EMOTIONAL PRESENCE**

the capacity to notice, name, fully feel emotion in your body while witnessing, then fully release or express your feelings on your own or in connection with another, as well as allowing others to have their emotional experience & skillfully resolve emotional conflict

the capacity to **notice & name** emotions in your own body, others or a group
the capacity to **fully feel** your own emotions in the sweet spot of 1) feeling the sensations in your body 2) while simultaneously witnessing, & noticing the tendency to **avoid** (numbing, dissociating, suppressing, distracting, addiction) or **attach** (getting stuck in, hanging onto, hysterically looping or partially feeling while verbally dumping on others)
the capacity to **release & express** (after noticing, naming & fully feeling) **on your own or in connection** with another
the capacity to stay present & connected while **allowing others** to feel their own emotional experience without trying to fix it, be hyper-positive to talk them out of it or needing them to feel anything different (to a point unless their process is overly aggressive &disrespecting your own healthy boundaries)
the capacity to **skillfully resolve emotional conflict** & continually return to emotional vulnerability & connection

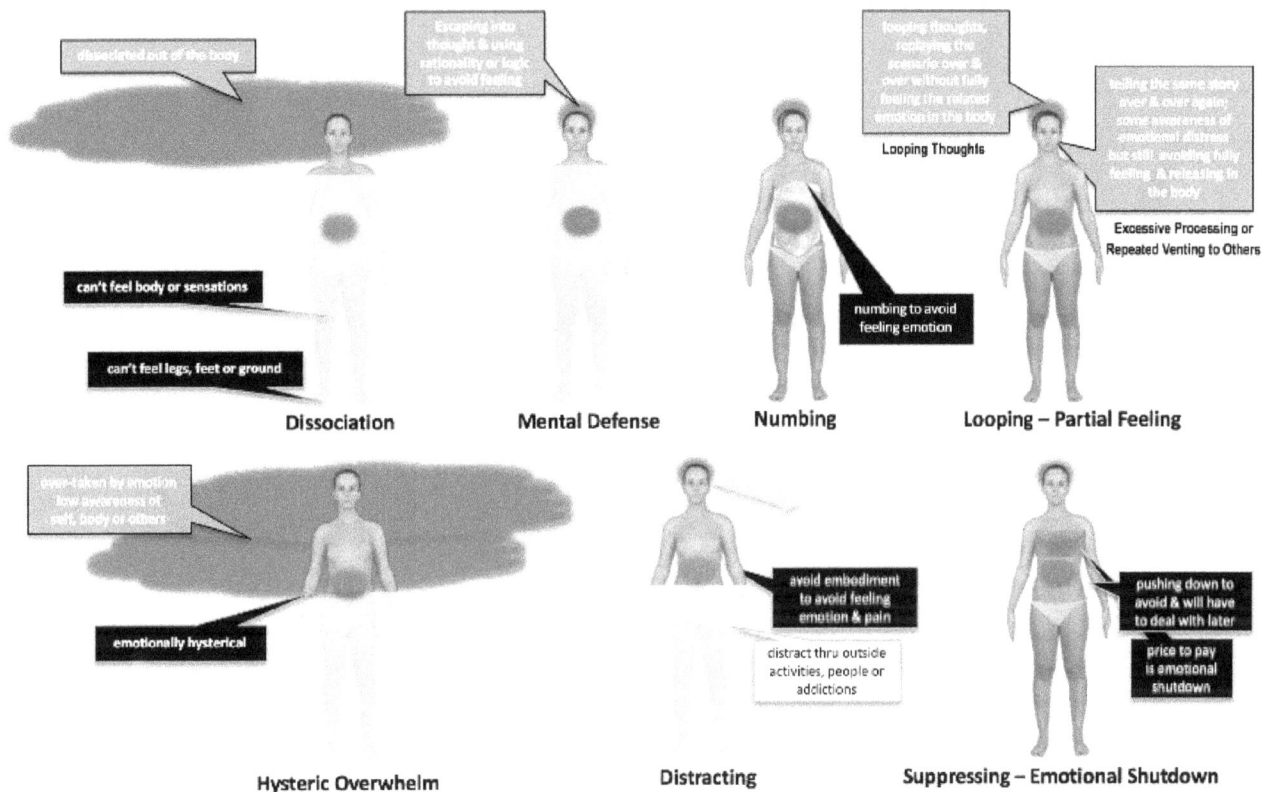

Dissociation — disassociated out of the body — can't feel body or sensations — can't feel legs, feet or ground

Mental Defense — Escaping into thought & using rationality or logic to avoid feeling

Numbing — numbing to avoid feeling emotion

Looping Thoughts — looping thoughts, replaying the scenario over & over without fully feeling the related emotion in the body

Looping – Partial Feeling — telling the same story over & over again; some awareness of emotional distress but still avoiding fully feeling & releasing in the body — Excessive Processing or Repeated Venting to Others

Hysteric Overwhelm — over-taken by emotion, low awareness of self, body or others — emotionally hysterical

Distracting — avoid embodiment to avoid feeling emotion & pain — distract thru outside activities, people or addictions

Suppressing – Emotional Shutdown — pushing down to avoid & will have to deal with later — price to pay is emotional shutdown

"Suppression is keeping a lid on our emotions, pushing them back down, denying them, repressing them and pretending that they don't exist. Any emotion that comes into Awareness and is not fully felt and expressed or released is automatically stored in our body-mind"

— Hale Dwoskin —

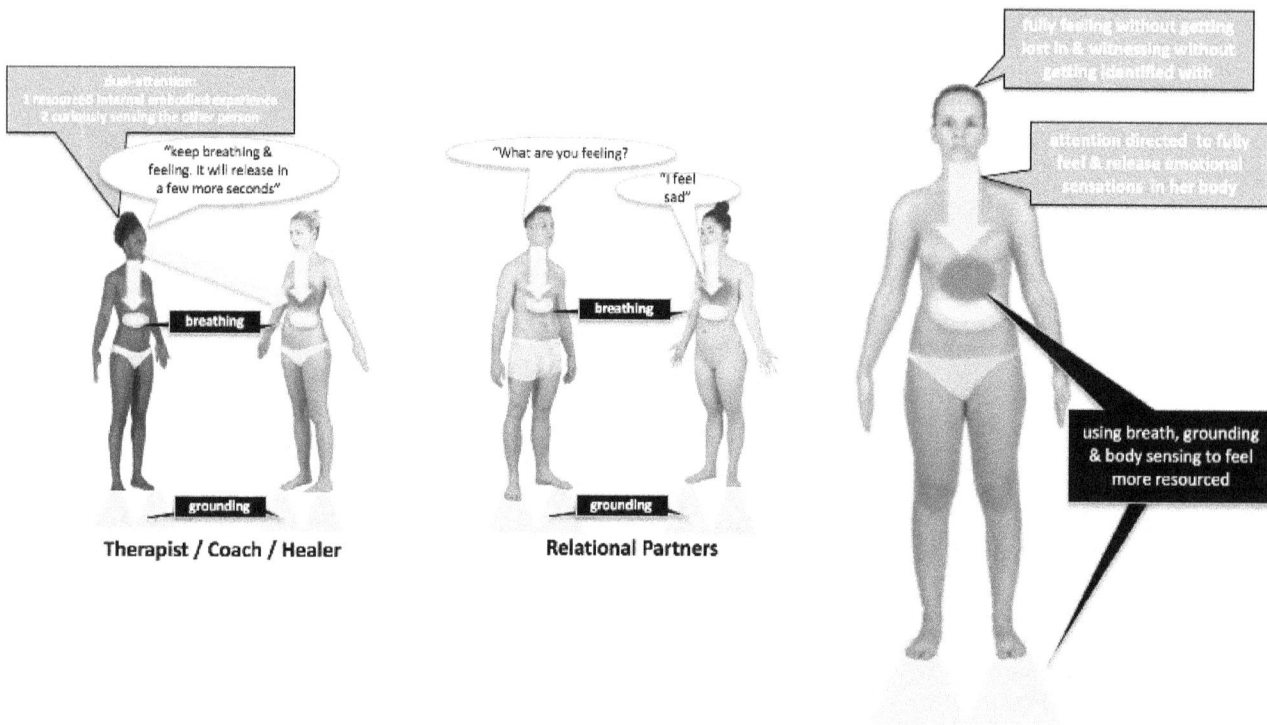

Therapist / Coach / Healer

"keep breathing & feeling. it will release in a few more seconds"

dual-attention:
1 resourced internal embodied experience
2 curiously sensing the other person

breathing

grounding

Relational Partners

"What are you feeling?"

"I feel sad"

breathing

grounding

fully feeling without getting lost in & witnessing without getting identified with

attention directed to fully feel & release emotional sensations in her body

using breath, grounding & body sensing to feel more resourced

WHY DOES **EMOTIONAL PRESENCE** MATTERS

Aliveness: allows us to feel life flowing through us

Guidance System: provides sensory information guiding our survival & functionality in the world

Decision-Making: an essential part of decisions & actions: informing & guiding interests, desire, motivation, inspiration & action

Connection & Intimacy: emotional awareness & vulnerability is the doorway to connection & intimacy

Empathy: emotional literacy & shared emotional resonance allows us to feel others & their experience

Group Coherence: sensing the emotional flavor & coherence of a group or room allows us share the resonance or redirect the state

Emotional Freedom: learning to fully feel the full spectrum of emotions & express or release into greater emotional freedom

Wholeness: learning how emotional triggers & shadows can point us to healing & awareness for greater love, freedom & wholeness

Conflict Resolution: skillfully navigating emotional conflict, faster recovery time, growing from each interaction & deepening in connection

BARRIERS TO **EMOTIONAL PRESENCE**

Dissociation: not feeling & inhabiting your body due to trauma, defense or hyper-mental

Hyper-Mental: excessive mental activity, overly theoretical, living in fantasy, lost in the past or future

Low Body Sensing: emotions are experienced in the body & insufficient body sensing inhibits emotional awareness

Emotional Distraction: using thought, devices, addictions, substances, or activities to avoid feeling body sensations

Emotional Numbness: numbing your emotional sensing due to past trauma or emotional overwhelm to avoid feeling pain

Emotional Overwhelm: inability to feel & release emotions, result in strategies like numbing & dissociation to reduce overwhelm

Emotion & Trauma: dead zones, suppressed emotions or body-stored trauma that keeps attention stuck in the body or dissociated

Emotionally Unsafe: not feeling safe as a child or in some past relations to feel & express your emotions

Pride or Disowned Emotionality: pride masking discomfort with emotion, staying mental, fear of or not allowing certain emotions

Gender Stereotype: believing or associating emotionality with a certain gender which could threaten identity

Invulnerability: ego-defenses & protection that prevent us from feeling

Hyper-Positive: disowning any thoughts or emotions other than positivity

Don't know how to Release: habitual suppression, believe supposed to manage or don't know how to fully feel & let go

Judging Emotions: judging certain emotions & believing you should not be feeling them

Spiritual Bypassing: using spiritual practices & beliefs to avoid your emotions, body, life & participation in the world

"One of the deepest feminine pleasures is when a man stands full, present, and unreactive in the midst of his woman's emotional storms. When he stays present with her, and loves her through the layers of wildness and closure, then she feels his trustability and can relax."

– David Deida –

EMOTIONAL PRESENCE DEVELOPMENT SUCCESS STORY

Cathy was an elite athlete who secretly had a habit of overeating and then excessively exercising to punish herself, burn off the calories and make up for it. In addition to enhancing self-care, we desensitized a major childhood trauma and helped her learn to be more aware of her emotions, to fully feel them in her body and to release them. Instead of using overeating food to numb her feelings or live a life in scattered chaos, she learned to ground down in her body so she could be more relaxed and resourced to feel and release her feelings. During our six months together, she ended up losing 30lbs., but it happened effortlessly, as for the first time in more than a decade of punishment, she started positively focusing on self-care, being more emotionally aware and loving to her body. Today she is a peak performance coach for professional athletes helping them optimize both their physical performance and emotional well-being.

Emotions are one of our primary information sources about ourselves, others and the surrounding world. In their most fundamental functional forms, fear helps keep us safe, desire helps us move towards goals, anger fuels determination and helps protect our personal boundary, joy allows us to celebrate, etc. The Latin root of **emotion** means to *"move through and out"*. Some, in the vein of Einstein's E=mc2, think of emotion as subtle *"energy (e) in motion"*. Emotions once thought to be random and irrational—which they can be at lower levels of emotional intelligence—are now understood to be an information signaling and processing system designed to quickly sense and reorganize behavior for survival.[1] Emotions can guide preferences, desires, needs, actions and are actually an important part of the decision-making process. Studies of people with damaged emotional brain centers show that they lose their discernment of direction in life as well as struggle with decisions due to a now evenly weighted multiplicity of options. Emotions were also once thought to come exclusively from the right brain, which is now considered an over-simplification. And while it's true, as commonly believed, that the female brain may experience emotions more intensely than the male brain, if men are not emotionally numb they too are potentially capable of experiencing the same emotions. Finally, different people have varying degrees of capacities for emotional presence and being with emotional intensity in themselves and others.

So, emotion if felt and expressed or released can be a transient information source that we experience through our bodies. We are emotionally more aware when: an emotion arises, we are aware of it, allow it to be, fully feel it for a short while and release it on its own or express it in relation with another. However, emotions are not always comfortable. Often with much tension, intensity and emotional discomfort in our bodies, it is easier to allow our attention to predominate in the mental world of looping related thoughts, past memory, future fantasy, conceptualizations, external distractions or addictions. Yet, we cannot get through the doorway of presence to our fuller potential, authentic happiness and embodied presence without greater emotional awareness and freedom. In order to experience really nourishing, authentic, evolving and connected relationships, we need to be more emotionally aware. Interpersonal relationships can be the domain in which we experience the most emotional beauty and distress: pleasure, gratitude, joy, attraction, personal love, as well as fear, sadness, disappointment, anger, hurt, rejection, and loss. Any emotions we are not willing to feel are parcels of power we bury in our bodies. The price for admission to greater presence is becoming intimate with everything that is arising in Awareness and for many of us, especially our bodies and emotions. The clearer and more attuned our emotional awareness instrument is, the more we can be aware of in ourselves, others and our surroundings. Sensations are the doorway to a deeper connection to ourselves, others and life around us. As our emotional awareness develops, we are increasingly able to maintain presence and feel the sensations of both the more pleasurable emotions and the less comfortable ones temporarily, before they are naturally expressed or released.

BECOMING MORE EMOTIONALLY AWARE

Sometimes it is not easy being human and emotionality is often flavors of the richest beauty, as well as the deepest sufferings in our human life experience. Compounding this, our culture has certain beliefs and ways of experiencing and expressing emotions, different genders have different biological and culturally conditioned ways of expressing emotions, and most of us were not taught emotional intelligence in school, nor by our families growing up. In fact, many of us probably got messages about suppressing or inappropriate expressions of emotions as children. So with all that considered, breathe a sigh of relief. Let us go easy on ourselves while remembering that we're all learning and that emotional awareness is a really important aspect of presence and becoming more fully human.

Ideally healthy bonding, attunement, empathy and verbal acknowledgment from our caregivers as children helped us to learn emotional intelligence. Since this probably did not happen so well for most of us and emotional intelligence was not taught in most schools in the 20th century, most us have had to do the best we could to learn greater emotional awareness and releasing. In reality, many of us are not aware of what we are sensing and feeling moment to moment in our bodies throughout our day. Emotions are not always comfortable or easy to *"deal with"*; sometimes we are unconscious of them, distract ourselves mentally, avoid feeling by engaging in activities, leave our bodies or use substances to numb the feelings.

With the latest fMRI brain imaging technology, we can now look inside normal brains and observe, in real time, when an emotion arises and how it can be processed. Dan Siegel notes that emotional self-regulation can be challenging for teenagers, particularly because the brain is still developing, especially the pre-frontal regions that allow fear emotional regulation, fear modulation, empathy and moral awareness, well into our mid 20's.[2]   Even as adults, emotional triggering happens when these more mature frontal regions go offline, losing blood flow and brain activity, and our reptilian brain takes over. Brain imaging research at UCLA by Matthew Lieberman demonstrates that the simple act of naming an emotion without further talking begins to reduce emotional intensity in the emotional limbic brain.[3] *"Name it to tame it"* Lieberman reminds us. Being able to name an emotion, is the first step in emotional awareness, demonstrates a capacity to notice, allow, and be with sensations rather than being overwhelmingly over-taken by, trying to dump on others or suppressing.

Many of us have a limited range of the emotions we allow ourselves to feel. Some groups that teach an introduction to emotional intelligence start with 5 basic emotions: joy, mad, sad, glad, and shame. For many of us, this is the appropriate starting place. Once we start to explore our emotional landscape and emotional past, we realize that there is a whole lot more than 5, each with varying flavors and intensities. We might have noticed certain unique tendencies that we have in relating to our emotions: ways in which we avoid, judge, suppress, numb, emotionally shut-down, leave our bodies, try to dump on others, go into the mental story, or overall bypassing feeling emotion in our body.

Initially, when we start to increase our feeling awareness, our limbic emotional brain region tends to flood with activity while our body floods with intensity. Because we experience emotions through our bodies, and our breath is often correlated with our emotional state, the development of emotional awareness is closely related with body sensing and breath awareness. As we increase our capacity for body sensing and emotional awareness, we can develop greater emotional presence which allows us to *intimately be with* emotional sensations in our body. For many of us, the moment we give ourselves permission that *it is okay to feel* is the most significant threshold on the emotional awareness and freedom journey. The more we practice allowing ourselves to temporarily feel whatever is arising—pain, discomfort, anger, hurt, vulnerability, sadness, joy, excitement, etc.—the more we strengthen our emotional intelligence muscles and attune our instrument to the ever-changing landscape of sensory experience and the more we open our systems to the vital flow of life through us.

Remember that learning greater emotional intelligence is a process. Especially as we are beginning to become more emotionally aware and allowing ourselves to feel, here are some helpful reminders:

- "It's okay to feel"
- "Men & women both have emotions"
- "It's safe for me to feel"
- "Stay out of the story; don't talk, just feel"
- "I experience emotions but I am not my emotions"
- "It's okay for me to feel this emotion & my whole body"

JUDGING EMOTIONS

Just as we can judge our behavior, we also judge our emotions, adding even more intensity to the original emotion. We live in a culture and time in which we are led to believe we are supposed to be confident and happy, all the time, so these feelings tend to be considered *"good"*, while states of sadness and vulnerability are often considered *"bad"* or *"weak"*. More neutrally exploring our emotional landscape and removing the good/bad labels from emotions is an essential step to greater emotional freedom. The judgments we have about our emotions are often linked to beliefs we have adopted throughout our conditioning from parents and teachers as children and or peers as young adults. *"Put on a happy face"*, *"put on your game face"*, *"don't worry be happy"*, *"it's all good"*, etc. are all cultural admonitions that encourage us to put on a mask over the authenticity of what we are feeling.

Because many people do not know that emotions naturally complete themselves when we fully feel them and express or release them, instead of ineffectively dealing with the discomfort, we use any number of the varying strategies previously mentioned to avoid feeling them. So rather than fully accepting without judgement, fully feeling even for a short time and then releasing, instead we judge *"I should not be feeling a certain emotion right now"* or that *"certain emotions are not acceptable to feel or express"*. These are important hindrances to greater emotional presence, range and freedom. Becoming aware of the judgments of our emotions and liberating those beliefs can be a huge emotional freedom breakthrough. One of the key points to remember with emotions is that we want to adopt a soft attitude towards them instead of taking a hard-core *"I have to get rid of it"* attitude; because in that approach often lies a lot of judgment and/or resentment that it is not okay to be feeling this right now. And when we apply judgment to our emotions, it takes us out of the direct experience of feeling, increases the intensity and adds another emotional layer on top of the original emotion. So, let us go easy on ourselves and remember to try to *"allow things to be"* as they arise, instead of forcing it and trying to immediately get rid of some feelings. Relax into them and start to enjoy the incredible power that we'll discover that comes from deeper awareness of the many dimensions of our emotional worlds.

AVOIDANCE

Many of us, perhaps without having the skills of more effective emotional processing, often choose to avoid the discomfort by engaging in activities, distracting ourselves, using substances to numb the feelings, or suppressing the emotions to store them for later. In one fMRI study at Stanford by James Gross, suppressed emotion built up and while the participants tried not to show any outward expression, their body became more tense, exacerbating future emotionally charged situations; in addition, their brain showed more stressed activation as opposed to the group that more effectively processed their emotions in real time. Despite our unconscious or clever subconscious attempts to suppress our awareness of emotions, they continue to affect us anyway. Dan Siegel confirms that *"research has shown repeatedly that even without conscious awareness, neural input from the internal world of body* and emotion influences our reasoning *and* our decision-making. *Even facial expressions that we're not aware of and changes in* heart rhythm we may not notice directly affect how we feel and how we perceive the world. In other words, you can run but you cannot hide."[5]

Alexander Lowen, a physician and psychotherapist who originally studied under Wilhelm Reich who developed *Bioenergetics* similarly confirms the numbing of body sensing and gets more specific as to why if a person cannot feel their body:

> *"it is because he is afraid to perceive or sense his feelings. When feelings have a threatening quality, they are generally suppressed. This is done by developing chronic muscular tensions that do not allow any flow of excitation or spontaneous movement to develop in the relevant areas. People often suppress their fear because it has a paralyzing effect, their rage because it is too dangerous, and their despair because it is too discouraging. They will also suppress their awareness of pain, such as the pain of an unfulfilled longing, because they cannot support that pain. The suppression of feeling diminishes the state of excitation in the body and decreases the ability of the mind to focus. It is the prime cause for the loss of mind power. Mostly our minds are preoccupied with the need to be in control at the expense of being and feeling more alive."* [6]

Our culture tends to encourage us to avoid our feelings by numbing ourselves with activities or substances. *"I had a rough day, okay? Leave me alone", "...I need a drink", "...I need a cigarette"*, etc. As an example, imagine on our computer desktop we have a program open and we can try to minimize it temporarily or put the computer on sleep mode, but as soon as we turn it back on, the program is still running in the background, slowing down its overall functional power. In other words, the emotion (program) is still there in our body (on our computer desktop). Interestingly, eating refined sugar provides an initial endorphin release that temporarily alters brain chemistry away from a primary focus on an emotionally charged event. However, in the not too distant future, this effect wears off and the event remains just as emotionally charged. Maybe we have noticed this in our own life. The experience of life happens in our bodies and so do our emotions, so not feeling our emotions is kind of like avoiding life or denying a part of ourselves—certainly moving in the direction away from greater presence. Yet, sometimes emotions can feel so intense, so overwhelming, so unsafe to feel or express, and so uncomfortable that there is usually there's a part of this that doesn't really want to feel these emotions in our body. Our culture makes it even more challenging by making it seem *"normal"* to avoid these feelings by distracting ourselves with technology or substances, suppressing *"bad emotions"* and remaining stoic or putting on a smile, mentalizing our emotions, taking a numbing medication at the slightest onset of pain, or soothing ourselves with substances like food, drugs, or alcohol. Yet, these distractions are temporary, because these emotions are information that is not being processed, not allowed to be felt and moved through. Remember the Latin root meaning of emotion is *'to move through or out"*; so to emote involves actual feeling and expressing or releasing. When we suppress, partially feel or attach to our emotions, they get stuck in our body-mind. Process with it now or store it for later reducing our power, energy, aliveness and openness until we do deal with them.

PARTIAL FEELING

In addition to suppression and avoidance, there are also partial feeling activities that we engage in such as mentally talking about our emotions, crying while we're still talking a.k.a. cry-talking, verbalizing and dumping on someone else, or blaming and lashing out aggressively at others. With partial feeling strategies we partially know we are emotionally distressed and there is more awareness than suppression and avoidance. However, instead of directing our attention into the sensations in the body and fully feeling it until it is allowed to be processed and released, we can escape into the mental domain, while only partially feel the sensations of the emotion in our body. Another way of partial feeling is through looping thoughts in which we have an unresolved, emotionally-charged event that by way of these looping thoughts is trying to get conscious attention in order to be integrated. This is a signal that we need to pause and fully feel in our body or do an emotional freedom technique, so the emotional charge can be fully felt, expressed or released and *then* the wisdom and understanding extracted from the emotion.

We can probably all relate to moments in our lives when we've used some of these methods or had one deeper-rooted unresolved trigger that snagged on and amplified lots of our smaller issues. Or, maybe we can remember times when we had partial awareness of feeling *"emotional"* or *"triggered"* without really being aware of what we were specifically feeling. Here, we are aware of a change of emotional state but are only able or choose to partially feel our emotions. Perhaps we *"felt triggered"* or *"just emotional"* or *"out of control"* or *"overwhelmed"* or tried to *"verbally dump"* what we were feeling on somebody else or got *"stuck in a loop"* of *"endless processing"*, etc.—all of these describe moments in which we were partially feeling emotions while still stuck in them. Whatever our primary means of emotional processing is, most of us are doing the best we can because usually we do not know another more emotionally skilled way.

Many conventional mental health professionals make up all kinds of cognitive diversions that help us be more rational or to mentally talk about emotions but ultimately they, too, are advocating avoiding feeling or partially feeling the emotions directly in the body. And if we do a cognitive technique or something else to temporarily distract ourselves from feeling— such as taking a walk—it might change our state temporarily, but when we think about the emotionally charged event, is it still there? The difference between using an emotional freedom technique or fully feeling and releasing as opposed to a distraction method is: *"when we think about that event, do we still feel an emotional charge in our body?"* If we are not fully feeling and releasing our emotions, they get stuck and at the end of the day we have lots of tension, stagnation, and emotionally charged baggage in our body-mind. Recent research suggests that emotions are an embodied phenomenon and actually originate not just in the brain (limbic emotional zone and the brainstem) but are more broadly dispensed in the body proper, especially the face, throat, chest and belly.[7]

RESISTANCE TO WHAT IS

Initially as we are learning to feel, there is disorientation as in *"What are these sensations in my body?"* or *"I don't want to be feeling this."* Sometimes we can fear it will be:

- uncomfortable
- too intense
- overwhelming
- out of control
- if we start feeling it will never end

These are tricks of the mind that keep us from actually fully feeling and then expressing or releasing. Ultimately life asks us to paradoxically accept the moment exactly as it is from an absolute perspective while we and everything we see in the relative world continues to evolve. The latter holds the evolutionary potential of life forms and in that we can evolve—in this case heal our past and learn greater emotional awareness. Each time we practice feeling, our emotional intelligence grows like a muscle as body and brain learn how to stay with and fully feel these sensations for a short period of time so that they can be registered, felt and released.

FEEL BEFORE THE STORY

Have we ever been triggered by something and then we told the same story to three or more friends, yet we still felt an emotional charge on the event? It is not that there is inherently anything wrong with recounting a story, but most people do it in a less than optimal order—too quickly going into the mental story, while their emotional brain and body are still triggered. Immediately after fully feeling and expressing or releasing, is a better time to really reflect, analyze, learn, extract wisdom and understand the experience. Staying out of the mental content of the story and first fully feeling the sensations in our bodies is probably one of the most important keys to gaining greater emotional freedom. For most people, especially as we are learning to feel more of our whole body awareness, any talking for more than a few words or a simple sentence while we are still emotionally triggered is an escape from really fully feeling our emotions, which paradoxically prolongs the process of the charged nature of these emotions.

Interpersonally, there's a way in which we can still be with someone and feel our feelings while staying connected with the other person but instead of going in a complete full story, actually just simply saying I feel _____, without initially continuing with more commentary or talking. Instead we can drop our attention down into the sensations in the body or in the cloud of emotion. Isn't that the opposite of what most of us do? We look for validation in the stories that bubble out of a partially felt emotion in an attempt to release the emotional charge; yet partially feeling and mentalizing first, actually prolongs the process.

When we express the same story to several different people, we are trying to get rid of the emotional discomfort related to the event but we're not fully feeling the uncomfortable feelings required to fully release the emotions and we're usually really making the suffering endure longer because we emphasize the content of our stories more than the direct sensory emotional experience. After all, it is the body that feels and stores all of these emotions; the body authentically knows how we feel and we will hold onto everything unintegrated or unprocessed unless we allow each emotion to be felt and flow through us via expression or release. Again, this is not to say that it is not important to extract wisdom and lessons from emotionally charged experiences but rather, feel and release first before trying to analyze them for meaning and wisdom.

The neurophysiological support for this is that when we are emotionally triggered, as much as 70% of our brain activity and blood flow activates our limbic emotional brain, rather than the front of our brain where we are more clear and relaxed. Research ^7 has demonstrated that emotional freedom techniques have been shown to relax the nervous system and decrease brain activity (particularly in the emotional limbic system, amygdala, and midbrain) involved in the stress response while restoring blood flow and brain activity to the front of the brain (prefrontal cortex and neocortex) where we think more clearly and calmly. The process of fully feeling is not always easy at the beginning as our ability to stay with discomfort until it is naturally ready to release must be developed. Let us remember if we are talking more than a few words, while we still feel an emotional charge in our body, we are probably not fully feeling it and it might not fully be able to release.

FULLY FEELING WITHOUT IDENTIFYING

Ultimately we want to be able to fully feel our emotions, but there's a subtle distinction to be aware of in feeling without identifying with the emotion. Consider the common statements in our language *"I'm angry"* or *"I'm sad,"* which are common phrases in our culture but we don't really consider the relationship to personal self-identification. For a common analogy, some sports fans talk about *"their"* sports team using the pronoun *"we"* as in *"we played well today"*. More precisely, the team played well while we watched on the couch, but such statements reveal that the person's identity is confusingly entangled with a team of which he or she is technically not a member.

Returning to emotions, consider that *"I feel emotions but my identity is not that 'I am my emotions."* It is essential to feel grounded in body and maintain our sense of self as larger than the emotion, whether that container is our whole body or spaciousness without boundaries. With *"hurt"* in the context of a relationship as the example, I might feel sensations related to hurt in the center of my chest or heart. However, rather than saying *"I am hurt"* and getting lost in the emotion, ideally we maintain larger witness or spacious Awareness as we breathe, while maintaining connection with our partner we can express *"I feel hurt"* (maybe even pointing to the area where we feel it while focusing primary attention on the direct sensory experience).

Sometimes we do not feel emotions localized in certain bodily areas but rather as clouds of emotion. This is common with sadness. Rather than becoming identified with and sucked into the sadness, we can feel the cloud of sadness with eyes open looking up and still maintaining larger bodily and/or spacious Awareness, naming it in saying *"I feel sad,"* and staying in the direct sensory experience until the emotion releases. On the shorter end of the spectrum this can take 30 seconds to a few minutes, or sometimes longer, but if fully felt will often release or feel like it is off-gassing. In the moment of intensity, remember that *"I am NOT the emotion but it is passing through me,"* and in order to do so, it needs to be fully felt and acknowledged. We recall the root of emotion is *"to move through and out"*, so neither avoid it, nor identify with the sensations.

GETTING STUCK IN A FEELING

On the other end of the spectrum from avoiding and distracting ourselves from our emotions is to actually hang on and get stuck in a feeling. If avoiding or suppressing is comparable to sticking our dirty clothes under the bed and pretending they are not in the room, then getting stuck in a feeling is like hanging on to it without letting it go and dragging it around throughout the day with us. When we have emotionally charged looping thoughts, mentally going over and over all of the details, endless interpretations, or what *"should"* or *"shouldn't"* have happened, we tend to feel even worse and it is a waste of a lot of mental and emotional energy which can feel draining of our overall vitality and resources.

Sometimes, we even tell ourselves *"I'm not ready to let this one go, because…."*. Have we ever noticed an inner dialogue saying that about someone or about something? Sometimes, in an interpersonal conflict, it is in the highest good to skillfully express the emotion in connected presence with someone else as we share the impact they had on us. Other times when the aggression is beyond reasonable, it might be better to disengage for our own safety and let things cool down before returning. But we can also hang on to an emotion as we try to subconsciously punish that person with underhanded jabs, sarcasm, judgment, biting comments, or passive-aggressive behavior. In such cases, when we choose to hang on to the emotion out of spite, not only are we hurting our partner but we are actually hurting ourselves. As we increasingly learn to enhance our emotional processing muscle, we become increasingly aware of the subtle choice points we have—to either stay attached to the emotion, avoid/suppress it, or fully feel and express it or release, which enables us to return to connection and then extract the wisdom.

FULLY FEELING, THEN EXPRESSION & RELEASING

We have discussed some of the detours we can take along the way of emotional processing; so now what do we actually do? As we said, the first step is always noticing an emotional state change and then naming it. Next we must develop a certain degree of presence from the previously discussed embodiment skills, *Breathing, Grounding* and *Body Sensing* to create enough resource to be able to stay present with the emotional intensity in our bodies long enough so that it can be felt, metabolized and expressed or released. Some of the more effective body-oriented psychotherapies like *Somatic Experiencing* spend significant time in initially working with someone to help their nervous system learn to breathe, ground and feel more safely resourced in their body. Once this is available and a person has passed the gauntlet of avoidance and partial feeling, then he or she can relax into fully feeling the emotion. This means simply directing the attention to the most intense sensations in the body and breathing in almost a meditative fashion, being careful not to get distracted by thoughts. Sometimes these sensations might be pain, tension, ache, heat, nausea, emptiness, numbness, etc. as the emotion is arising out of the body and becoming more consciously aware.

As we are learning greater emotional intelligence it can be very helpful to do this in the presence, of someone who can offer their relaxed quiet open presence. We are social organisms and in childhood need to learn to regulate our own bodies and emotions in relation with resourced caregivers. In Interpersonal Neurobiology there is a saying that it takes two brains to regulate one. Of course, at higher levels of embodied presence and emotional intelligence we can learn to feel and release emotions on our own but it can be very helpful and much faster in the safe relation of another's presence. Sometimes an emotion might only require being felt for 30 seconds while others might take a minute or two but there is usually a moment when the emotion is ready to release, like when the toast is done and it pops up. Similarly, when an emotion has been fully felt it can off-gas naturally, or release through crying, shaking, sighing, changes in breath, yawning and even burping. If you ever see me yawning when working with someone in emotional presence it is not because I am bored, but rather it is a gentler way of discharging emotional residue after it has been sufficiently felt.

Watch out for subtle attempts to try to get rid of the emotion before feeling them; they can get offended and tend to stick around. To better understand this dynamic think of it like a Chinese finger trap: if we try to pull our fingers out they get stuck, but if we relax them and actually move closer to the center, then the trap releases and in life so too will the emotion when it is ready. Sometimes an emotion can be felt and released quickly in a minute or two of presence, while other times we might need to really accept the feelings as if we would feel it for a long time and then at some point in minutes or an hour later it might spontaneously release. In general, if an emotion lasts for longer than hours or a day, it might be helpful to contact a body-oriented coach, healer or therapist, or even a trusted friend skilled in presence to help us feel the emotion at a deeper level. Another important note here is that current emotions tend to be more on the surface and can be felt and cleared more easily while sometimes emotions stored from the past can be deeper, take longer to clear and really benefit from the additional support of someone skilled in emotional presence.

It is important to note the difference between **emotional expressing** and **emotional releasing**. Emotional expression is a more external cathartic style characterized either by crying, journaling, expressive dance or doing real-time authentic expression in the moment. We might use one or more of these as our emotional go-to and can be quite effective in certain situations. There are also newer types of emotional releasing modalities that are more subtle and less traumatic such as embodied or somatic psychotherapy, *Somatic Experiencing, Sedona Method, Luminous Awareness* and subtle energy work that support feeling and releasing. Most of these methods again are quite subtle and oftentimes tearless but allow us to actually focus our attention, go into the sensations in our body and then release it so there is no longer an associated emotional charge on the person or event an hour, day, week, or month later on. While these methods can help us safely and effectively release unintegrated emotions from the past, which is essential for deeper presence and openness, but ultimately they can help us learn to engage in greater emotional presence and the ability to feel and express or release emotions in the immediacy of the moment.

MULTIPLE EMOTIONS - ASPECTS & GETTING TO THE CORE

Sometimes emotions can be overwhelming and sometimes they can feel so uncomfortable that we just do not want to deal with them. They can feel like a heavy stagnant weight pressing on us or a jumbled conglomeration of painful sensations and discomfort. We humans are complex beings and often we feel multiple emotions, yet sometimes we feel like such a mess we do not even know where to start. However, as with most things we start small by taking the first step. In this case, as we scan our body for the most intense sensation, starting by simply naming the sensations that feel most pronounced or intense, and continuing to do so one at a time until we get to the core. Often underneath is an essential spacious freedom and peace. So this brings us to the concept of surface versus core/primary emotions.

As an example, sometimes when we feel hurt, instead of vulnerably showing that and feeling the pain of the hurt, anger arises secondarily on the surface to protect our vulnerability. That anger might be justified in helping to protect our boundaries when we were hurt or the anger can turn into aggression manifest verbally or physically toward another person. In the later case, we feel aggression on top of anger on top of hurt. Ideally, we can notice the hurt the instant it is felt and vulnerably share that with the other person or at least name that we feel anger, and in being intimate with that without verbally trying to dump it on the other person, as we feel and release the anger. Only then can we then get to what might be the deeper core as we fully feel, express and share the core vulnerable hurt.

The other major concept with multiple emotions is past trigger versus present emotion. Perhaps we have had the experience where we get really triggered by something that seems mentally quite trivial yet our bodily reaction seems disproportionately intense. When this occurs we realize, it might actually be triggering something deeper that is unresolved from the past. We could work with whatever was presently arising in the body, but at a certain point we might ask *"does this remind me of anything from the past?"* In this moment, I am feeling _____ (*whatever the current experience is*). After we have felt and released the present triggered emotion, sometimes just going back and scanning our body will connect us to the past event or root. Powerful questions we can ask to get to the deeper core are as follows:

- *"Is there a pattern of recurrent feelings here?"*
- *"When was the worst or the first time I felt this?"*
- *"What does this remind me of from my past?"*

Now remember working with multiple emotions is a more advanced aspect of the emotional processing skill, but it is important to lay the foundation and plant the seeds of understanding for more in-depth future capacities. For now, just start the most predominant pattern of sensations or emotion at a time, and slowly but surely, peel away the layers, past and present, to experience greater emotional freedom, openness and presence. Letting go and clearing the past takes a little time and we go event by event, but our overall real-time emotional awareness, fully feeling and expressing or releasing in real time in everyday life is what this process is all about. So be patient, go easy, and allow ourselves to be in the learning process. Imagine that it is like learning a new athletic move and it takes a little time and there's a little bit of a learning curve, but eventually we all can learn greater emotional awareness and realize freedom from the past and in the moment.

RECOVERY TIME

We are probably all aware of situations when we felt emotionally triggered by someone or something, but did not pause and properly process it. Instead we spent the next few hours or rest of the day with looping thoughts about it, partially ruminating on it, partially feeling lingering discomfort and partially trying to distract ourselves or focus on something else. One goal of emotional presence is to focus on Recovery time—meaning taking less and less time to fully feel, express or release and return to openness, connection, and emotional freedom—and to increasingly process emotions in the moment to so that we do not take emotional residue in our system with us into the future. Thus we aim for less and less moments with leftover emotional remains. We should scan our body and ask if we still feel a charge on a particular person or event, and if so work on our emotional processing skills. The more unprocessed emotional baggage we carry with us the less presence and free-attentional energy we have for our work, relationships, and future situations. Our practice is to increasingly keep our emotional body clear and our loving heart open. If not, life has a way of poking us in the places we resist, have a yet unhealed an open wound or feel stuck.

It should be briefly mentioned that the goal is to focus on recovery time, not necessarily to never be emotionally triggered, although as we continue to develop, conflicts might bother us less and happen less often. However, just as the tension between Earth's tectonic plates can periodically create earthquakes, on a larger level this is part of the Earth's growth and development. So too, some amount of relational conflicts can create greater awareness, foster needed communication or serve at least one person's development. Sometimes healthy anger can fuel our determination to rise above our circumstances, illuminate something that was previously unconscious interpersonally that needs to be looked at or maintain healthy boundaries. The healthier more integrated version of ourselves should neither fear conflict nor necessarily seek it out. If we find ourselves continuously processing, generating fights or avoiding possible conflict of important conversations, perhaps this is something to look at more deeply and perhaps enlist some outside support of a therapist.

Ultimately, emotional processing is not about never feeling certain emotions and always being happy but rather more importantly to fully feel everything and then to be able to express or release it. Therefore, let us focus on recovery time and increasing the speed and skill with which we become aware of emotional charge, fully feel it, name and express it or release it before returning to openness, connection and peace—that is emotional freedom.

TRAUMA & CLEARING THE PAST

As we discussed in the *Body Sensing section*, we tend to falsely think of trauma as severe PTSD with abuse victims and war veterans, but most if not all of us humans have emotions from the past that were not fully felt in the moment and instead we numbed our body or dissociated out of the body to avoid feeling the discomfort. Also, remember in that in a previous section, we discussed the related research and book *Your Body Keeps Score*, so know that our body holds our unfelt, unintegrated, unreleased emotional past. Sometimes this has us want to avoid feeling certain emotions or all emotion by closing down our emotional body, because if we did allow ourselves to open and feel it might touch in on a jumble of that emotion stored from our past.

Our emotional past does not go away because we talk about it; we cannot heal and resolve past emotional charge with our mental world alone. It requires a more integrated nervous system, including body sensing, emotion and mental thoughts, and in some cases can be greatly quickened when done relationally. In one trauma desensitization method, they have something called a **Personal Peace Process** in which we recall and make a list of all of the significant emotionally charged events from our past and using certain techniques to help us safely feel, metabolize and then release the related emotions in our body with a trainer therapist one event at a time.

Some of us might feel overwhelmed or daunted imaging tens or hundreds of memories flashing through our minds (especially in cases of ongoing abuse over a number of years). The good news, supported by thousands of successfully desensitized therapeutic cases are living proof of a phenomenon called the *generalization effect* which refers to a system-wide phenomena in which after a few significant events of a core issue have been cleared then the intensity of the other aspects tends to be less. In other words, clearing one *emotionally charged specific event* tends to have a positive effect in decreasing the overall intensity on other remaining *emotionally charged specific events*—especially those that are related. Whether it is with *EMDR, EFT Tapping, Trauma Release Exercises (TRE)*, body-based psychotherapy, *Somatic Experiencing, Luminous Awareness* healing, medicine-assisted healing ceremonies or grace, releasing our emotional past is one of the most liberating, power-reclaiming, and presence enhancing things we can do over the course of our lives.

We are going to get a little technical in this paragraph for the scientifically minded or skeptical. James Lane PhD, a Clinical Psychologist specializing in trauma resolution, relationship counseling, and anxiety disorders conceptualizes an explanatory theory calls *"Reciprocal Inhibition"* as a mechanism used to *"desensitize"* or *"counter-condition"* the emotional stress-producing stimulus and then to replace it with the relaxation response.[10] As opposed to mentally talking about our past, while disconnected from our emotional and physical body, and leaving a session or conversation all stirred up, some of these more effective body-based trauma desensitization and emotional releasing methods leave us feeling more safe, relaxed, open and emotionally free. Lane notes that Brain research has shown that body-based trauma desensitization creates brain changes by increasing the release of internal opioid chemicals such as endorphins (*feel good molecules released after exercise and other activities*), serotonin (*happy, peaceful mood*), GABA (*calming anti-anxiety*) and reducing the stress hormone cortisol by up to 50%. Basically this process releases our own internal feel good, peaceful, calm compounds, decreases our heart rate and shifts our nervous system from the stress response *Sympathetic Dominance* to a greater relaxation response *Parasympathetic Dominance*. Also, in our brain, when we are emotionally triggered, anxious, afraid, etc., brain imaging research indicates that there is more blood flow and neural activity in the limbic emotional brain and that up to 70% of blood flow is redirected there rather than the frontal brain where we think more clearly and calmly. However body-based trauma desensitization has been shown to decrease brain activity (particularly in the limbic system, amygdala, & midbrain) involved in the stress response and restores blood flow and brain activity to the front of the brain (prefrontal cortex and neocortex). These biochemical and physiological factors are important aspects of the desensitization counter-conditioning process combining of the benefits of body-based stimulation with psychological tools to reprogram the emotionally charged conditioned response with a neutral conditioned response of safety, calm, and relaxation. After using effectively using methods to desensitize specific body-stored emotions related to a specific previously distressing emotionally charged event, when the person thinks about the event memory they often report it no longer has any related emotional charge. In other words, it has been felt, integrated and released so that no associated stress or discomfort remains, but instead the person's body feels parasympathetic dominance and bloodflow/neuro-stimulation having returned to the neo and prefrontal cortex which allows the person to authentically cognitively reframe a new reference creating new neural pathways with neutral psychophysiological responses to the stimuli which now more safely allows new behavior change. Once the loop is broken if all aspects have been desensitized, it usually stays broken so that when we think of the event our body feels little to no stress response or emotional charge, months and years later as demonstrated by follow-up research on recipients.

EMOTIONAL PRESENCE & FREEDOM

The Latin origin of the word emotion is *"to move through or out"*, but in order for this to happen, we have to be aware of emotions, so we can fully feel them, before expressing or releasing them. Unfelt and unintegrated emotions create congestion in our system, looping ruminations and mental chatter, body numbness or dissociation, attraction to or avoidance of similarly emotionally charged people or situations. Emotional presence is our capacity to feel and maintain presence amidst emotional intensity, whether pleasurable or painful. Ultimately, this involves fully feeling emotional sensations until we can either express or release them. This emotional presence requires staying in the sweet spot of feeling—neither avoiding feeling nor getting overwhelmingly lost in or attaching to them. Emotions unfelt from the past or emotions too intense to feel and integrate in the moment, are stored in our body leaving us numb or dissociated and remaining in subconscious or unconscious awareness. Sometimes, when we seem to become emotionally triggered to a disproportionate degree, it might be pointing us to previously unintegrated emotional charge or trauma. The more inner emotional and somatic based healing work we do, the less emotional charge from the past we have to get hooked or triggered, which in this context, means less emotional content to process.

So, in addition to releasing our emotional past with effective trauma desensitization, we each have varying degrees of capacity developed to be able to process emotion in real-time. When we avoid feeling or we stay stuck in an emotion, it significantly decreases our overall presence. The more hijacked our attention is in a emotionally charged looping thoughts from an earlier event, the less free attention we have available. The more we can enhance our capacity to fully feel and express or release our emotions in the moment, the greater the emotional presence we embody. Greater presence enables us to stay with the intensity of our own feelings or those of others without reactivity or contracting our potential aliveness. In a relational conflict, if one person can stay present, open and resourced it allows space for the other person to work through their emotional process, but if both get triggered, it makes it much more challenging. Of course it is natural to get emotionally triggered but the virtue of the skill of emotional processing is the amount of recovery time and how skillfully we can fully feel, express or release, reopen and reconnect, whether in solitude or connection. Emotional Intelligence is at the foundation of a civilized society in being able to feel empathy, morality--the moral impact of words and actions on others—and compassionate action for a better world. Overall, limited capacity for emotional processing is THE most significant inhibition to deeper presence for many humans.

EMOTIONAL PRESENCE KEY SUMMARY & KEY TAKEAWAYS

➤ Emotion is a rapid sensory information signaling & processing system to guide behavior related to physical survival.

➤ Emotional feeling, expression & empathetic receiving is the language of connection thru our bodies.

➤ Emotion means "to move through and out" & can be felt or sensed as subtle "energy (e) in motion".

➤ Emotions can inform & guide preferences, desires, needs, actions & decisions.

➤ The female brain experiences emotion more intensely, but if males are not emotionally numb they can feel all the same emotions.

➤ Our culture including many psychotherapists encourage emotional unintelligence by distracting, addiction, numbing medication, suppressing "bad emotions", stoicism, fake smiling, & mentalizing our emotions.

➤ Our Body Keeps Score & emotions that are not fully felt & released or expressed in the moment they arise, get stored to be processed later when we have developed more emotional presence to be resourced enough to fully metabolize the emotion.

➤ Brain imaging research shows that naming an emotion begins to reduce emotional intensity in the emotional limbic brain.

➤ Allowing is being with sensations in our body—resting in the sweet-spot of feeling rather then strategies to avoid feeling like judging, wishing it were different, wanting to get rid of it, suppressing, avoiding, numbing, dissociating out of the body, mentalizing or talking too much.

➤ Partial feeling lies on the other end of the emotional presence spectrum from more avoiding & suppressing strategies, we can also become stuck in a partial feeling loop including hanging on, cry-talking, telling the same story over & over again, or trying to dump on others without fully feeling the sensations in the emotional presence in our body.

➤ False stories our mind can use to trick us into avoiding feeling include that the emotional sensations will be uncomfortable, too intense, overwhelming, out of control, never ending or cause me to be judged.

➤ Fully feeling requires 1) grounding, 2) breathing, 3) body sensing & especially as we are learning, 4) the safe attuned relational presence of another person, until the emotion has been metabolized & is ready to release.

➤ A good way to check to see if you are fully feeling in embodied presence is if you are talking for than a few words you are probably not fully feeling the emotional sensations directly enough for the emotion to be effectively metabolized.

➤ We can't attune to & empathize in others what we are emotionally unaware of in ourselves.

➤ The more expanded Awareness becomes the more we deeply we feel in ourselves, others & the world. Learning to ask "Is this mine or someone else's?" is an important advanced practice, although ultimately we would want to be able to fully feel & release whatever arises in our embodied experience.

➤ In general & especially for those who identify as being "over-sensitive" or "too empathetic" it can be that they are also more dissociated out of the body & can benefit from being more grounded, embodied & self-referencing in their own center axis, allowing them to still be empathetic & then more quickly feel & release while staying resourced in their own grounded center.

➤ Some smaller emotions can be felt & released or expressed on our own, however other past experiences or more intense emotions can be better metabolized & released in the attuned presence of another.

➤ Sometimes when we seem to become emotionally triggered to a disproportionate degree, it might be pointing us to a previously unintegrated emotional charge or past trauma.

➤ The more we feel & release from our past plus the more able to feel & release or feel & express while staying in relational connection, the more emotionally free our is our system.

PROGRESSION OF EMOTIONAL PRESENCE

UNCONSCIOUS: NOT FEELING & UNAWARE

AVOIDING SUPPRESSION: RESISTING FEELING & HOLDING
Avoiding
Distracting
Numbing
Dissociating out of the body
Hyper-Mental
Addiction to Substances: Food, Drug, Alcohol

RELEASE	↑ increasing Awareness
EXPRESSION	↑ increasing feeling
PARTIAL FEELING	↑ increasing letting go
AVOIDING SUPPRESSION	
UNCONSCIOUS	

PARTIAL FEELING: PARTIAL FEELING HOLDING or LOOPING
"Emotional"
Out of Control
Overwhelmed
Looping Thoughts
Externalizing: Blaming, Verbal Dumping
Endless Processing
Crying while Talking without Body Sensing
Hysteric Process

EXPRESSION: FULLY FEELING & EXPRESSING
Crying while feeling whole body
Journaling while feeling whole body
Expressive Dance while feeling whole body
Noticing, Naming, Feeling, Expressing
Expressing Feeling through Sound
Authentic Relating / Getting Real

RELEASING: FULLY FEELING & LETTING GO
Moment to Moment feeling & releasing
Embodied Release (*Sedona Method, Luminous Awareness, Somatic Experiencing, Trauma Releasing Exercises TRE*)

HEART

How often does your open heart feel &
express joy, gratitude, passion & loving?
Does your heart receptively allow you to take in &
receive compliments, love & connection?

Are you aware of when you are opening & closing your heart? When do you close your heart to guard or protect yourself?
How do you avoid connection?

How much can your heart open right now,
opening as the moment, as the fabric of Love itself?

"Your task is not to seek for love, but merely to seek and find all the barriers within yourself that you have built against it."

– Rumi –

WHAT IS **HEART OPENING**

the capacity to openly feel, give & receive gratitude, joy, passion & love

Left figure labels:
attention mainly in busy mental thoughts
guarded & protected
low awareness of body sensations

Right figure labels:
open to give & receive love, connection gratitude & joy
heart open & undefended
body sensing feels alive & relaxed

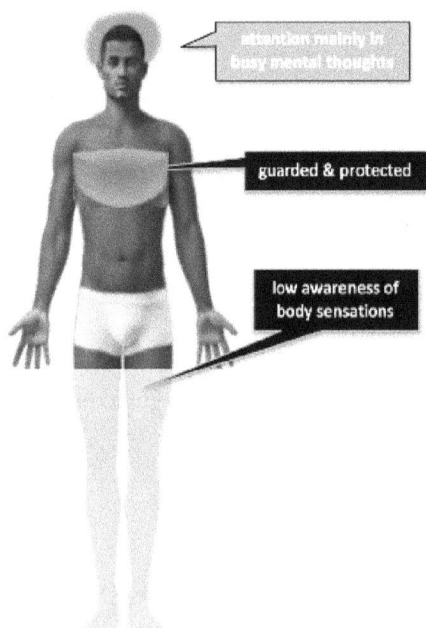

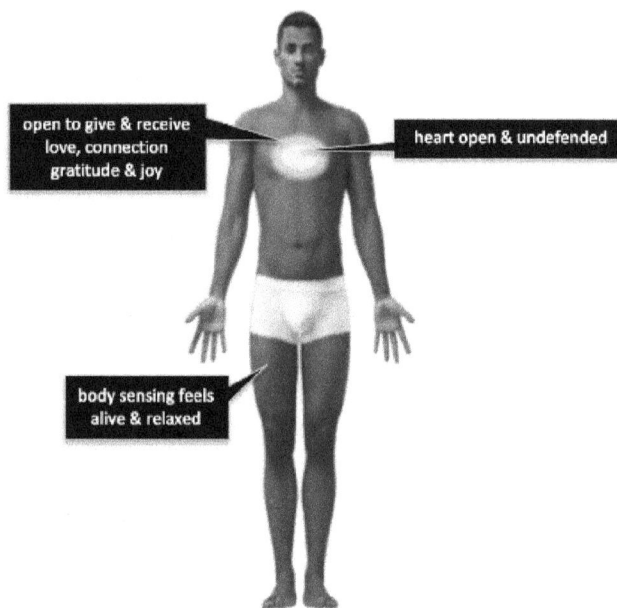

WHY **HEART OPENING** MATTERS

Gratitude: allows us to express gratitude

Receiving: allows us to receive compliments, affection, love & connection

Acceptance: gateway to greater love & acceptance of self, others & the moment

Joy: allows us to experience & express joy

Passion: source of living, loving, working & communicating with passion

Generosity & Giving: allows us to offer love through words, touch, service, gifts & presence

Compassion: allows compassion for self, others & life

Connection: emotional vulnerability & an undefended open heart are the gateway to connection

Intuition & Wisdom of the Body: heart has 40,000 neurons (brain cells), enhances intelligence, intuition & decision-making

BARRIERS TO **HEART OPENING**

Hyper-Mental: excessive mental activity, overly theoretical, living in fantasy, lost in the past or future

Emotional Numbness: numbing your emotional sensing due to past trauma or emotional overwhelm to avoid feeling pain

Emotionally Clogged Heart: unreleased sadness, anger, resentment, hurt

Emotion & Trauma: dead zones, suppressed emotions or body-stored trauma that keeps attention stuck in the body or dissociated

Lack of Joy/Passion: signal to reconnect with passions, make life changes or unclog the heart of past emotions

Lack of Gratitude: ungrateful, negative or sense of entitlement

Fear of Connection & Intimacy: fear of emotional closeness & connection

Anxious Heart: fear or worry about losing closeness & connection

Unable to Receive: unreleased shame, feeling unworthy/unlovable & blocked receptor site to receiving love/compliments

Empty Heart: younger unmet needs or unfulfilled love exchange

Trust Issues: need to dominate & power-over to feel safe, past betrayal hurt or rejection

Judgmental: critical, negative, or condemning point of view about others or the world with fixed attention & closed heart limiting alternate perspective taking, empathy, compassion & connection

HEART OPENING DEVELOPMENT SUCCESS STORY

After 10 years and with two young children, Katarina's marriage was on the brink of collapse. While she originally came in citing her husband's behavior as the problem, it always takes two to tango, and upon deeper exploration, Katarina realized her own heart was also part of the equation. Not uncommon in our human complexity, her own patternings of love had her heart stuck in a cycle of 1) needy yearning to be filled—which she sometimes felt too vulnerable to express to her husband, so she shut down emotionally and withdrew from connection or 2) when the very thing she wanted most – his loving presence and attention—came close, her own heart's receptor site blocked her from receiving love and pushed him away in some way. He was thoroughly confused and frustrated by this and started turning away from the relationship. Exploring the subtle inner terrain of her heart, we helped re-pattern some past limiters, open her heart to receiving healthy human connection and love, helped her learn to fill up and re-source herself and to re-integrate her emotional vulnerability, loving affection and healthy desire for connection. Her connection and marriage is "better than it's ever been" and she feels more loving fullness and passion all throughout her life through movement, dance, quality time with friends and through her greatest passion: painting.

"If you are waiting for anything in order to live and love without holding back, then you suffer. Every moment is the most important moment of your life. No future time is better than now to let down your guard and love."

- David Deida -

EARLY HEART TRAINING

There is a beautiful preciousness and innocence to the young infant's heart. We are wired for love and connection, and our caregivers attunement literally contributes to wiring the neurological architecture of our brains and nervous systems. We are conceived, carried, birthed, held, fed, attuned to and loved to varying degrees based upon the capacities of our parents and caregivers. Although not all children had the ideal infancy and young home environment, we all have the same hardware for an aperture in the center of our chest. Artists, poets, lovers and lay folk alike call this the human heart. Some of us learned open-heartedness and felt love, care, compassion and kindness from our parents, while others received it modeled by movie actors, teachers, mentors, friends or their parents. Some were resilient and learned how to have a healthy heart aperture, when to open and close, when to express and receive love, gratitude, joy and passion. Others learned it was safer to protect their heart and keep their heart aperture closed.

LEARNING TO FEEL & OPEN THE HEART

Whatever our past experiences and wiring have been, all we can do is start with the current capacities we have, and learn to open our heart more and more, release past hurt and reopen when we close. It's no mistake that the *Emotion section* preceded this one, because oftentimes the doorway and opening of the heart occurs through greater emotional awareness and vulnerability. Some say it's a common human proclivity to go towards pleasure and avoid pain, however the paradox with the heart is that in numbing and putting up shielding to protect ourselves from hurts, we also block the beauties of joy, appreciation, love and ecstasy from being expressed outwardly by us and received inwardly from others.

For many, the pathway back to rewiring and living with an open heart is being courageous enough to be willing to increasingly feel the full range of emotions: denumbing, relearning to feel and releasing the past. As a metaphor, ice is frozen water. Freezing perishable alive food preserves it for the future. Reptiles also use the survival strategy of holding still and freezing in place in hopes of preserving their future, while we humans can freeze or numb emotion as a survival strategy of storing it in our body for a later time when we feel safer, more resourced or have the emotional capacity to effectively feel and release them without being overtaken or overwhelmed. In all of these cases, freezing and numbness can be helpful temporarily useful protection strategies, but anything we do not feel in the moment but instead store for later can clog our aliveness pipes. Over the long term, the benefit for humans in denumbing past frozen emotion we weren't resourced enough at the time to feel is that we can increasingly live with our beautiful, passionately powerful and sensitively tender loving hearts more and more open so that greater magnitude of love and aliveness can naturally flow in and out of our amazing hearts.

HEART, FACE, & EARS – THE POLYVAGAL CONNECTION

We all have a network of nerves called the poly-vagal system that connects the muscles of our chest (heart), emotional expression in our face, and ears. Stephen Porges, psychophysiology expert who we will get to know better in the *Connection section*, describes this as the reason why music can have such an emotionally moving and heart opening effect as well as why when our heart is tense, guarded and closed so too our facial muscles go flat and we can't listen as effectively and take in what someone else is expressing. When however, we feel safe, our system can open, our chest muscles relax and our heart can open, our facial muscles can reflect this inner openness through greater emotional warmth. All of these subtleties are part of what Porges calls our **Social Engagement System**, which can cue others that we are open and safe to connect with.

ACCEPTANCE

Acceptance is another powerful doorway into presence—accepting ourselves, accepting others, accepting the moment exactly as it is now. *"I don't like my body," "I'm not pretty enough." "she is getting fat." "I don't make enough money, yet."* Can we love through the current circumstances, radically accepting everything exactly it as it is right now with an open heart? Everything in the world of form is in constant change—some say the only constant in life is change. Life in form is movement, motion, change, arising, being born, growing, evolving, dying, the cycle of life and death. So yes, we can evolve, change, choose a different future, harness our intention, mobilize new actions and move in the direction of new possibilities. But closure and resistance to what is now blocks the flow of aliveness and new possibility. First, let us except everything exactly as it is right now; and then put our attention on voting for the future possibility of what we do want.

Judgment of ourselves or others closes the heart. Don't try to block judgment though as it points to hidden power in the form of shadow aspects we see in others and have disowned in ourselves. We can use these shadow judgments to reclaim buried power and greater range of ways of being—as we will learn more about in the *Behavioral Flexibility & Shadow section*. Also, judgment is on the lower end of the wisdom spectrum. Discernment is judgment plus the compassionate wisdom of an open heart. So don't throw it all away; keep the discerning wisdom that comes with judgment, let us just open our heart a little more. Mindfulness is the nonjudgmental noticing of what's arising in the present moment—radical open-hearted acceptance from the Witness vantage. Byron Katie has a practice called **loving what is** which involves open the heart and accepting this now just like it is. From the relative view maybe some aspect of this moment could evolve and be better than it has and right now from the absolute vantage, can we open into radical acceptance of everything, now exactly as is. Embracing and accepting ourselves, others and the moment exactly as it is now can be very healing and heart opening—and some of our hearts are craving this acceptance.

HEALING & FORGIVENESS

For some, fear has destabilized the safety of our systems to live with an open heart as we learned to protect our precious hearts the best we could from physical danger, emotional rejection or mental judgment. Some have lived in war-torn regions, others in homes with constantly warring parents; some boys had to guard against getting made fun of or getting beat up; some girls protected from cattiness and reputation-slandering gossip. While in other cases, a buildup of scar tissue from past hurts, betrayals, and unfelt sadness, anger or other suppressed emotions clouds our heart openness. Some of us interacted thousands of times with so many guarded closed hearted people that their nervous system registered the wiring of **closed guarded heart, emotionally shut down** or **emotionally numb** as normal. Paradoxically, underneath some of our desperate yearning for love, we can have blocks around receiving love from others related to our own feelings of worthiness or scabs from past pain and unmet developmental needs. Notice how our own body responds as an indicator of its threshold of receiving which can be indirectly related to self-love (via sensation, emotion, energetics, eye contact or staying in connection) when someone offers us a compliment, an act of love or an open-hearted expression.

Shame is probably one of the emotion we humans most avoid feeling. A certain degree of healthy shame is essential for interpersonal relating because it allows us to feel the negative impact we've had on ourselves or others. A small dose of healthy shame plus emotional vulnerability empathy and connection are all essential ingredients in a sincere apology. Healthy shame can be thought of as related to *"I have done something wrong,"* whereas core shame is more related to *"I am fundamentally unlovable, unworthy or flawed."* Sometimes when people have a complete blind spot and don't even know what shame is, it can indicate a deeper buried bundle of core shame often associated with feeling not enough, not good enough, unworthy or unlovable at their core. In this case, we are unable to feel even small doses of healthy guilt and shame because it hooks the big unresolved garbage bag in our bellies and initiates a toxic shame spiral. Healthy shame enables us to feel the impact on others when we have hurt them; and without being able to feel even a small amount of shame, it makes it very difficult to sincerely apologize. The first step towards increasing self-love and opening our heart to receiving love is to desensitize emotional charge on past shame related experiences—especially looking for the first and worst charged experience of feeling rejected and unlovable, not good enough or shamed.

There is a big difference between mentally saying we have forgiven because we think we are supposed to and actually having released any related emotions and feeling true forgiveness and open-hearted love again. The true test of forgiveness is do we feel any remaining emotional charge related to the person or event and have we reopened our heart. Take an event from the past, when we made a mistake, didn't keep our word, or hurt someone. How much emotional charge to do we currently feel in our body on a scale of 1-10? Chances are if we thought of it there is still some emotional charge, so consider that that emotional charge could be a conglomerate bundle of emotions like guilt, shame, disappointment, anger, etc. To completely clear the emotional charge on a past event, we can release each of these past emotions related to the event; eventually the memory will remain but the event will be emotionally neutral and in our heart we feel true lasting peace, acceptance and openness, then this is the measure of real self-forgiveness and forgiveness of others related to that event. This is a thorough forgiveness process, not just mentally saying *"I forgive."* Some people mentally say the words *"Okay I forgive you"* but in their heart, maybe resentment and anger may still remain. In this case, if we want to hang on to the past and keep our own heart covered, we are free to do so, but let us understand that it come with a cost of inhibiting our heart openness to feeling, giving and receiving even deeper love, gratitude, passion and joy. The true test is do we feel any remaining emotional charge on the event and is our heart reopened.

We can do the same thing with transgressions by other people or situations in which we still hold a grudge, resentment or anger. Sometimes a clearing conversation needs to be had between us and another person, other times we can do the inner forgiveness clearing process on our own and it can shift the dynamic. Sometimes we need to forgive ourselves, sometimes others and sometimes we can forgive life: who are we mad at, are we mad at the world, feeling like a resentful victim, angry at God? Forgiveness is a process and sometimes we actually need to touch into the anger that would have been used to healthfully protect our boundaries or let someone else know that what they did was not okay, etc. Sometimes this is an important, yet overlooked aspect of really feeling everything, learning all the related lessons and fully completing the forgiveness process. We can progressively release more and more of the emotional clouds and heart congestion related to past events until we increasingly heal and forgive ourselves and others for the past, reclaiming our bound up power and freeing up our life force for deeper openness, presence and connection. Forgiveness work, healing and clearing the past heart congestion is one of the most powerful and important practices for living with a more open heart and increasing our capacity to love.

GRATITUDE & HEART COHERENCE

In many spiritual traditions, gratitude along with love, compassion and wisdom are considered among the highest of human virtues. In positive psychology, some consider gratitude to be one of the qualities most associated with mental health and human happiness. Numerous research studies confirm that people who feel gratitude more often are less stressed, less depressed, have better relationships, are more resilient with life challenges, and are more satisfied with their lives.[3][4] Gratitude is a skill that we can learn, but for most of us it requires a little practice. While gratitude does have an accompanying positive mental perspective, the essentials of gratitude comes from the heart. Gratitude is an open-hearted feeling of appreciation. While we can initially start by *counting our blessings* or mentally thinking of qualities within ourselves, our connection with other people or aspects of our life, ultimately gratitude is a state of being radiating out of our hearts. As we will learn in the next section, this grateful state of heart coherence is something we can train and develop.

HeartMath Institute in Northern California, has performed pioneering research since 1991 on *"heart-coherence"* and the physiological effects of emotions—especially gratitude. They have been developing scientifically based technologies and techniques to help people bridge the connection between their heart, breath and minds, as well as the connection with others' hearts—commonly using gratitude or compassion as an essential heart emotion. Let us define coherence as rhythmic, organized, harmonious connectedness between parts of a system, in this case between internal human systems although two or more people could also share heart coherence in connection with each other. Their research suggests that the electrical field of the heart (measured in an electrocardiogram (ECG) is around 60 times stronger in amplitude than the amplitude of the electrical field of brain waves (measured in an electroencephalogram (EEG) and the magnetic component of the heart field—which can be measured several feet away from the body—is about 100 times stronger than that generated by the brain. Fascinated with the impact of mental attitudes and emotions on heart coherence, their research has demonstrated that experiencing different emotions produces distinct rhythmic patterns in beat-to-beat heart rate variability. Simply stated, thoughts and emotions can change not only our heart-rhythm patterns, but these changing states and resulting heart rhythms affect our entire physiology. This emotional rhythmic heart activity, again specific to different emotions, has been shown to impact (or can be felt by) every cell in our body through changes in electromagnetic, blood pressure, and sound pressure waves which they hypothesize as supporting the heart's role as a global internal synchronizing signaling system. A state of heart-centered coherent presence marked by relaxed emotional positivity with mental clarity and alert attention can also be a gateway to higher level decision-making, creativity, problem-solving, and wisdom. Heart coherence not only provides immediate benefits including helping people learn to reduce stress, change their state and enhance their emotional mood, but it has been shown when used over a longer-term to repattern some of the maladaptive heart closure tendencies mentioned earlier in this section. The big-take away from their research is that by synching our breathing while intentionally experiencing positive heart emotions such as gratitude, care, compassion, and love creates the coherence of overall well-being but also activates the heart-centered doorway to some of the most virtuous human states or presence.

QUESTIONS FOR HEART EXPLORATION

Whatever our past experiences have been, every human has the same heart aperture in the center of their chest. Awakening, opening and closing the aperture of the heart, moment to moment

What is the quality of its openness now? How do you know when your heart is open? What does that even feel like?

Is your chest tense or soft? Does it feel numb, or feel like nothing?

How open is your heart at work? How open is your heart with loved ones? What situations do you hide or shut down?

Is your heart shielded or by scar tissue covering past hurt?

Is there someone you need to forgive to reopen your heart again? Someone else? Yourself?

Do you have blocks to receiving: love, connection, or compliments?

Can you feel massive love & joy blasting out a gaping hole in the center of your chest?

How does your personal heart and Big Heart feel different? Can you feel infinite heart openness in all directions?

Whatever the flavor, texture and span of your heart this moment, can you feel acceptance for it exactly as it is?

HEART OPENING KEY SUMMARY & KEY TAKEAWAYS

➢ In emotional numbing & shielding our hearts to protect ourselves from hurts, we also block the beauties of joy, passion, awe, gratitude, love & connection.

➢ Emotional vulnerability & an undefended open heart are the gateway to connection.

➢ Stephen Porges Poly-Vagal nervous system connects the muscles & emotional expression of our belly, chest (heart), face & ears, which explains why when we feel fearful or aggressive our heart can become tense, guarded, closed & our facial muscles go flat, versus when we feel safe & available for connection, the social engagement system of our face can reveal emotionally attuned responses that are synchronized with an relaxed open-hearted chest. And because our ears are enervated & connected to our hearts, we can listen in conversation best when we feel safe & open-hearted as well as why certain music received through our ears can emotionally move us & open our hearts.

➢ Judgment of ourselves or others closes the heart. When the heart is open, judgement combined with higher clarity can be discerning wisdom.

➢ Emotionally Clogged Heart: a buildup of subtle scar tissue from past hurts, betrayals & unfelt sadness, anger or guilt can cloud our heart openness; sometimes forgiveness work is needed to feel & release past emotions that can cover our heart.

➢ Receiving: an open heart allows us to receive compliments, affection, love & connection whereas a blocked receptor site to receiving love compliments can be related to unreleased shame, feeling unworthy/unlovable & trauma.

➢ HeartMath Institute research on heart-coherence & related wearable biofeedback technologies help train people to develop greater open-heartedness, compassion & gratitude.

➢ It is thru an open-heart that we express & receive joy, passion, acceptance, love, closeness & connection

AUTHENTIC EXPRESSION

Do you notice when you hold back, avoid, hide, lose your voice, check-out or get rigid in your **expression**?

Do you notice when you compromise yourself or become **inauthentic** to please others or avoid criticism?

On a scale of 0-10,
how **authentic & freely expressive**
do you feel in your life in the ways you
speak, dress, make a living & move in your body?

"Authenticity is a collection of choices that we have to make every day. It's about the choice to show up and be real. The choice to be honest. The choice to let our true selves be seen."

– Brene Brown –

WHAT IS **AUTHENTIC EXPRESSION**

The capacity to allow your uniqueness to be expressed thru body, emotion & voice in a real, transparent, attuned & related way moment to moment

voice & thoughts disconnected from body & emotion

emotionally shut-down

blocking authentic expression of emotion, voice, movement & sexuality

Body feels tense & locked down

VOICE

EMOTIONS

BODY

unique aligned expression of thought, emotion & energy thru body & voice

body sensing feels alive & relaxed

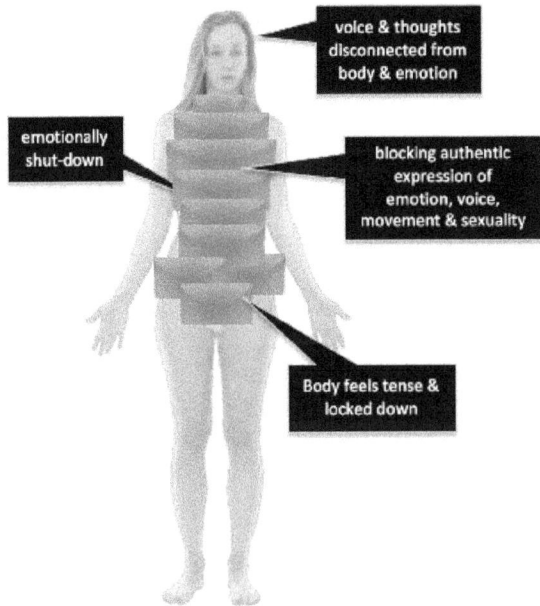

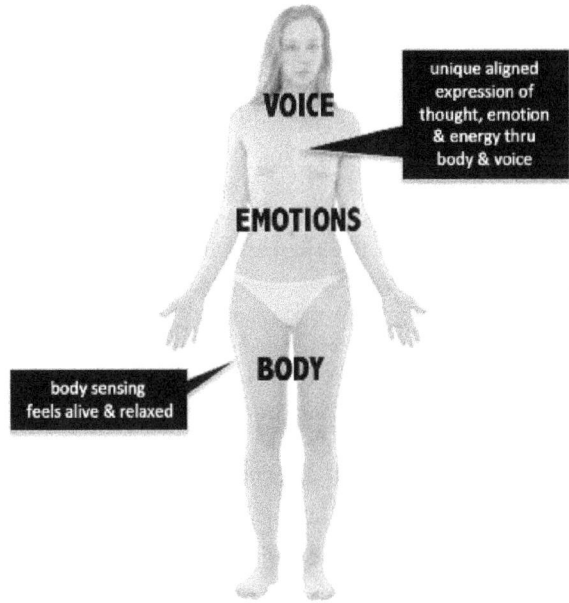

WHY **AUTHENTIC EXPRESSION** MATTERS

Uniqueness: allows your uniqueness to be heard, felt, seen & known by yourself & others

Communication: an open uninhibited voice allows you to communicate & share your unique experience with others & the world

Question & Answer: allows you to ask clarifying questions, offer feedback to others, or responsively answer

Request: allows you to make requests, delegate, ask for help & voice your opinion

Enhancement & Clarity: enhances oral & written communication at work & in your personal life

Connection: clearer & more authentic communication in relationships enhances connection & reduces conflict

Expressing your Message: the medium for you to share your unique embodied voice & message with the world

BARRIERS TO **AUTHENTIC EXPRESSION**

Dissociation: not feeling & inhabiting your body due to trauma, defense or hyper-mental

Self-Referencing: part of healthy boundaries, the ability to self-reference from central column rather than others

Gender Stereotype: believing or associating emotionality with a certain gender which could threaten identity

Hyper-Positive: disowning any thoughts or emotions other than positivity

Image Positioning: hiding something or trying to say something to be seen in a certain way or meet an expectation

Hesitation or Withholding: guarded, hiding, fear of being judged or criticized, fear of saying the wrong thing

Emotional Numbness: numbing your emotional sensing due to past trauma or emotional overwhelm to avoid feeling pain

Fear of being Seen: hiding or blocking real expression to avoid criticism, disapproval or rejection

Shame: unreleased from past experiences of feeling flawed, not enough, rejected, judged, disconnected or not belonging

Fear of feeling Shame or Punishment: lying or morphing your real expression to avoid feeling these emotions

Unworthy of having a Voice: shy, muted or struggle to communicate what want to say

Fear / Terror: believing "the world is not safe", "it is not safe to be you", "it is not safe to be in your body"

Stoic / Rigid: closed, defended, emotionally numb, or playing tough

Superficiality: avoiding depth, afraid of intimacy or feeling deeper emotions

Clichés: speaking habitual phrases from memory can be funny in context but can also be a protection, avoiding unique expression

Pleasing: compromising your authentic expression to be liked, validated, or belong, being too nice in fear of conflict or disapproval

AUTHENTIC EXPRESSION DEVELOPMENT SUCCESS STORY

Jerry is an attractive 6'4" ex-college-football-player, known by his friends as being a big-hearted, positive, inspirational man. While this may be his social persona & is often in joyful charismatic mood, sometimes he feels "blah", not good enough & overly concerned about what others think of him. At a certain point he realized that he would experience situations interpersonally, in which he would lose his voice, feel emotionally constipated or feel like he needed to run away. Upon deeper exploration, together we discovered that based on his vow of being a source of positivity and inspiration at work & for his friends that certain parts of himself weren't being allowed to be authentically expressed such as "negative' emotions like anger, frustration or shame. While at times he can be a passionate expressive man, if any of these emotions arose in situations with others his system would feel blocked in his ability to express himself & stay in connection with others. Afraid of not being liked by others, damaging his persona of being the positive guy or fear of hurting others, Jerry would freeze in the moment or flee without responding for days. Through experiential exercises in sessions & practices in between, he increased awareness of his inner state, allowed himself to express a fuller range of thoughts & emotions through his body & voice while staying connected to others. He realized that what others most wanted was to know, see, hear & feel his authentic experience & that in doing so it actually increased their mutual sense of closeness. And that he could also allow himself to feel socially relaxed, sexy, & confident as well as anxious or angry!

"When a child's creativity is not seen and received by the parents, blockages may result in the expression of the core intelligence... We each have a core intelligence which is the creative or evolutionary impulse within us – our purpose in life is to express this unique intelligence."

– Thomas Hubl –

HOW AUTHENTIC EXPRESSION DEVELOPS

Developmentally as children and teenagers, we tend to be more impulsive in expressing ourselves in our best attempts to get our emotional bonding and physical survival needs met. As we are mature we have an authentic impulse to explore, experience and express ourselves in the world, as we are learning how to be in a body and relate with others in the social fabric of our family, friends and culture. During this time, there is a natural tension between the unique expression in the world of our developing authentic self while simultaneously staying connected in relation with others as a coherent part of our surrounding social environment. We are learning to be more aware of the impact of our words and actions on others. Mystic Thomas Hubl calls this relationship between essential human drives, **becoming** and **belonging**—two sometimes seemingly conflicting motivations to honor our own authentic expression in the world and our needs for **human connection**. Many of our inner conflicts revolve around this tension to become—to evolve and uniquely express our unique self in the world—and to belong—to feel accepted, loved and connected to others.

Sometimes, and especially when we are younger in the inevitable family value assimilation, social conditioning and enculturation processes, there were likely moments for all of us, in which our young selves in our natural growing up processes, were being self-absorbed, impulsive, inconsiderate, and unaware of our impact on others. In these cases, we ideally needed some loving acceptance combined with attuned feedback and healthy limits to provide greater awareness and guide us in this growing up process. Yet there were likely other moments when we unnecessarily had our authentic impulse criticized, shamed or squelched. And in response to these we learned to use defenses, to dampen our voice to keep quiet, to suppress the emotions we really felt, to use seduction to be liked or get what we want, to compromise our integrity or change our way of being to get our needs met, to avoid getting in trouble, or to protect against the loss of love. Often, there was a key moment when we learned to suppress or compromise our authentic expression to align with our external environment and maintain safety and love—in essence we traded our authenticity for approval and/or survival. As this continued some of us learned to tell little white lies, withhold the truth, or please others. For some it was a crafty ability to get what we want, for others a way to avoid punishment or disapproval and for some a way to survive.

EXPRESSION & CONNECTION

As we age, some of us continue to develop and become less impulsive by learning greater self-regulation and taking on the beliefs and values of our family, institution or religion, seeking to belong to the group we most trust. In this process, many of us align or subvert our own beliefs, values and opinions with those of our in-group. Some people stay in this stage, much of their lives while others go through the confusing, uncertain and destabilizing process of breaking away from the group-think and increasingly learning to question social morays and think for themselves. As greater self-reflection comes online in our brains and as another level of authenticity emerges, this process can not only be unsettling internally for the person who continues to evolve but it can create moments of conflict and dissension with people whose identity is still more intertwined with the values and rules of the group. While this tension of becoming and belonging continues throughout our lives, the transition out of this absolutist or fundamentalist stage marks an important milestone for authenticity, we tend to develop more capacity for self-reflection a more mature sense of personal responsibility and self-determination, an interest in individualism, financial success and personal freedom. Even at this stage though our belonging is still important and our values tend to shift to living the good life with self-esteem needed for success, *"keeping up with the*

Joneses" and being respected by those who have *"made it"* in a worldly sense. Relative to the previous stage, this mentality marks an important advancement toward the greater individuation needed for truer authenticity, yet people at this stage still tend to be primarily satisfying self-esteem needs, which creates the tendency to subjugate authenticity in favor of fitting in, achieving a certain perceived social status and idealized success. Eventually, some realize their original hopes for lasting happiness did not come along with greater external *"success"*. In the next wave of becoming and belonging we actually consciously seek authenticity and connection.

AUTHENTICITY, DIVERSITY & SENSITIVITY

As we begin to externally develop a more multicultural worldview, celebrating diversity, acknowledging relativity, valuing equality and harmony, supporting sustainability, and seeking connection, it is here that we also can increasingly appreciate more internal awareness and sensitivity as we increasingly value self-expression, emotional vulnerability and authenticity. And as we increasingly honor our own interior world, likewise our honoring of everyone's voice and feelings being heard and acknowledged also tends to increase. Some more consciously notice the gap between allowing full expression and layers of protective or socially appropriate filtering—many of which have become habitual. It is common to hear people refer to *"sharing my truth"*, *"expressing my truth"*, *"speaking my truth"*, again emphasizing the value of each person's voice and their *"right"* to be heard. As a counter to all of the previous filtering and inhibition due to worry about what others will think, fear of judgment, fulfilling self-esteem needs, maintaining good social graces and conforming with the group, now some people begin focusing on *"unapologetic expression"*. This impulse to be freely expressed and liberated from social constructions and self-imposed inhibitions due to external perceptions is an important step along the way towards greater authenticity; however it is inherently still egocentric and the *"unapologetic"* part is usually not able to be in relation with ourselves and another person simultaneously. At a deeper level we are interdependent beings continuously impacting our shared world. Whereas before, some degree of awareness of others inhibited authenticity, with the new intention of unapologetic expression we attempt is to disregard others so we can feel express ourselves. While this is an important part of the process, the ideal communication would include awareness of self and others. If we deny our own self or our connectivity/impact on others we limit our mutual communication. Ultimately, the answer is to allow oneself to be authentically expressed AND simultaneously feeling connected to others with greater presence and consideration.

SELF-ACTUALIZATION

Eventually, as we continue to develop greater systemic awareness and desire for integration—both externally and internally—we develop greater self-awareness of the diversity of parts, paradox, and ways of being within ourselves and with others. Realizing that all authentic perspectives do indeed have some degree of truth, but that some are more inclusive, a strong impulse emerges to be an Integral or integrated functional, self-actualized human being[3] —which becomes our predominant concern and our deepest fear is no longer death but the fear of unfulfilled potential.[4] Here authentic integration and self-actualization are the primary personal motivations as we realize both are required to live an integral life as desire to be an integrated functional participant in the world actualizing our unique gifts in service to others from a much larger span of consideration and awareness.

ALIVENESS & CONGRUENCY

Ultimately let's define *"authentic"* expression in two dimensions: **unique aliveness** and **vertical congruency**. Unique aliveness is a gauge of relatively how fresh and unique the emergent expression is, and vertical congruency refers to relatively how synchronized our voice, body, emotion and energy are in their expression. It is sometimes easier to sense via incongruence when someone's expression—words or body language—is inauthentic. In the previous stages discussed above we tend to speak more from memory, cliché, or habitual phrases from our past or from exclusively mental content. When there is congruency between body language, energy, emotions, and words, others can perceive a subtle sense of authenticity. Each of us has a truth meter or authenticity sensor, although some of us have not tuned our instruments to pay attention.

BARRIERS TO AUTHENTIC EXPRESSION

Some of the biggest limiters to authenticity involve protecting our self-image by 1) **posturing** (wanting to be seen in a certain way), 2) **hiding** (not wanting something to be seen) 3) **worrying what others will think**. The first, wanting to be seen in a certain way, requires an effort on behalf of the ego to create pretenses in order to have others perceive us in a way we imagine will earn or maintain respect, social esteem and worth validation. This effort can have a flavor of trying, falseness, or effort which can override authentic being and expression. Not wanting some quality or event from our past to be seen prompts the ego to defend or hide certain parts of itself or past events with unresolved shame. Sometimes when someone speaks there might be the underpinning of a desire to present him or herself in such a way as to be perceived as successful, smart or spiritual. Authenticity is experienced as a relative synchronization of emotion, energy, and body along with our voice as we speak, and some people are able to sense an incoherent resonance or gap in authenticity. On the other end of the spectrum, someone might respond "I am good" out of habit to the question *"How are you?"*. Yet if they didn't take a moment to scan their body to authentically assess how they are feeling, their answer might have been, *"I am feeling tired"*, *"I am feeling relaxed"* or *"I am feeling sad"* or *"I feel spacious"*. Meanwhile, if the listener was perceptive enough, he or she might sense that there is, for an example, an underlying sadness on the heart which reveals a lack of authentic congruence between words, emotion, energy and body language. The greater the gap between these elements the more incongruence and inner tension, because one or more parts are not integrated; whereas the more integration, the less the gap, and the more authenticity and synced resonance between elements. So authentic expression refers to the relative synchronization of mental, emotional, and energetic elements as they are expressed through body and words.

SELF-TRANSCENDENCE & AUTHENTIC INCLUSION

The next phase of the authenticity journey takes on a whole new factor as for the first time, the ego begins to become transparent to itself. During the initial phases of this "**ego-dismantling**", as Susan Cook-Greuter, Harvard developmental physiologist calls it, it can be quite disorienting as the limits of the human mind are increasingly realized and the ego, the previous central organizing function of the human mind, is increasingly known to be a construct.   Peppered with peak states and sometimes extrasensory perception, people going through this stage increasingly experience the constructed nature of all language and meaning. A deep existential questioning of nature that personal self and true authenticity ensues. Paradox and polarity are seen to be irreconcilable, mutually necessitating and defining each other, so are increasingly allowed to become integrated. Additionally, throughout our lives, via implicit learning, we have been subconsciously assimilating how to be embodied and express ourselves by absorbing and mimicking how our peers, friends, idols, mentors and especially primary caregivers or parents move, speak, and emote. It is here, in this phase of construct-awareness and greater self-transparency that we tend to be more aware of liberating ourselves from past unconscious habituation while integrating various parts of ourselves into a coherent expression in the world. As this relates to authenticity, this feels like the resonance of vertical synchronization of thoughts, emotions, and energy through our body and voice.

Eventually as the **awakening process** continues, **immediacy** becomes the key feature of authenticity as the habituated nature of the mind's automatic conditioned responses from memory and cultural conditioning are seen to be one of the remaining veils obscuring a more emergent, truer authentic expression of aliveness. The person is more comfortable with spontaneity, uncertainty and mystery as they increasingly allow unconditioned authentic expression to experientially arise out of the immediacy of the present moment. Authentic expression not just of a separate ego mind but of a more emergent congruence within a unique human being also intimately related with others and embedded in the totality of life, a process of life expressing itself moment to moment.

There are more than 7 Billion human beings on our planet, each with a unique fingerprint and personality. But there is more to our uniqueness than the personality of the individual self. Each of us has a unique essence beyond our personality, conditioning and habitual ways of being. First, our unique essence includes our special gifts and life purpose, and as we increasingly live with greater authenticity, life is able to activate, cultivate and express these gifts and missions through our unique life as opposed to compromising our deepest desires to please others, living someone else's dreams, or wearing social masks to cover our deeper, rawer realness. Whatever previous experiences stifled our authentic expression, for many it has become a habit and is often a source of much power that can be reclaimed and the gateway to reconnecting with our deeper authentic expression while simultaneously remaining connected to others and life. However, the less energy we waste trying to be seen in a certain way, hiding parts of ourselves or worrying what others will think, the more free, available attention and energy we have to simply be or allow the moment to express itself through us. Without putting up a façade, pleasing, hiding or censoring, and realizing that nothing needs to be noticed or rejected, we are free to allow the fresh authenticity of the moment to arise—and it is here in the naked transparency and unconditioned authenticity of the eternal Presence that life is allowed to express itself, to evolve as something new and to intimately, know Itself on this great canvass of aliveness through each and every one of us.

AUTHENTIC EXPRESSION SUMMARY & KEY TAKEAWAYS

- Authentic expression allows our uniqueness to be heard, felt, seen & known by yourself & others.
- Authentic expression allows us to make requests, delegate, ask for help, voice our opinion or ask clarifying questions.
- Vertical congruency refers to relatively how synchronized our voice, body, emotion & energy are in our expression while unique aliveness is a gauge of relatively how fresh & unique is the emergence of our expression.
- As social creatures we also have a drive to feel connected to others, together these essential drives becoming (authentic expression) & belonging (connection) although in some cases or at some points in our lives, we sacrifice one or the other, which must later be reintegrated.
- Some of us had our authentic impulse criticized, shamed or squelched, or we learned to use defenses, to dampen our voice to keep quiet, to suppress the emotions we really felt, to use seduction to get be liked or get what we want, to compromise our integrity or change our way of being to get our needs met, to avoid getting in trouble, or to protect against the loss of connection.
- The biggest limiters to authenticity involve protecting our self-image by 1) posturing (wanting to be seen in a certain way), 2) hiding (not wanting something to be seen) 3) worrying what others will think.
- Others sacrificed belonging, friendship or community in order to continue to authentically develop.
- As some develop a more multicultural worldview, they increasingly celebrate diversity & honor an authentic voice in us all.
- Self-actualization is the drive to realize our full potential, creativity, expression, spirituality & contribution in the world.
- The more comfortable with spontaneity, uncertainty, body sensing & emotional vulnerability we are capable of being, the more we can allow unconditioned undefended authentic expression as a more emergent embodied congruence to experientially arise out of the immediacy of the present moment, that can also be intimately related with others & embedded in & as the totality of life.

ATTUNEMENT

How often do you attune with yourself & scan your body
"What am I feeling?" "Is there anything I need?"
"Am I hungry, thirsty, tired or do I need to move?"

Would your romantic partner & children say you attune to them, sense their state, check-in with their needs?

When you enter a room or new group, do you attune: scanning your own system, sensing others & the vibe or needs of the group or space?

The greatest gift a parent has to give a child—and a lover has to give a lover—is emotionally attuned attention and timely responsiveness."

--- Sue Johnson ---

WHAT IS **ATTUNEMENT**

the capacity to intimately tune into, sense, see, hear & respond to the current state, wants & needs of yourself & then in doing so to be resourced enough to effectively do the same with others such that they feel genuinely seen, felt, heard & understood

self-absorbed mental noise unable to attune to self or other

self-absorbed mental noise unable to attune to self or other

hearts are emotionally defended inhibiting connection

low awareness of body sensations; if you can't feel your body, you can't feel others or life

dual-attention:
1 scanning internal embodied experience
2 curiously sensing the other person

heart open

heart open

breath aware

body sensing feels alive & relaxed

grounded stable base

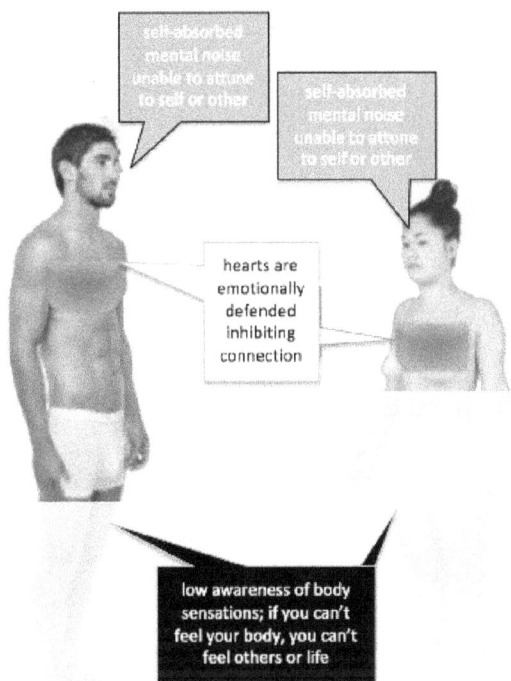

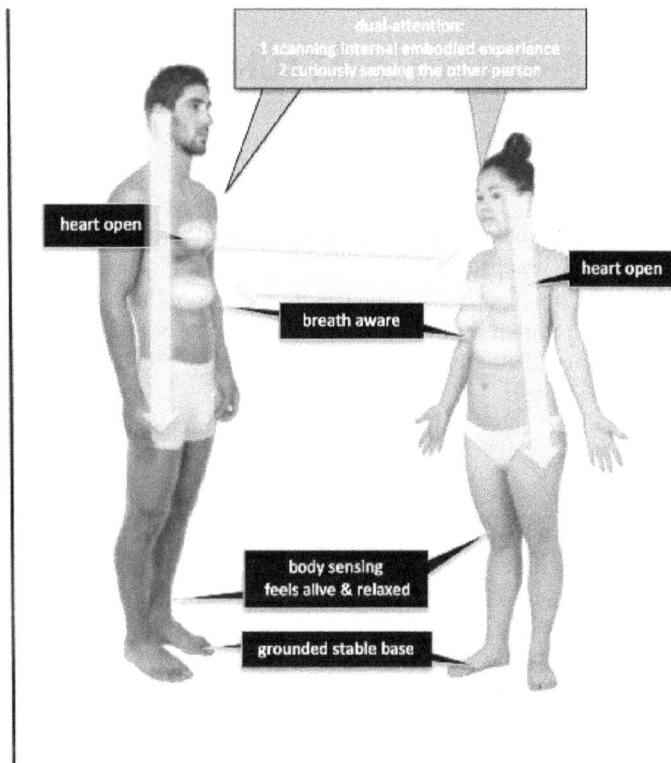

WHY **ATTUNEMENT** MATTERS

Infant Development: adult attuning helps infants know themselves, get needs met, regulate their state & feel securely connected

Self-Care: the ability to attune to ourselves, our states & needs underlies self-care & the ability to ask for help

Bonding: attunement to our partner or child is an essential component of healthy relational bonding

Nourishment: enables us to recognize, reach out for & take in physical & emotional nourishment

Attunement & Connection: able to be in relation without self-sacrificing your own needs

Perspective-Taking & Empathy: attunement is the first ingredient skill in perspective-taking & empathy

Rapport: in conversation, attunement is the first ingredient in creating rapport

Business: sensing the needs & taking the perspective of clients, team-members, investors, end-users, the entire supply chain, etc.

Group Dynamics: enables reading a room & skillfully navigating group dynamics, states & needs

BARRIERS TO SELF-**ATTUNEMENT**

Dissociation: not feeling & inhabiting your body due to trauma, defense or hyper-mental
Unaware of Own Needs: unaware of what you need
Emotional Overwhelm: inability to feel & release emotions, resulting in strategies like numbing & dissociation to reduce overwhelm
Pain: you can avoid self-attunement to avoid feeling physical or emotional pain in your body
Self-Referencing: part of healthy boundaries, the ability to self-reference from central column rather than others
Pride / Shame: pride in not having needs or shame for having them
Low Body Sensing: emotions are experienced in the body & insufficient body sensing inhibits emotional awareness
Self-Sacrifice / Self-Neglect: feeling undeserving of care & having own needs met; self-sacrificing your own needs to please others or earn worth
Codependency: over-tending to others, worth through helping, rescuer, consummate caretaker

BARRIERS TO OTHER **ATTUNEMENT**

Poor Attention: requires intimate attention to focus & sense ones' own plus another's experience
Distracted: internally by your own mental-emotional noise or externally by digital stimulation or the environment
Emotionally Shutdown: it is difficult to sense others when our own sensing system is shut down, closed or numb
Self-Absorption: overly focused on having your own needs met before being resourced enough to attend to someone else
Low Emotional Literacy, Empathy or Perspectives: unable to interpret what might be being sensed

ATTUNEMENT DEVELOPMENT SUCCESS STORY

Self-attunement is the prerequisite to self-care. Initially, Brenner, a computer genius, wasn't too competent at either attunement or self-care. As a late 20's millennial & after a couple of unsuccessful attempts at college primarily due to poor attunement (self-care, time management, sleep schedule, etc.), he was still living at home, isolating in his room & spending so many hours on the computer that his mother had to make a time restriction. We did processes to really see into his world & honor his unique gifts, turning up the self-appreciation & turning down the self-criticism (including desensitizing some past events & limiting beliefs) in order to make space for self-attunement scanning. "What do I need today physically (food, exercise, computer breaks to maintain vitality)?" "What do I need emotionally & socially?" "What do I need for mental stimulation & moving in the direction of my desired career?" We started identifying 3 priorities each morning that needed to get done by the end of each day. At the time of publishing, he was almost finished with his computer science degree & is interviewing in a very specialized niche technology field.

"We have the ability to listen to life in two channels simultaneously – the outside channel and the inside channel (when we are tuned into our core intelligence). We can tune into people like a radio station...Higher attunement means listening to others without our personal filters."
- Thomas Hubl -

HOW ATTUNEMENT DEVELOPS

As infants, we were less self-reliant and communicative than we become as adults. From an infant perspective, it is a big, new world and we need a few essentials in order to survive, but we can't talk, walk, feed ourselves or even wipe our bottoms after elimination. Infants are completely dependent on our adult caregivers to attune to their needs for safety, shelter, sleep, nourishing milk, burping, touching, connection, soothing emotional state regulation, etc. So without being able to talk, we as infants need to have all of our needs met in order to survive and develop. As an infant, we must receive physical liquid nourishment and emotional connection nourishment for our developing bodies and brains which, in addition to the need for these developmental nutrients, are learning to regulate our emotions and nervous systems via this attunement process. Allan Schore PhD, pioneering UCLA neurobiology researcher and psychotherapist first described in 1994 how an attuned parent, in the back-and-forth attunement dance with their infant amidst the swirling sea of emotions in the baby's brain, is actually helping the baby begin to develop the neurological capacity to regulate his/her own emotions, states, body sensations and biological processes.[1]

Again attunement refers to the ability to tune into our state and needs (physical and emotional) to help our system restore balance and then to be able to tune into the state and needs of others. Frequent eye contact is one of the most important initial attunement methods of connection between infants and adults. Touch through skin contact, secure holding and breastfeeding are also important ways we feel attuned with and connected as infants. From infancy to 18 months, our connection with our primary caregivers is the main regulator of our nervous system. Prior to this we are unable to self-regulate, and this ability must be learned and wired into our nervous system through thousands of what Dan Siegel calls *"micro-moments of interaction"*: the continual, subtle, body-based, interactive exchanges of eye contact, facial expressions, body language, tone of voice, emotion and other subtleties that *"reveal otherwise hidden states of mind"*.[2] Each time a mother effectively attunes to her baby and the baby feels seen, felt, heard and soothed, it helps regulate her baby's nervous system and in doing so the baby's nervous system is learning how to eventually self-regulate.

To use a metaphor to help us understand being self-resourced before taking care of others, consider an airline flight attendant's suggestion that in case of an emergency it is suggested that we put on our oxygen mask first to make sure we are not in chaos or survival mode but instead are relaxed and full of life. As we will explore more deeply in the *Connection section,* a mother who has not in herself developed a capacity for self-regulated relaxation and secure attachment inhibits her ability to provide secure attachment to her own child {**emotionally available** (open and comfortable with closeness), **responsive** (able to receive another's reach for support, comfort, and reassurance) and **reliable connection** (secure base and safe haven to freely venture out and return)}. Not only does she need to be physically present, but also emotionally available and attuned. In fact, an essential part of misattunement is that some parents could benefit from more presence (groundedness, breath relaxation, emotional intelligence, heart open connection, etc.) so they are resourced enough to be able to effectively attune to their children...and each other as well...(wink, wink) romantic partners.

One important point here is that we humans need to learn to **self-attune** (to be aware of our own needs and practice good self-care) or when to **ask for support from others**. Ideally, we can learn this from a parent who is decently enough attuned. It is not easy being a parent, but this practice of intimately tuning into, sensing and responding to the state, wants and needs of our children, others and frankly ourselves first so we can be resourced enough to attune to others, is a very important human skill. Some mothers, who themselves as children did not receive the attunement they needed, can be unable to attune to themselves and therefore their own child—a pattern that can be passed down generationally. The adult is intended by nature to be the more resourced party who is supposed to attune and take care of the child. However, in sometimes the roles can be reversed where a parent is too **emotionally imbalanced** (chaotic) or **depressed** (shutdown),[3] even more than their child, so the parent can unconsciously use their own child to meet their own emotional needs, help the parent calm down or take the love form their own child that they never received. In these circumstances, a child can grow up too soon by being the one who attunes to their parents or other family members, which can either lead to the child being codependent in over-tending to others while sacrificing themselves, becoming hyper self-reliant in taking care of their own needs at the expense of their own joy, play, and childhood.

Dan Siegel who has pioneered the enhanced scientific understanding of interpersonal neurobiology to help us understand what is happening in our brains and nervous systems during interpersonal relating describes another possible negative result of chronic lack of parental attunement:

> *"When we need to be seen and understood by others our attachment circuits are revved up; we are in a state of seeking connection. And when our (attunement) need is met, we move forward happily through lives. But if we are not seen, if our caregivers do not attune to us, and we are met with the experience of feeling invisible or misunderstood, our nervous system response with a sudden activation of the break position of its regulatory circuits. Slamming on the brakes creates a distinct physiological response: heaviness in the chest, nausea in the belly and downcast or turned-away eyes. We literally shrink into ourselves from a pain that is often beneath our Awareness. This nauseating and jolting shift occurs and is experienced as a state of shame. Shame states are common in children whose parents are repeatedly unavailable or who habitually failed to attune to them."* [4]

Psychotherapists Laurence Heller and Aline LaPierre in their work *Healing Developmental Trauma* describe another way we can adapt to ineffective parental attunement by emotionally numbing or learning to limit own needs:

> *"Babies learn to match the amount of nurturing available. There's intelligence to the strategy because it's the only way dependent babies can cope with a deficit over which they have no control. At the onset, this response reflects a healthy capacity to adapt. However, if the nurturing and attunement deficits continue for too long, the body-mind of the developing infant is negatively affected. Babies begin to ignore their own needs. Again, there is intelligence to this response because it's too painful for babies to continue feeling their needs when satisfaction is not forthcoming. Babies disconnect from their own needs and eventually lose touch with them. The reaction not to need leads to a numbness to sensations and feelings."* [5]

MASLOW'S HIERARCHY OF NEEDS

Abraham Maslow was a prominent pioneering U.S. psychologist in what later became known as the *Human Potential Movement.*[6] He was interested in personality and motivation, as well as specifically why some people experienced different degrees of happiness and thriving. Working with thousands of people over his lifetime he came to understand that humans are in a developmental process of satisfying specific essential human needs. If we are freezing cold, severely dehydrated or starving, our fundamental human survival instincts or **physiological needs** will preoccupy us so we can satisfy these needs first and foremost. Next, assuming that we do have enough *food, shelter, warmth*, etc. but our lives are threatened by living in a war zone, we then are then motivated to ensure our **safety needs** of *protection, security (personal and financial), and boundaries*. Once we are safe, we seek to fulfill our deep human **belongingness needs** for *respect, acceptance, relation, connection, common bonding and affection often in social organizations such as gang, clubs, sports teams, religious groups, work teams, professional organizations*, etc. Next, we humans seek to satisfy our esteem needs through behaviors motivated by *achievement* and *status creation* for respect and acceptance by self and others. Maslow identified two orders of esteem needs: *the 1st esteem need* is for the **respect from others**: *recognition, attention, status, and prestige*; the *2nd esteem need* is for **self-respect**: the need for *self-confidence, strength, competence, mastery, independence, and freedom*. Maslow collectively classified as deficiency needs these basic *physiological, safety, belongingness*, and *esteem needs*.

While a deficiency in *physiological needs* manifests as noticeable symptoms in the body the only signs of deficiency in *safety*, belongingness, and *esteem needs* are *anxiety, stress, and tension*. Once these fundamental **Deficiency Needs** are met, Maslow observed that people move into the second tier **Being Needs** and are motivated to *grow, evolve, authentically express themselves, cultivate and share their unique gifts in service, etc.* Maslow describes this motivation for self-actualization and expression of one's full potential in contribution as *"the desire to become more and more what one is, to become everything that one is capable of becoming."* With even a basic understanding of *Maslow's Hierarchy of Needs*, open us up to much greater compassion for ourselves and fellow humans. It is easier to understand how someone without food might be more motivated to steal; how someone whose life was threatened might be more motivated to kill to secure the safety needs of themselves or loved ones; how someone looking to fulfill belongingness needs might join a gang or exclusive membership group to satisfy a sense of family and connection which they might not have previously experienced sufficiently; how someone with unmet self-esteem needs might sacrifice their integrity and authenticity in behaviors or even work jobs not aligned with their deeper values to achieve status or possessions to subconsciously bolster their self-esteem. Furthermore, we can now better understand why the inner motivation for authentic expression and self-actualization needs manifests differently amongst different individuals.

ATTUNEMENT TO OUR OWN PERSONAL NEEDS

Perhaps the above description of how our attunement skills developed or not was useful for our understanding. Perhaps we don't care about all that developmental stuff. Either way, the only choice we have is to start where we are.

Self-attunement enables us to recognize, self-regulate or reach out for support and take in physical and emotional nourishment. The first step of this is that we have to be able to internally scan and be aware of our own needs. Some people have a yet unresolved conflict between having essential personal human needs and rejecting them. Again some of us learned to be very attuned to others' needs while suppressing awareness of own needs. Some feel prideful about not having needs, others feel shameful about being needy or do not feel like we deserve to have our needs met; any of which can inhibit this natural self-attunement process and contribute to poor self-care or sabotage us from fully receiving support from others. Ultimately the first step in the whole needs fulfillment process is allowing ourselves to have essential human physical and emotional needs and then being aware of them. There is a strong human impulse to have our needs met, to feel relaxed in our body, to be emotionally regulated, and feel connected to others, yet when we feel imbalanced we use all kinds of strategies from avoidance, distraction, self-medicating, addiction, etc. to soothe the best we can. We all have varying degrees of ability to attune to our own needs and self-care or ask for support. Sometimes these strategies are unconscious or semi-conscious, but we are sometimes aware of only the tip of the iceberg above water, strategic behaviors, rather than going deeper below the surface to the underlying discomfort, distress or needs.

ATTUNEMENT & SELF-CARE
Self-care requires self-attunement; these questions can offer us a starting point in our ability to attune to and take care of ourselves. Whether we had good modeling and instruction for self-care as a child or not, we all have to learn it some time or another.

Do you regularly attune to your body, needs, and overall state?
Do you feel comfortable in your skin?
What are you feeling? How often do you check in with your body as to what you are feeling?
When you are tired, do you sleep?
Do you take breaks at the computer when you need to so you stay productive and vital throughout the day?
When you are thirsty, do you drink?
When you are hungry, do you eat?

Do you know how to attune to the type and quality of foods your body instinctually wants to eat or does impulsivity or dissociated theory override this knowingness?
When you feel tense or stressed do you have supportive ways to relax?
What is the quality of your breathing and overall state right now?

WHEN TO SELF-REGULATE, WHEN TO ASK FOR SUPPORT

The life-cycle of attunement begins with a self-awareness scan, and from here can go in two directions, self-regulation (physical and/or emotional) or asking for support from others. It is a good thing to learn to both self-regulate and to ask for support. Ultimately, we all need to learn self-regulation of emotions and physical bodily processes; some already have this integrated, some can learn it on their own with biofeedback technology, while others do better learning in the attuned presence of another person. Some people who are disconnected from their body, when asked what they are feeling in their body, feel confused, anxious, speechless or unable to answer the question; these people fall into the latter category of those who could benefit from the attuned presence of another to help them learn greater self-attunement and self-regulation.

Some people have beliefs or blocks around asking for help from others. Some are proud of having become hyper self-reliant due to a lack of trustable caregivers, mentors or lack of effective attunement. As we are learning to become more trusting of others' reliability and to ask for help, some of us have trouble verbally expressing our requests. Some have a fear of being denied, perhaps from the remaining pain of repeated unsuccessful attempts. Some secretly want other people to intuit their needs and come to the rescue. Just like when children sometimes react to unmet needs with frustration, anger, or emotional manipulation, some adults who are learning how to verbally express requests for help, when they try it can come out in younger frustrated ways. This actually happened to me, as I was learning how to be more aware of my needs and ask for support, as an adult. Heller and LaPierre, cautioned that this can push people who they actually want to attune to them, away even further, potentially reinforcing the loop that if they do express a need it won't be reliably met.[7] Like most things, this takes practice to be aware of our inner landscape, to be okay with what we notice, to be in connection with another and make appropriate, clearly communicated requests.

SCARCITY

Other people have become hopelessly numb or unconscious to this whole attunement process, which might show up as a prideful minimalist or a person continuously struggling in survival mode with barely enough. Raina DeLear and Anna-lisa Aldeberg from *Luminous Awareness Institute*, observe some people have developed a survival defense when they became accustomed as children to living with unmet needs, in which they learned the pain of unsuccessfully asking was too great, so it seemed a better strategy for adapting to scarcity and learn to make do with the minimum to want no more from their surroundings, others and life, than was available.[8] Their work suggests that this needs compensation can go in of collapse or hyper-self-reliance. While from one perspective the later adaptation can be functional especially in the short term, but when scarcity or just barely enough is a chronic pattern it is also a chronic stressor that limits joy, pleasure and thriving. Some people have a block around receiving which can sometimes be related to this pattern and for some, it seems as if they have a hole in their bucket such that they either block themselves from taking in enough or can save enough resources.

SELF-CARE & RECEIVING ALLOWS PLEASURE & THRIVING

What is the benefit of self-care, receiving and all this attunement stuff? Well, taking care of ourselves and our human needs, allowing pleasure in our body and thriving in our lives, of course. Sometimes we need to learn to be grateful for what we have and be happy amidst scarce resources and on the other end of the spectrum sometimes we need to learn to experience greater pleasure, fullness and well-being. If we don't attune to our own needs and take care of ourselves or effectively get support, eventually our body and life tend to fall apart. The benefit of attuning to and tending to our body and life while opening our giving and receiving channels is that we can allow the experience of support, pleasure, love, and fullness so that we can live with greater ease, joy and thriving.

ATTUNING TO ANOTHER

As soon as you engage with another person, do you instinctually attune to their overall state, mood, physical comfort, sense of safety, openness or closure for connection and authentic congruence?

Attunement and emotional openness are doorways into feeling connected to others. This always starts with self-attunement as I need to be able to be centered, resourced and aware enough to be able to attune to another. If my own mental-scape is so noisy and chaotic, or if I cannot feel my own body, it is nearly impossible for me to be quiet enough to sense into the subtle nuances of another's inner landscape. While some people struggle with self-absorption, others have difficulty with staying centered inside while simultaneously connecting with another—losing awareness of their inner landscape and needs, while going over onto the other person's side and overly attuning to the other. Ideally, we are able to **self-attune** and **other-attune** to our own inner state AND the state others, simultaneously. Again we can learn to better attune and self-regulate on our own through biofeedback training or in the safe, dependable, empathetic, and attuned presence of another—whether a romantic partner, spouse, friend, therapist or coach.

To some this might bring up worries about doing it right or being not good enough, but here is some real, in the trenches research from Harvard, retold by bonding expert Sue Johnson in noting that we just need to be attuned just enough of the time (in this case 30%), so that the other person overall feels seen, heard, felt and gotten.

> *"Misattunement is inevitable and normal; in fact, it is startlingly common. Ed Tronick of Harvard Medical School, who has spent years absorbed in monitoring the interactions between mother and child, finds that even happily bonded mothers and infants miss each other's signals fully 70 percent of the time. Adults miss their partner's cues most of the time, too! We all send unclear signals and misread cues. We become distracted, we suddenly shift our level of emotional intensity and leave our partner behind, or we simply overload*

each other with too many signals and messages. Only in the movies does one poignant gaze predictably follow another and one small touch always elicit an exquisitely timed gesture in return. We are sorely mistaken if we believe that love is about always being in tune." [9]

ATTUNING TO LIFE

In deeper states of Presence with greater Vantage of Awareness, it might seem as though there is less of an exclusive focus on personal states and needs—although of course they are still included. However, as Awareness expands, the attunement function extends to include a greater span of consideration. Although healthy interpersonal boundaries could also still be included, the ego inside and Life outside distinction begins to relax and blur as Awareness is seen to include all of these. From this Vantage, vastly Open as if the moment itself were the body-view, the attunement process can sense the greater needs of the group, room, or moment and can equally accept everything to be exactly as it is or allow itself to be skillfully animated in service of that. If this does not resonate, please focus on attuning to our own physical and emotional self-care, then focus on attuning to the state and needs of others. Ultimately, these are all included in the greater attunement to self, others and Life Itself—to whatever Vantage of Awareness we can inhabit.

ATTUNEMENT SUMMARY & KEY TAKEAWAYS

➤ Attunement involves sensing or tuning into the state (energy & emotion) & needs (physical & emotional).

➤ We can learn to attune ourselves, others & our surroundings.

➤ As infants, caregiver attunement helps young ones know themselves, get needs met, regulate their state & feel securely connected.

➤ Some adults have difficulty attuning to others when their own unmet needs or emotional static is so loud, while others lose themselves in connection, self-sacrificing their own needs or taking the attention off their own emotional pain.

➤ Healthy self-care comes from self-attunement to our states & needs, which allows us to receive & thrive in our lives.

➤ We can learn when to self-regulate or take care of our own needs & when to ask for support versus more wounded patterns of helpless collapse, overly self-reliant can't trust others.

LISTENING

How would your friends & loved ones rate your **listening**? Can they get your full attention or are you often too busy, ignoring, preoccupied or multitasking?

Do you try to fix, control, give unsolicited advice, interrupt, or talk-over others when **listening**?

How open, empty & spacious
can Awareness feel
while **listening**?

"If I appeal to you for emotional connection and you respond intellectually to a problem, rather than directly to me, on an attachment level I will experience that as "no response." This is one of the reasons that the research on social support uniformly states that people want "indirect" support, that is, emotional confirmation and caring from their partners, rather than advice."

- Sue Johnson -

WHAT IS **LISTENING**

The capacity to be quiet, receptive, curious & attuned enough to hear what is being expressed

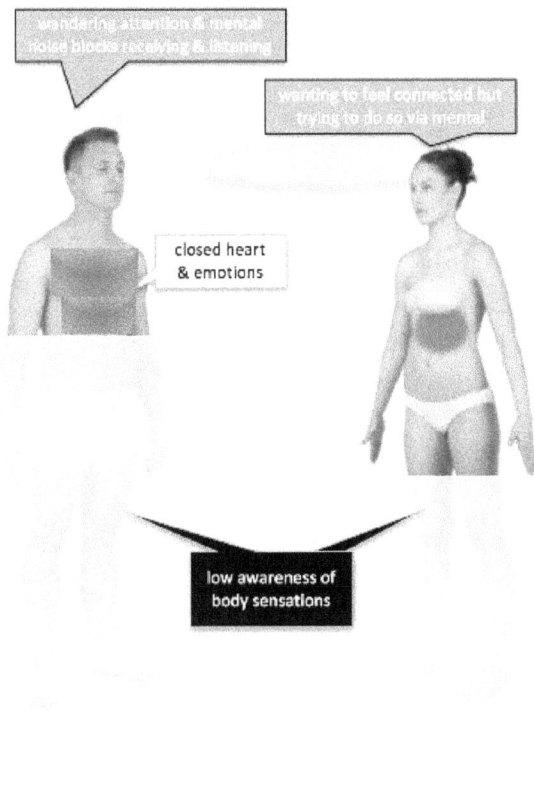

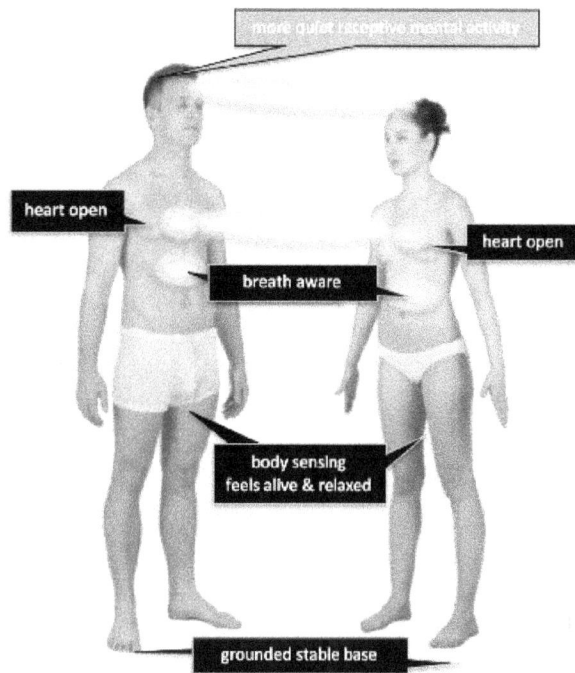

WHY **LISTENING** MATTERS

Communication: essential for effective communication

Rapport: listening with genuine curiosity & attunement supports shared resonance of rapport

Empathy & Perspective-taking: enables feeling emotional resonance with others & understanding their perspectives

Connection & Relationships: essential to develop, maintain & deepen connection & relating

Work: essential for effective conversation, correspondence, managing people, training & motivation

Clients: enables better service, understanding, sales & satisfaction

Getting Other's World: allows speakers to feel heard, understood, appreciated & seen for who they are

Safe to Express: allows speakers to feel safe, accepted, & freer to open & express a greater depth & range of themselves without feeling self-conscious, feeling pressure to present themselves in a certain way or hide things for fear of others knowing

BARRIERS TO **LISTENING**

Distracted: internally preoccupied with your own mental-emotion noise or externally by digital stimulation/environment

Emotional Overwhelm: redirecting attention to own internal experience or easier to dissociate than stay in connection

Poor Attention / Busy Mind: requires intimate attention to focus & sense ones' own plus another's experience

Self-Absorption: focused on your own needs, anxiously waiting to talk or thinking of what you want to say

Interrupting: talking over or always having to speak the last word

Ignoring: disregarding or pretending to not care as a power-play

Multitasking: task-switching while splitting attention between 2 or more things

Advice or Fixing: giving unrequested advice or trying to problem solve when the person simply wants you to listen

Bias: judgment, prejudice, filter, or fixating on first impression

Selective Perception: I can only hear what I want to hear

LISTENING DEVELOPMENT SUCCESS STORY

Tanner's main focus was his professional objectives, but upon further exploration, he realized that he had a deeper "need to be heard" & a "need to be seen as knowledgeable" that had him do most of the talking in most of his relationships in business, with friends & especially with his fiancé. Further, he realized that with his fiancé, he never actually listened to her, asked her questions nor asked her what she was feeling or thinking. It was as if he was using her as an object to fulfill his needs rather than interacting in real time with another equal human being. Through a series of progressive embodied connection & communication practices, Tanner wired his nervous system to be able to be aware of himself & another person in conversation so that there are two unique humans relating with each other in a communication dance. Learning to really quietly & curiously listen to her, value her contribution to a conversation, appreciate her perspectives by feeling himself & her simultaneously, they have dramatically deepened their presence & connection.

"Look man, you can listen to Jimi (Hendrix) but you can't hear him. There's a difference man.
Just because you're listening to him doesn't mean you're hearing him."

- Wesley Snipes White Man Can't Jump -

Listening is a crucial part of our ability to communicate and thrive in relationships and at work. It affects how well we understand, acknowledge, and appreciate others as we create, maintain, and deepen relationships as well as the way we engage, correspond, sell, inspire, instruct, and manage in our workplace. Better listening enhances communication, understanding, and appreciation of others. More advanced listening enables empathy and compassion, as well as enhancing relationships and connection with others. The masterful listeners listen from a depth of openness that allows speakers to feel heard, understood, appreciated, seen for who they are and feel freer to express a greater range of themselves. There is always an Awareness within us that is listening; what we consciously hear requires the safety and relaxation of embodiment with the curiosity and attunement of connection.

THE EMBODIMENT OF LISTENING

As children up until the age of 7 years old, we are in a highly receptive, almost hypnotic state. Our predominant brain state is theta, which is common in dreaming, flow states, creativity, and learning.[1] It is a highly suggestible time in our lives, ripe for learning and assimilating the beliefs, worldview, and behavior of our parents, caregivers, teachers and friends. It is only later as our brains continue to develop that we learn to better discern relative truth from fiction. Yet in this young period of infancy and childhood, is our first introduction to listening, during which time our capacity to take other perspectives tends to be limited to our own experience. In the first stage of listening, we tend to either be self-absorbed In our own Me-Map perspective or get distracted by our own experience and have limited resources to pay attention to the other person's experience. This can show itself as being overly distracted by the volume and static of our own inner experience (sensations, thoughts, emotions) or distracted by the sights, sounds, movement, or technology in the external environment. Classic barriers that commonly get in the way of better listening include trying to fix the other person, problem-solving, giving advice, or focusing more on the outcome than a mutual exploration of the immediate conversation. Sometimes emotions can arise in conversation and if the listener can't stay present with those emotions or discomfort in the speaker or themselves, some uncomfortable listeners can try to pep talk the person out of feeling that way with hyper-positivity. This dilutes the mutual depth of presence by retreating to the more superficial safety of the mental world.

When we get stuck in the Awareness of only our own skin-encapsulated world, we can sometimes also interrupt others, try to feel more powerful by talking over others, be preoccupied thinking of what we want to say, or anxiously waiting for our turn to talk without really even hearing the other person. In other cases, some people's focus remains on themselves because either they are overly consumed with satisfying their own self-esteem needs or they haven't yet developed the ability to care about others. Even a personal agenda to be heard can capture the majority of our attention and limit our ability to receptively listen and actually hear others. Sometimes we ignore others, give them the blocking *"yah yah yah"*, or pretend to partially listen, while dividing our attention on something else. With partial or selective listening, sometimes we only allow ourselves to hear what we want to hear to reinforce our own beliefs, feeling of safety, and self-image.

And yet some of us less qualified listeners have actually heard requests to be better listeners, however many of us do not actually know how to be or what to do to enhance our listening skills. The basic skill of listening is partially a 1st person embodied hardware issue—meaning a brain and bodily capacity to relax and become quiet—and partially a 2nd person relational software component—meaning the ability to be curious and attune to others. Stephen Porges explains the science behind why we literally have to feel safe and be relaxed to effectively listen.[2]   His Poly Vagal research shows that the vegas nerve fibers connect our brain with muscles and bodily functions that control facial expressivity, vocal intonation, breathing, heart openness and even the muscles in the middle ear that control listening. So when the person across from us, all of a sudden gets emotionally reactive, muscularly tense, raises the tone of their voice, has their face go flat or starts avoiding eye contact, know that the capacity to listen and receive what we are saying has declined. When this happens, focus on restoring safety, body relaxation and connection before trying to continue communication.

The first step in becoming a better listener is a more **internal personal process** and starts with increasing our **relaxation** with breath and body sensing and training our ability to be empty of mental chatter by concentrating our attention. The muscular tension, shallow breathing, restless leg, fidgeting, or insufficient activity of a sedentary lifestyle can manifest in our bodies as either tense stagnation or restless hyperactivity. And because the experience in our body is intimately related to the quality of our mental and emotional world, the lack of relaxed readiness in our bodies mirrors the lack of quiet alertness in our mind. As discussed in the *Body Sensing section* the latest biofeedback research on mindfulness demonstrates that being more relaxed and mindful starts in the body with increasing attention on breath and body sensing. Sometimes there is simply too much static inside of our own system to be quiet enough to attentively listen to another person. Learning to tune out background noise and technological distractions by concentrating our attention inside our bodies allows us to become more quiet, relaxed and alert within ourselves, physically, emotionally and mentally. This is the first step to enhancing our capacity for presence and listening, because it is when we are relaxed, empty, quiet and aware within ourselves, no longer stuck in our own stuff or distracted by static that our system can now be available to receive multi-channel information and sense the empathic impact in our own body, emotions, thoughts, subtleties, and intuition while listening.

THE INTIMACY OF LISTENING

The next evolution in the development of listening becomes **interpersonal**, as we intentionally move beyond exclusive awareness of our own world and metaphorically move out into another's world (You-Map perspective—which we will learn about in more detail in the *Empathy, Perspectives, Impact & Compassion section*). Ideally we want to maintain awareness of what is happening inside of our body, while also feeling connected and being aware of someone else's experience, yet as we are learning, what tends to happen is we either get stuck inside our self (Me-Map perspective) or leave our own perspective and can get lost in someone else's world (You-Map perspective). Rather than one or the other or merging, ultimately we want to train our nervous system to maintain awareness of Me-Map, a You-Map, and a third co-created We-Map. As we increasingly develop healthy boundaries, as opposed to merging and are able to stay resourced at home within ourselves AND openly reach out with genuine regard for others, we are able to maintain our own center, stay grounded and quiet, while listening inside to our own inner world AND attentively to others. **Curiosity** and **attunement** are the two most important ingredients for moving from "I" or "you" and switching focus to a more expanded focus or "me AND you". Curiosity has an open, receptive, non-judgmental quality of availability to it. When we are listening without defensiveness, judgment, or with ulterior motives to *"get something"* from someone else, our mind-body system possesses the empty openness to really listen and openly receive the other person's expression and experience. When curiosity has an active flavor, it comes with a genuine desire to know more deeply and often asks powerful questions. It is the same curiosity that has our minds want to go out and explore our external environment, other countries, and even outer space that has our hearts want to reach out to connect, know and feel others. Once curiosity is activated, we can learn how to *"attune"* to someone else's system, which is the capacity that underlies connection, rapport, and empathy. As we learned in the previous section, the origin of the word attune is the combination of *"at"* and *"tune"*. The tuning process of one musical instrument with another as musicians are warming up is similar to the attunement of one human nervous system to another in real human connection. There is a lot more information being exchanged in human relating than just mental words. Just like a good musician learns to listen and Deeply "feel" the music, so to an attuned human learns to deeply sense another. Attunement involves allowing one's body to be relax, open and alive so it can sense the deeper body language, movement, tonality, emotion, energy, etc. being expressed moment to moment. This is not a purely mental analytical process, but an embodied resonant awareness that creates the deep human connection. Through this attuning process, deeper connection, energetic rapport and emotional empathy align to help us really sense and understand someone else's world in a much deeper and more nuanced capacity. Listening to the momentary fluctuations in the tone of voice reveal much more than merely deciphering the binary data from the surface content of the words as if it were in computer programing language. The same phrase can be spoken in varying tonalities, each revealing differing underlying meanings, and emotionality. In Japanese, speaking is a combination of the content of the words plus intention via *ki* (energy). So listening with more presence has a two-way channel of being more present and receptive in my own 1st person Me-Map system and more curiously attuned to our 2nd person You-Map system.

THE AWARENESS OF LISTENING

Finally, the very best listeners have the added advantage of being more relaxed and resourced in an even deeper open presence, attuned to everything arising in the environment. Some have cultivated an open, receptive, spacious, nonjudgmental ability to receive and allow the range of emotions, thoughts, sensations, and perspectives within themselves and others. Allowing the moment to unfold, discerning when to be receptive and when to ask a powerful question, they are okay with silence and words, emptiness and fullness, yet being attuned to far more than just words and thoughts they often savor pauses and might notice unspoken underlying emotions, sensations, or beliefs. When someone with this capacity is listening to us, we might feel really heard and understood with a sense of safety, openness, acceptance, and spaciousness to receive whatever arises in us or needs to be expressed. Listening from this depth of presence has a way of drawing out deeper authenticity, insight, underlying beliefs and emotions. From this depth, speakers sometimes realize and mention something to the extent of *"WOW! I can't believe I am telling you this"* or *"I feel so safe and accepted. I feel like I could tell you anything"* or *"I really feel like you get me"* or *"I feel like I can share parts of myself and learn things about myself just by the way you listen"*. Speakers might feel free to express more of themselves without feeling self-conscious, trying to be perfect, feeling pressure to present themselves in a certain way or hide things they are afraid of others knowing. Some listen to the world around them as an extension of themselves—personal, interpersonal and transpersonal are all included. Ultimately, Awareness includes the listener, the one being listened to, and the act of listening itself.

LISTENING SUMMARY & KEY TAKEAWAYS

➤ Effective listening, first requires becoming more relaxed in our body which allows us to quiet mental & emotional static to become more empty & available to listen & receive someone else's experience.

➤ Then with genuine curiosity to know someone more deeply & a openness to connect, we can passively receive them or ask a curious question.

➤ Staying resourced in our body (grounded in our legs & centered in our center axis) when listening to others prevents us from leaving ourselves & getting lost in their world.

➤ Most people are either self-absorbed ("Me" focused) or lose their own center in connection ("You" focused without awareness of "Me") or merge (an amorphous blob or It) in connection but healthy connection with mutually individuation ("Me AND You") allows the meeting of two & the creation of a third "we space".

➤ Listening without defensiveness, judgment, hidden motives, giving advice, trying to fix, or to "get something" allows the speaker to feel safer to express more of themselves.

➤ Attunement with another person's system while listening allows rapport, resonant connection, empathy & multi-channel information to be sensed & received thru words, sensations, emotions, body language & tonality in the other person's system.

➤ A skilled listener discerns when to be silent, when to empathize, when to relate, or when to ask a deeper question.

➤ Deeper listening occurs from deeply relaxed, spacious & open presence attuned to everything arising, allowing the moment to unfold & something new to emerge, drawing out deeper authenticity, insight, underlying beliefs, intentions, embodied sensations, emotions, energy & presence.

CONNECTION

How do you tend to feel more anxious about losing **connection** or tend to avoid **connection**?

When you feel **disconnected** from your partner do you tend to be the one who pursues or withdrawals?

Would your current or last romantic partner say you were easy to **connect** with, emotionally available, responsive, reliable & verbalized your inner world?

"We seek out, monitor, and try to maintain emotional and physical connection with our loved ones. Throughout life, we rely on them to be emotionally accessible, responsive, and engaged with us. We reach out for our loved ones particularly when we are uncertain, threatened, anxious, or upset. Contact with them gives us a sense of having a safe haven, where we will find comfort and emotional support; this sense of safety teaches us how to regulate our own emotions and how to connect with and trust others. •We miss our loved ones and become extremely upset when they are physically or emotionally remote; this separation anxiety can become intense and incapacitating. Isolation is inherently traumatizing for human beings. We depend on our loved ones to support us emotionally and be a secure base as we venture into the world and learn and explore. The more we sense that we are effectively connected, the more autonomous and separate we can be."

--- Sue Johnson ---

WHAT IS **CONNECTION**

the capacity to be open, emotionally available & feel connected to ourselves, others and life around us

attempting to connect mentally

heart guarded

heart guarded

If you can't feel your own body, you can't feel connected to others

fear

heart guarded

anxiety

dismissive avoiding connection

asnxious reaching for connection

ungrounded

felt sense of connection thru heart openness & emotional vulnerability

heart open

heart open

body sensing feels alive & relaxed

grounded secure base

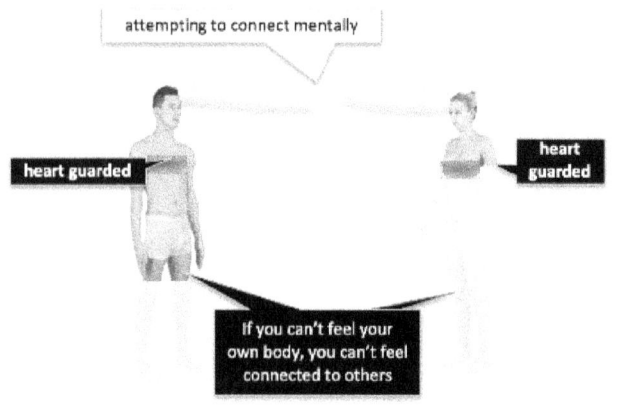

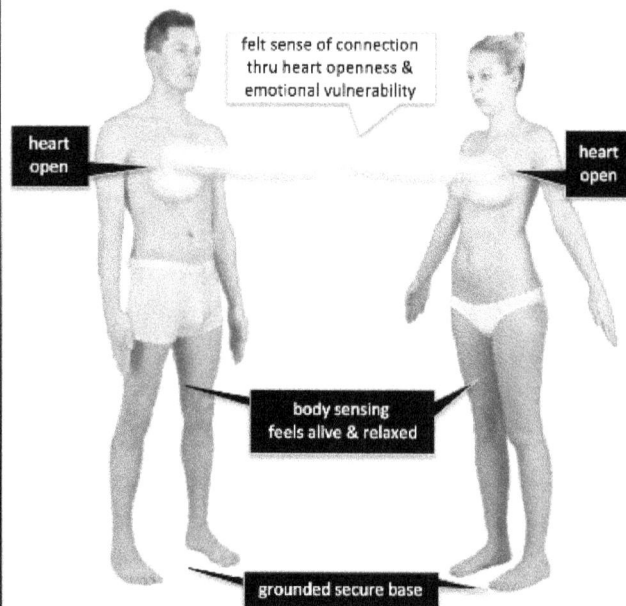

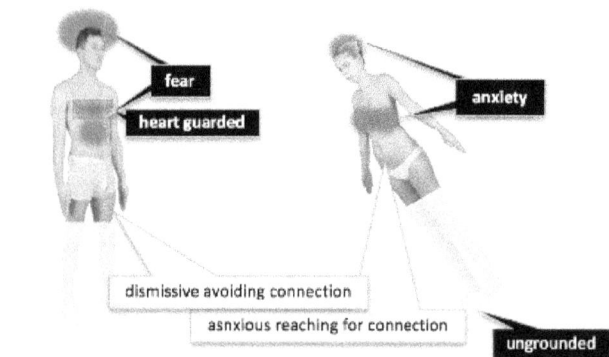

WHY **CONNECTION** MATTERS

Social Beings: humans are social creatures, wired for connection with others, primary partners, family, friends & community

Health: research shows strong social connection enhances immunity, heart health, stress-buffering, well-being & longevity

Nervous System Development: from birth, attuned connection from our caregivers literally wires & builds neuronal architecture

Connection Circuitry: our early bonding & attachment patterns with caregivers whether secure, anxious, avoidant, or ambivalent wires our tendencies & capacities for connection as adults

Impulse to Bond: infants need to feel securely bonded with caregivers, as do adults have related drives to feel securely connected

Primal Panic: our primal survival circuits, evolutionarily wired for bonding with a secure partner, can get tripped when threatened

Transparent Communication: with emotional vulnerability is the essential doorway to closeness & connection

Closeness: emotional vulnerability & an undefended open heart are the gateways to feeling connection & intimacy with others

BARRIERS TO **CONNECTION**

Dissociation: not feeling & inhabiting your body due to trauma, defense or hyper-mental

Self-Absorption: overly focused on having your own needs met before being resourced enough to attend to someone else

Hyper-Mental: excessive mental activity, overly theoretical, living in fantasy, lost in the past or future

Unwelcomed: not feeling wanted or welcomed during conception or as an infant by parents or socially at school

Self-Referencing: part of healthy boundaries, the ability to self-reference from central column rather than others

Fear of Connection & Intimacy: fear of emotional closeness, connection, rejection, judgment, hurt, or betrayal

Empty Heart: younger unmet needs or unfulfilled love exchange

Judgmental: critical, negative, or condemning point of view about others or the world with fixed attention & closed heart

Image Positioning: hiding something or trying to say something to be seen in a certain way or meet expectation

Hesitation or Withholding: guarded, hiding, fear of being judged or criticized, fear of saying the wrong thing

Fear of being Seen: hiding or blocking real expression to avoid criticism, disapproval or rejection

Superficiality: avoiding depth, afraid of intimacy or feeling deeper emotions

Low Body Sensing: emotions are experienced in the body & insufficient body sensing inhibits emotional Awareness

Trust Issues: need to avoid or dominate/power-over to feel safe, past betrayal hurt or rejection

Not Good Enough: unreleased shame, feeling unworthy/unlovable, emotionally charged unreleased from past memories

Closure: being closed & not allowing life or others into inside, afraid to allow emotional vulnerability or others to know, see, feel you

Merging: Lack of individuation & healthy boundaries can lead to merging rather than meeting in connection

Isolation: Feeling of not belonging, rejection, pride in being a loner, not needing others

Attachment Style: early & unhealed bonding patterns (anxious, avoidant, ambivalent)

CONNECTION DEVELOPMENT SUCCESS STORY

Elieen loved closeness & connection. She was passionate about all forms including touch, massage, sex, communication, conflict resolution, etc. As much as she loved connection, deep down she also really feared the loss of it. Eventually, she realized she was using multiple relationships to hedge her anxious style of attachment, fear of loss of connection & difficulty being by herself. She started doing attachment healing work, was offered a more secure bond by a loving partner & we worked on helping her learn how to stay in her own center so she could meet in connection as two individuated beings as opposed to losing herself through merging as a single blob. "Teach what you want to learn," they say; well today she has traversed much of the spectrum of the human connection & intimacy terrain & as a professional relationship therapist skillfully supports couples into a deeper connection, embodied self-love & secure bonding.

"We are biologically, cognitively, physically, and spiritually wired to love, to be loved, and to belong. When those needs are not met, we don't function as we were meant to. We break. We fall apart. We numb. We ache. We hurt others. We get sick."

– Brene Brown –

HOW CONNECTION DEVELOPS

Connection implies a bodily felt sense of relation, a link or bond between one or more people or objects. Even though in our most isolated, self-absorbed states it can feel like we are an island unto our self, we really are not. If we notice some part of us wanting to isolate our personal self and escape to some other moment than what is here now, we are going in the direction of less presence. Even in moments of solitude, we can feel connected to the totality of Life. The essence of Life is interdependence and connection; life forms arise in mutual dependence—sometimes called dependent origination or dependent arising.

Humans are social creatures and we have banded together in tribes and communities for hundreds of thousands of years to support each other in living. Sue Johnson, a renowned relationship therapist and foremost expert on adult bonding and connection, sites the finding of research in evolutionary biology and the latest neuroscience that the primary instinct of humans is neither sex nor aggression—it is to seek contact and connection.[1] Yes we do have aggressive and sexual drives: the former is an inherent property of the impulse to compete on the field of life and improve, and the latter is essential for procreation and to ensure the propagation of our species. But just as we are interdependent parts of life on Earth, in relationship and community, we come together to bond, live, and experience life together. Connection is not all touchy-feely; in some cases, it is a matter of survival. Athletes, soldiers, warriors, firefighters, law enforcement officers and even gang members can develop incredibly strong bonds and connections with each other after having proved their trust and reliability through challenging situations. They want to know they can count on each other and trust their comrades to have one another's backs in a tough circumstance, a life-threatening situation or a competition.

Bonding and connection begin in the womb with our mother and is especially essential because we are born into the world, small and dependent on her for our survival. Not only do we require feeding, nurturing and protecting as we grow, but we literally require connection through eye contact, touch, emotional resonance and loving heart connection for our development. We humans are social organisms, and our brains and nervous systems are wired for integration both within ourselves as individuals and in relational connection to others, and our first couple of years developing bonding, attention, attunement, mirroring, emotional responsiveness, etc. with our primary caregivers lays the foundation in our developing nervous systems for a lifetime of connectivity. Evolutionarily, we have been bred and are designed for connection and bonding. While some species in the animal kingdom leave their newborn soon after birth—as some humans can also do—human adults, especially mothers seem to have an innate drive to care for and connect with their young perhaps because our human species requires it for healthy development, which is enhanced by the precious infant's reaching, gazing, crying, cueing, and smiling. When we in our human infant vulnerability reach out, even yet without words, it is our caregivers' responsiveness, eye contact, emotional attunement and open heart that signals a felt sense of connection.

BONDING & ATTACHMENT

There are 4 specific styles of connecting with others in close relationships with varying degrees of secure connection, avoidance or anxiety, that are predominantly developed during the first 2 years of bonding patterns with primary caregivers based on their own attachment style and capacity for emotionally available, attuned responsiveness and reliable connection.

Research on attachment styles since the 1950's—especially pioneers John Bowlby and Mary Ainsworth's work with mother-infant bonding and later in 1980's as attachment theory was increasingly applied to adult relationships—has shown that the type of relating and connecting we had with our primary caregiver as infants, and especially our mother, has a profound impact on the type of connections, intimacy and relationships we develop with others as adults, unless we have done some inner rewiring and healing. Infants have obvious needs for nourishing milk, safety, and sleep, but research in the past century confirms that infants also have a primal human need for physical touch and developing a bonding connection through emotional attachment with at least one adult primary caregiver in order for healthy brain, emotional and social development. Lack of emotional connection and isolation can stunt this development, activate dysfunction or even be deadly. According to Sue Johnson, older studies of institutionalized orphans in the 1930's and 1940's who were provided shelter and nourished sufficiently with food, yet deprived of sufficient touch and human connection showed that 31-75% died before the age of 3, while newer studies of Romanian orphans who spent more than 20 hours per day alone suffer from brain abnormalities.[2]   Again, early connection with caregivers is literally forming our brain architecture and pathways for later connection.

John Bowlby noticed that infants separated from parents would use all kinds of strategies from desperate visual searching, to clinging, crying and even hysterical screaming to reestablish physical and emotional closeness with their primary caregivers who are their attachment figures.[3]   Rather than dismissing this as some neurotic infant thing, knowing these behaviors are common to a variety of mammal species, he searched for the evolutionary function these behaviors might serve. Like human infants, other species of mammals are also dependent on adults to feed and protect them, unlike reptiles like frogs, fish, and others who have an older brain structure and nervous system without the limbic-emotional brain region—and so lack the attachment system that mammals have.

So, Bowlby reasoned that infants who were able to maintain physical proximity and a special emotional connection to an adult attachment figure, via what at he called the attachment behavior system, would serve the evolutionary purpose of being more likely to survive and develop into reproductive age, as it does for all mammals. University of Illinois Professor of Psychology and attachment expert, R. Chris Fraley, who has written a great summary of attachment theory notes that according to Bowlby:

> *"the attachment system essentially asks the following fundamental question: Is the attachment figure nearby, accessible, and attentive? If the child perceives the answer to this question to be "yes," he or she feels loved, secure, and confident, and, behaviorally, is likely to explore his or her environment, play with others, and be sociable. If, however, the child perceives the answer to this question to be "no," the child experiences anxiety and, behaviorally, is likely to exhibit attachment behaviors ranging from simple visual searching on the low extreme to active following and vocal signaling on the other. These behaviors continue until either the child is able to reestablish a desirable level of physical or psychological proximity to the attachment figure, or until the child 'wears down,' as may happen in the context of a prolonged separation or loss. In such cases, Bowlby believed that young children experienced*

profound despair and depression." [4]

Mary Ainsworth initially, and numerous researchers since, who have studied infant and child development have identified several distinct infant attachment styles (secure, anxious, avoidant, disorganized)[5] resulting on our parents or caregivers' sensitivity, responsiveness and attachment security particularly during times of emotional distress during our first one to two years. Recent advances in neuroscience and fMRI technology have allowed us to look inside the brain while we are connecting and relating with one another, which has enabled us to have a much better scientific understanding of human connection. This field is referred to as Interpersonal Neurobiology, and pioneer Dan Siegel at UCLA emphasizes that in order for a child to feel securely attached to his or her parents or caregivers, a child must feel safe, seen and soothed.[6] Our parents' responsiveness to our physical and emotional needs, is largely based upon the parents own attachment orientation, yet this is a major factor in establishing our view of self as well as our wiring for emotional regulation and connection. We use **wiring** as a metaphor because the nerves in the front of our body (face, chest, and belly) literally develop based on how relational interactions usually occurred with our primary caregivers—which establishes the foundation for our patterns of relating in later life. In other words, as children our view of our caregivers, combined with our self-perception of how deserving we are of receiving good care from our caregivers, form our working models of attachment which help us anticipate caregiver responsiveness. These early interactions wire our nervous system to lay the foundations for our mental maps and body capacities for the ways we experience and how we believe *"connection works"*.

In a practical example, when we are standing across from someone in conversation, the nerves and muscles in our face, chest, and belly are either 1) relaxed and open to connection, 2) numb, guarded or closed avoiding connection 3) or anxious. So, our infant attachment patterns literally wire in our connection style for the rest of our lives, unless we heal and rewire our attachment and connection style. Although our adult romantic relationships do have obvious differences compared to our infant-caregiver dynamic, since they are also bonding relationships and excite the same bonding circuitry in our bodies (face, chest, and belly) and mental maps in our brains, the same core principles apply to both. Although we can be part of a larger community and have a variety of friends, we humans are designed to have a few close relationships and also be wired for the potential of a secure bond with a primary partner. Similar qualities that make an attachment figure *"desirable"* for infants (emotional openness, attunement and responsiveness, the reliability of connection) are the same essential bonding qualities we adults want in our primary romantic partners. Note this is bonding, not sexual attraction—a woman might be sexually attracted to a man, but complain he is not **emotionally available** (emotional openness, attunement and responsiveness, reliability of connection) so she might not want to continue dating him if she is looking for a **long-term bonding partner**. We humans are social organisms designed for connection and the architecture of our nervous system is literally wired and built by the attuned connection with a primary attachment figure—someone who provides protection, support, and care. After the second year of life, children typically begin to use the adult as a secure base from which to explore the world and develop greater independence. And as we continue to grow and develop, eventually becoming working professionals and perhaps even parents ourselves, these two polarities of independent exploration and secure bonding, freedom, and love continue to interweave as natural and healthy human needs. As Bowlby beautifully stated, "all of us, from cradle to grave, are happiest when life is organized as a series of excursions, long or short, from the secure base provided by our attachment figures."[7]

Below are more detailed summary descriptions of the 4 ADULT ATTACHMENT STYLES:
Secure, Anxious-Preoccupied, Avoidant-Fearful and Avoidant-Dismissive

SECURE

Infants who had secure attachment, or adults who have repaired/healed (from anxious or avoidant) are considered earned-secure attachment

- believe in & tend to have relatively **loving, satisfying & enduring** relationships
- have healthy **self-esteem**, tend to have a positive view of self, partners & relationships
- are comfortable feeling **open, connected & emotionally close** to others
- are comfortable **disclosing** inner thoughts & feelings with friends & partner
- are able to **trust & depend** on others that are close to you & have others rely on you
- can count on the **emotional availability**, responsiveness & reliability of loved ones
- undoubtedly know that you & your partner love & **matter to each other**
- feel **safe in your bond & do not worry** constantly about being abandoned or rejected
- able to **reach & receive partner's reach**, in times of distress, for support, comfort & reassurance
- both you & your partner are **secure** in the independence of **solitude** & in the **closeness** with each other
- your partner is a **secure base** from which to freely go out to explore the world on your own & safe haven to return to
- can be securely **individuated in connection** without merging, able to be committed to freedom & healthy boundaries
- your life probably feels more **balanced**

ANXIOUS-PREOCCUPIED

Infants who had an ambivalent/anxious attachment, as adults tend to have *preoccupied* attachment
- **worry a lot** about your relationships
- worry whether partner **really loves you** or values you as much you do them
- fearfully worry about being **rejected, abandoned or not loved**
- have **difficulty being alone**
- have a **strong desire to be very close to others**, but often others don't want to get as close as you like
- want to be in **constant proximity or communication** with your partner
- can be **clingy** & **overly dependent** on your partner
- frequently **crave** & **seek** connection, **constant** closeness & **confirmation** that you are loved
- are **overly-pleasing**, **seeking reassurance** & approval from others
- tend to **view others more positively**, but can be **insecure & self-critical** with yourself
- insecurity perpetuate **desperation, doubt & preoccupation** with your relationship
- though you want feelings of security with a partner, you can sabotage or **act in ways that push your partner away**
- your **anxious, needy, clingy or possessiveness** can make your fears of abandonment come true
- your life probably does **not feel balanced**

AVOIDANT-FEARFUL

Infants that had traumatic or disorganized attachments, tend to be *fearful-avoidant* detached from self, emotions & others as adults
- **mixed feelings toward attachment**: both fear of being abandoned & struggle with being too close
- it feels like the person you want to go towards for **safety** could be the same person that **hurts you**
- may **ambivalently** be in a relationship or **avoid** connection, closeness & relationships altogether
- limit relational closeness in an **ambivalent state**: fearing to be both too close & too distant
- as a child, you felt afraid, unsafe, or were harmed so you **learned to detach from feelings** or limit emotional closeness to prevent getting hurt
- **fear of being harmed, rejected, or abandoned** so maintain emotional distance with others
- **confused & unclear strategy for getting your needs** met by others
- **invest little emotional energy** in social & romantic relationships
- show **little preference** between your romantic partner & acquaintances
- **reluctance opening** up to others, unable or **unwilling to share deeper feelings**
- **less comfortable depending** on others
- your life probably does **not feel balanced** & may feel like your **timing is off**

AVOIDANT-DISMISSIVE

Infants that had unavailable or avoidant attachments, or had to parent themselves, tend to be *avoidant-dismissive* attachment as adults

- may feel like you don't want to depend on others or it is **better to not need others**
- prefer **not to depend on others** or have others depend on you
- relationships & emotions are **less important** to you than to others
- on some level, you probably **avoid or limit emotional intimacy & connection** with others
- you tend to **avoid or subtly get out of prolonged intimacy** or emotional closeness
- you **do not fear** being abandoned or rejected
- you **can detach relatively easily**
- you may be now or have been in a romantic relationship but **can be fine on your own**
- are relatively **independent, self-focused & self-reliant** & take care of your own needs
- you highly value **freedom & self-reliance**
- able to **protect yourself, hide your feelings** or shut down emotionally

WHY ADULT ATTACHMENT MATTERS

Whether child or adult, having secure connections is literally like having a secure base from which we can be more open to new experiences and confidently venture out to explore this great mysterious world, as opposed to feeling anxious due to a wobbly foundation, confused due to ambiguous signals or avoiding connection altogether. Adult Attachment style refers the particular way that we relate and connect with other people. Not only does understanding our style of attachment offer us insight into our own childhood bonding history, but as adults it impacts how we relate in close relationships, romantic partner selection, depth of connections, how we attach to our own children, relationship progression, our relationship template for how we navigate our connection needs, our strategies for getting them met and even how open and connected we can be when meeting someone for the first time. In a sense, we set ourselves up by attracting relations and partners that confirm our models or heal our models. On the positive side, it is never too late to heal bonding wounds and develop more secure bonding capacities. Although, our infant attachment patterns built our early neural wiring in our brain and body, we humans are amazing evolutionary beings with neuroplasticity in our brains so we can grow, develop, and learn new ways. In the domain of relating and connecting, becoming aware of our attachment style tendencies, through healing connection anxieties or defensive avoidances, while learning presence and connection skills like breath and body relaxation, emotional intelligence, attunement, transparency (heart openness and emotional vulnerability), etc. we can actually rewire our nervous system and develop the skills necessary for healthy emotional connection and an *earned secure attachment* and a more satisfying, loving relationship.

SAFETY & TRANSPARENCY

Renowned family therapist, Salvador Minuchin reminds us that as important as the early mother-child bond is, the stability of the early childhood environment offers a vast range of important human influences that also need to be considered in contributing to a person's connection style and capacities.[8]   These can include safety of the home, community, and culture the person is born and raised in—for example, a relatively stable economic and political environment is a lot safer than a gangland neighborhood, area of genocide or warzone. The secure connection of the parents during pregnancy and childhood as well as the safety and connection styles of the entire family, peers in school and close community can also be formative, but again not permanent with bonding repair work.

Safety, both physical and emotional, is the first essential feature of connection. Again drawing upon our primal ancestry, even amidst very challenging survival conditions in hunting and gathering food, avoiding animal predators, preventing illness without modern medicine, as well as avoiding animal predators, the leading cause of death for our Paleolithic ancestors was being killed by another man.[9]   Therefore, it is deeply wired into our human nervous system, upon meeting a new person, to sense whether this person is safe or going to physically harm me. Although it is a lot physically safer for most people in many first-world cities, rape is sadly still occurring at high levels high on our planet, millions of humans live in poverty or war zones—all of whom must focus on survival in navigating physical danger on a daily basis. Two samurai warriors or knights in full armor and weapons, can often barely see each other's eyes and while they can share words, it is not until they lay down their weapons and shield to take off their armored defenses, that they can feel safe enough for more of them to be seen, felt and known. I love the scene in Braveheart in which the English army hires the Irish infantry to fight against the Scottish. With anticipatory music climaxing, both sides of male warriors are running at full speed charging each other to attack, yet both sides slow down just steps before what would be the center collision point. First, they lay down their shields and weapons, then embracing in a handshake or strong masculine hugs, smiles abound as they show each other the openness of undefended friends.

It is here from this safety, in the undefended openness of friendliness that we are able to connect with each other in the authentic aliveness of presence. Learning to experience other people as *"friend"*, as supportive human beings, as opposed to dangerous threatening objects, can require some attachment healing, trauma desensitization and reprogramming with increasingly safe examples of healthy connection. When our defensive shields are down in the physical safety and emotional safety of open transparency and acceptance, we humans can have powerful, loving and tender hearts. However to drop down out of the mental protection of our thoughts and guarded chests can some be frightening or simply an avoidance of true connection habit. As discussed in more detail in the *Authentic Expression section* as well as *Transparency section*, we have a variety of parts designed to help us function in the world, strategically get our needs met and emotionally protect our more vulnerable parts. We have to have released and desensitized enough shame from past experiences so that we no longer feel defective, unlovable or unworthy such that we can allow others to see inside—which can really compromise intimacy and interpersonal connection because the closer someone comes to the real undefended essence beneath our persona masks efforting to be seen in certain ways and hiding other parts we don't want to be seen, the more we fear they reject us. Plus, we have all of the previous wiring connections from infancy and childhood—the multitude of moments when the emotional openness and responsiveness programmed our own openness and anticipation of attuned connection. All of these moments in which growing up in later years that we felt judged, criticized, shamed, etc. by family, friends or peers, could have also affected our aperture of heart openness and capacity to experience a real alive connection with others. So, for some of us to experience a deeper connection with others might require unlearning some past habits and learning some new ways of relating.

Some people say *"it takes me time to open up to people"* which reflects their process of feeling emotionally safe enough to open. Others have so much emotional numbness and calcified protection over our heart that they may not even remember what it felt like to have the front of their chest and core relaxed and open for connection. Others have learned to open and close their connection aperture with ease, and for these connectors, it takes merely an instant to lovingly open in connection to those closest to them or to be able to meet even *"strangers"* with open, warm, welcoming connection.

FACE, CHEST & BELLY RELAXATION FOR CONNECTION: STEPHEN PORGES & POLYVAGAL THEORY

Stephen Porges PhD, proposed the Polyvagal Theory[10], which links human connection to body sensing states in our nervous system, especially in our face, chest, and belly. Dr. Porges directs brain-body research at top psychiatry departments (University of North Carolina Chapel Hill and University of Chicago) and has been Professor Emeritus at the University of Maryland, where he chaired the Department of Human Development and directed the Institute for Child Study. Porges is the first person to ever quantify heart rate variability conducting nearly 20 years of research measuring the heart rate patterns and vagal function of babies and fetuses. He is an expert in how our bodily state affects our psychology, especially in relation to safety and connection. Until 1994, textbooks said the autonomic nervous system only had a sympathetic branch (fight or flight) and parasympathetic branch (rest and digest). However, Porges' research discovered a third neural circuit that regulates the muscles of the face and head that he calls the **Social Engagement System**. Related brain imaging demonstrates that we are able to effectively feel connected to others via eye contact, emotion, touch and communication when our breath and the front of our body (face, chest, and belly) are relaxed. Said in another way, the felt-sense of connection registers in our body and if we want to feel connected to others, we need to learn to relax the frontal sensing regions of our body (face, chest and belly) so we can register feeling real human connection In our bodies

Porges, who is both a professor and researcher, has studied everything from reptiles and mammals to human children and adults. Integrating brain, body and social relating from an evolutionary perspective across species and has published more than 200 scientific articles across disciplines. Because he has studied both evolution, development and social engagement, Porges understands that each organism, whether reptile, mammalian animal or human has developed various protective survival defenses of such as fighting, fleeing, freezing, or freighting in response to fear, panic or life-threat.

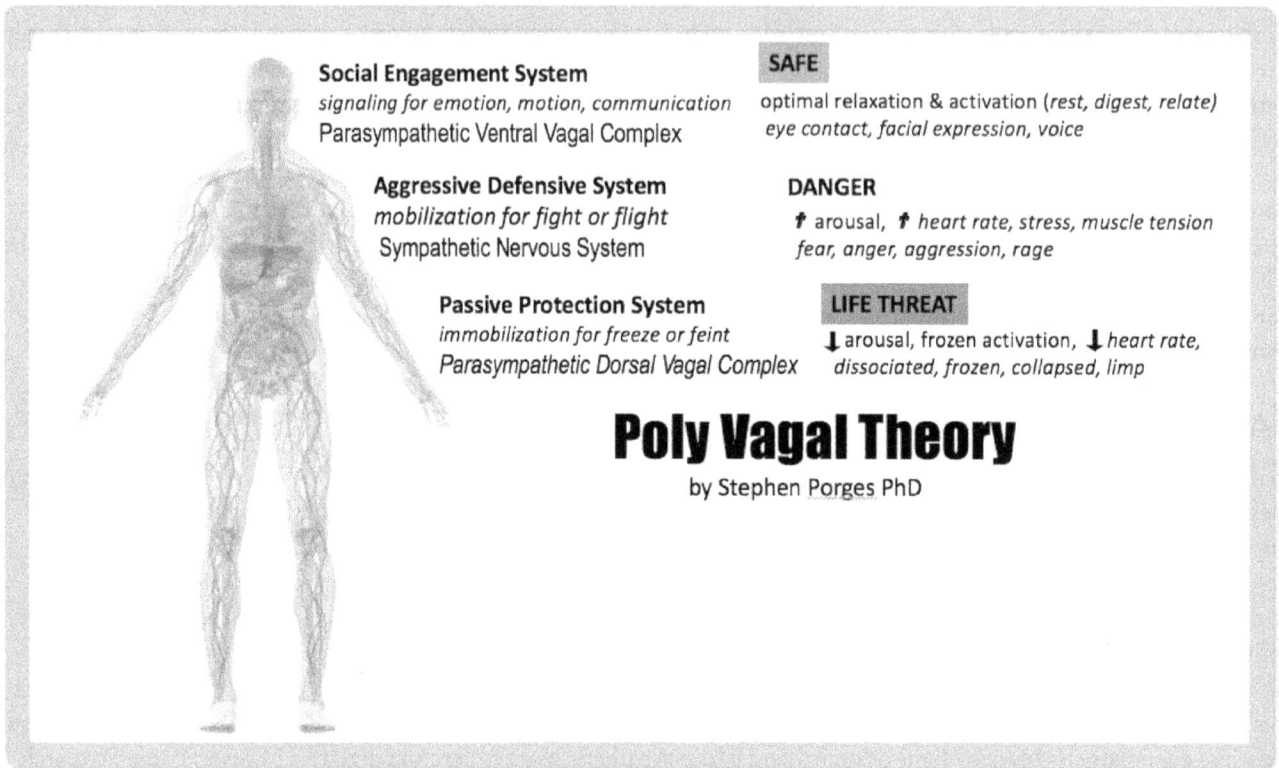

Social Engagement System
signaling for emotion, motion, communication
Parasympathetic Ventral Vagal Complex

SAFE
optimal relaxation & activation (*rest, digest, relate*)
eye contact, facial expression, voice

Aggressive Defensive System
mobilization for fight or flight
Sympathetic Nervous System

DANGER
⬆ arousal, ⬆ heart rate, stress, muscle tension
fear, anger, aggression, rage

Passive Protection System
immobilization for freeze or feint
Parasympathetic Dorsal Vagal Complex

LIFE THREAT
⬇ arousal, frozen activation, ⬇ heart rate,
dissociated, frozen, collapsed, limp

Poly Vagal Theory
by Stephen Porges PhD

When we feel safe and relaxed, then our nervous system puts the brakes on these defense responses that protect the vital organs in our chest (tension in the chest to mobilize fighting or fleeing to protect the heart) and gut (tension or numbness in the gut to immobilize. The old model of the autonomic nervous system was that when people were stressed they were sympathetically over-stimulated and when they were relaxed they were in parasympathetic mode, but Porges says this is overly simplistic. He cites trauma and PTSD cases in which people's body goes into depressive numbness, dissociation or shutdown in response to stress; similar to our ancient reptilian ancestors who used this freeze/immobilization tactic as their primary social defense system. If we feel afraid or unsafe and fight/flight doesn't get us to safety, our neurological system hijacks us and forces us back into our third, most primitive response: freeze, aka immobilization or dissociation (using the reptilian unmyelinated vagal system). For example, when a mouse is in a life-threatening situation of being eaten by a cat and it can't escape by running away, another strategy it can use is passing out (faint) or playing dead by freezing and in going limp and losing muscle tone, the cat loses interest. Have we ever felt nervous and all of the sudden our body felt frozen or we lost our voice—this is that same freeze defense for us humans. This immobilization survival defense actually comes from our reptilian lineages. The turtle can pull its head and limbs back into its shell to freeze and hide in protection or the lizard can immobilize by being very still hoping to blend in with its environment to survive by going unnoticed. Similarly, we might recall a time when we fearfully wished we could be invisible or retract deep inside to protect ourselves. So, evolutionarily we have developed protective defenses like immobilization, in addition to fighting or leaving. Many of us know the term fight or flight in relation to stress responses. Porges classifies this as the mammalian defense system that developed as a more functional option—instead of simply freezing in immobilized fear, mammals could now also fight or run away. In the chart above this is called the *Aggressive Defense System*. Our nervous system is subconsciously continuously sensing to evaluate danger or safety cues both physical or emotional in our surroundings and prioritizing behaviors, a term Porges calls **neuroception**.

Polyvagal theory emphasizes that potential protection systems are operating beneath conscious control inducing a range of physiological indicators such as sweating hands, increased heart rate, voice inhibition, emotional numbness, facial stoicism, etc. These responses are involuntary, meaning it is not like people want to feel afraid, but some more primal nervous system detection alarms might have been triggered. That guy does not want to feel frozen and speechless when the attractive woman speaks to him, and the public speaker does not want to feel stiff and monotone but their nervous system and muscles in the face and front of their bodies are in fearful protection mode. When we feel safe, we get access to the **Social Engagement System** of the integrated emotional expressivity of the face, eye contact and relaxed chest with an open heart via the relaxed front of the body and we get fuller access to emotion, vocal range, facial expression, and connection. Porges notes that the breath is the primary integrator of safety, relaxation, and social connection because it literally turns on and off the myelinated vagus nerve that relaxes the more primitive protection mechanisms in our nervous systems in the fight/flight and immobilization/dissociation systems. When our body feels safe, the vagus nerve is activated in comfortable homeostasis and it basically slows the heart rate down and calms the body down. Porges declares that when our nervous system feels safe, and our body is relaxed and available for connection (social engagement) and from this state we can do lots of our basic human skills as well as higher-level human potentials. When our nervous system detects risk and fear, we can't even sit in a room without being hyper-vigilant. When we feel fear danger or life threat whether physical or emotional, the vagus nerve surges in imbalance either too much activation (fight or flight) or too little activation (in the extreme response people can pass out, urinate or defecate themselves, but in lower levels of a person could experience psychologically oriented constipation, diarrhea or hundreds of other physiological symptoms that Porges and other psychophysiological researchers have demonstrated and documented. So it is NOT just all in our head, on the contrary, our body and mind are inseparably linked and emerging research by Porges and other Interpersonal Neurobiology researchers are showing how essential physical embodiment is for healthy human connection.

When we feel safe, the muscles of the chest and belly are relaxed, the defensive shield is down and our system is available for connection, which is reflected in the relaxation and emotional expressiveness of these 3 frontal areas of the social engagement system—which enables us to smile, express emotion and respond via facial expression to communications from the other person, modulate the range of our voice, relax open our undefended hearts and even be relaxed enough for our ears to really listen and receive communication from others. The front core of our body (belly, chest, and head) are literally 2-way sensing and transmitting instruments for connection and communication.

In contrast, when we feel afraid of connection, afraid of someone seeing something inside, afraid of being judged, afraid of not belonging, etc. we put our defenses up and either activate an immobilized freeze/numb/collapse response in the belly or a more aggressive mobilized fight/flight response in the chest—in either case, the protective defenses are activated and the social engagement system of connection is deactivated. While eye contact is often the first channel of connection people use, research indicates that our inner state when making eye contact can positively or negatively signal availability for connection and affect our state. Ray Castellino, an expert in family connection in pregnancy and infancy, cites research that when we look into another's eyes in a *"mutually supportive and cooperative state"* it releases feel-good bonding hormones (oxytocin) but when a couple look into each other's' eyes in stress, they transfer stress hormones.[11]

Connection is not just a mental state; it is a felt sense of connection in our bodies. This requires our body to have a certain degree of sensing awareness in order to be able to register a receiving connection and to send signals of safe availability for connection to another. When we are in a reactive defense state of fight, flight or freeze, our connection instruments are not online for connection. Our own defenses increase our blood pressure, breathing and heart rate while inhibiting our connective eye contact, vocal cords and ears from effectively hearing what someone else is saying. Porges explains that deeper breathing and calming external sounds via music or someone else's soothing voice can also help relax some of these defensive functions. The intonation of voice not only signals whether it is safe to come closer but also can stimulate our *recurrent laryngeal nerve* to signal our myelinated vegas nerve (part of the polyvagal system) to calm down and relax our body muscles. Since we are not all walking around hooked up to biofeedback equipment, we read and sense other people's friendliness and *"availability"* for connection by their facial expressions, tone of voice and how comfortable they seem in their skin as they stand or move—and for those more skilled sensing instruments the degree of relaxed openness of the chest and the energy they give off.

CHANNELS OF CONNECTION

We humans are pretty incredible and complex organisms—and in our complexity, we have a variety of channels of connection. As an infant, **touch** is the first channel of connection we utilize. When we go through the birth canal in a traditional vaginal birth, the process is designed to begin to activate sense receptors in the skin as we discussed in the *Body Sensing section* and even babies with high-stress cortisol levels at birth who were massaged for several days following birth showed lower baseline stress levels as they grew. Research of Romanian orphans that were not physically touched during infancy developed a range of physical, psychological and interpersonal issues.[12] So, we humans need safe, loving touch from early infancy, through childhood and into adulthood. Affectionate physical touch not only decreases stress hormones, but it also increases endorphins, natural internal painkillers, and the connection hormone oxytocin. Obviously, inappropriate or unwanted touch can be creepy, smothering or overwhelming to some people in certain moments, so we still need to be attuned to others' responsiveness and respectful of others physical boundaries.

Attention is the most foundational channel of connection. Although babies have a film over their eyes from the first number of days or weeks, beyond that frequent eye contact is one of their other primary means of connection. Part of our nervous system tracks the presence of engagement in connection with the other person by the quality of their eye contact—among other things. Can we recall a conversation in which the other person's attention was checked-out or an instance in which we were touching someone but their attention was lost in thought? Neither of these probably felt like the person was present with us. While people with highly developed subtle perception can direct their attention and connect with someone else to the back or side of them, as well as close their eyes while still tracking externally with their attention, for most of us, our attention is correlated with our engaged eye-contact. We might also notice increased eye contact with securely attached adult romantic couples. In some more violent circles, eye contact can be used as intimidation and as a means to show power-hierarchy but in most cultures, in relationships in general and especially the business world, it is a sign of respect, confidence, and connection.

Mental-Verbal Connection is probably the most commonly used channel for most human adults. We use our words, stories, concepts, humor, projected identities, and attempts to find common interests to try to create a felt sense of connection. Some people do not like to discuss anything personal, real or of any depth or emotion. Others say *"it takes me a long time to open up"* or they tend to avoid human connection. All of these are legitimate expressions along the spectrum of human connection, but in the brain, they do not register as connection and do not release oxytocin. Our advanced mental capacities (critical thinking, logic, abstraction, systematic thinking, multi-variate complexity, discernment, etc.) are a virtue of our species and one that hopefully continues to evolve along with an equal portion of moral impact awareness. However, mental and verbal exchange does not register the same in our nervous systems as the physical and emotional connection channels.

Emotional Vulnerability is often cited as the doorway to connection because it is through this transparent disclosure of our inner world that we subtly open and allow our systems to open for connection and closeness with others. Naming emotions also releases oxytocin and can only be done by relaxing our protections so we can allow the other to see and feel our inner world. This channel really draws upon our attachment style: three important markers of which include self-disclosure, emotional closeness, and reliable responsiveness. In regard to emotional responsiveness and approachability, part of this registers as *"Are you there for me?" "If I reach will you respond?" "Am I important to you?"* In regard to disclosure, for some of us, this involves learning to turn towards each other, open up and reveal our inner emotional worlds including fears, sadness, desires, and celebrations.

Sexual Connection is another channel, simultaneously the most pleasurable although probably the most confusing and emotionally charged. We will be exploring this in more detail in the *Sexual Essence & Gender Polarity section*, but for now, let us simply note that for some it is the only connection and intimacy channel they know. Many people erroneously confuse intimacy with sex but intimacy means closeness, which includes emotional, physical and sexual closeness. Integral Psychotherapist Robert Augustus Masters reminds us not to use sex to create intimacy (closeness), but that great sex comes from an existing cultivated emotional closeness and connection. Some women use their sexual energy to get attention and accumulate worth points or manipulatively get what they want. Some men use sexual energy while mentally-verbally when trying to connect, which may not be wanted or feel safe—every person is different and attunement offers insight into the best moves, but sometimes there is a preferred order of intimacy and connection, so sometimes the safety of feeling an open heart unlocks deeper connection channels. Some men's systems have been trained through masturbation to open sexually without necessarily having an open heart and some have to learn or relearn to powerfully inhabit their physicality, activate their breath and sexual energy while opening their hearts in deep intimate sexual connection. Some couples

113

have lost their sexual polarity and they are attracted through sexual connection. This channel is a beautiful, sexy, playful, passionate part of life, but we can probably use it with more attunement, consideration of impact and awareness.

Heart Connection, feeling connected in mutual heart openness is the channel we utilize to feel most connected to others. The aperture of our heart protects our deepest vulnerabilities and reveals our most beautiful treasures. Advanced connectors practice living with an open heart and so can create heart connection relatively easily while the majority of people walk around with varying degrees of protection. In the latter case, the majority of people have emotional vulnerability is intertwined with heart openness and it is the doorway to the richest heart connection.

Transpersonal Connection, *"trans"* also means beyond and in this context, it refers to beyond exclusive identification with the personal self; thus enabling connection to occur from a higher vantage like Spacious Openness, Ever-present Witness or Non-Duality (see *Vantage section* for more info). These include and transcend self, others, and life. Some are able to volitionally access more expanded body-views through grace and/or practice, while others access more expanded states through authentic relating in deep presence, transcendent sex, or in the group field and presence of a master.

RESONANCE & RAPPORT
When musicians are preparing to play together, in addition to individually warming up, they often also tune their instruments so that they are in resonant harmony with each other. While they certainly could play a cacophony of chaos, it is more pleasing to the audience, when they are playing in a shared resonance. Likewise, we are free to communicate and relate to any degree of resonance, and although some of them have wounding or incomplete circuitry wiring for connection, when their connection circuitry is working most people experience incredible pleasure in shared resonance, rapport, and connection. Masters of rapport are able to sense the dominant channel another person is using to connect and meet them there initially and then through increasing relaxation and safety inviting the person into opening and connecting through one or more channels. (Note that this is different from some people who use linguistic manipulation without consent to influence others.) As the resonance of feeling felt, seen, heard and understood increases, so too does the felt sense of connection. In this palpable sense of aliveness and connectedness, feeling felt by another person gives us the sense that our internal world is shared—that in this sharing of inner worlds we feel a shared resonance. Through signaling via facial expressions, tone of voice, emotion, energy, and body language, we can share in an ongoing dance of attuning and misattuning, reading cues and missing cues, meeting and pulling away, communicating and miscommunicating, connecting and disconnecting we can dance in relative resonance, moment to moment.

INTERDEPENDENCE & RELATEDNESS
The felt sense of closeness (intimacy) and connection is a huge area where we can lose presence and an essential threshold in our journey towards greater intimacy and presence with all things. A felt sense of being in connection with our body, others and life is an essential pathway to the flow of aliveness, vitality and thriving. When experiencing life only from the personal mental perspective, a person experiences isolation from others and separation from Life itself. Yet the essence of Life is interdependence—there is a fundamental felt sense of interdependent connectivity between all living things and we are impacted by everything around us. In some traditions, this experience of separation is considered to be the root

of suffering, and in others, it is compared to hell. As we will learn in the *Vantage section*, as our BodyView of the world expands we feel intimately connected or unified with the totality of life—not just as a mental concept, but in a felt sense.

Thus at any point throughout our life, any relationship is a fractal feature of our ultimate relatedness. Presence is a 24-hour practice and just as we practice meditation on the cushion, yoga on a mat, or mindfulness at work, so too our quality of intimate connection in relating is an essential element of presence. Just as we practice returning our attention to our breath or the deeper purpose and priority of our work; so too, we practice reconnecting in a relationship as well as making our system open and available to relate with Life. Our relationships can also be powerful and insightful teachers, illuminating closures, avoidances, graspings, areas we are not free or our limits of love—offering moment to moment opportunities to open and deepen into the great openness of Presence and felt-sense of unified loving connection with all.

CONNECTION SUMMARY & KEY TAKEAWAYS

- ➤ Humans are social creatures & we have banded together in tribes for hundreds of thousands of years to procreation & ensure the propagation of our species, in relationship & community, we come together to bond, live, and experience life together.
- ➤ Bonding begin in the womb with our mother & not only do we require feeding, nurturing & protecting as we grow, but when we, in our human infant vulnerability, reach out, even yet without words, it is our caregivers' responsiveness, eye contact, emotional attunement & open heart that signals a felt sense of connection.
- ➤ Because our infant attachment patterns (0-2 years old) built our early neural wiring in our brain & the front of our upper body, it lays the foundational map for how we believe & feel bonding works which affects how we attract relationships & partners that confirm our prior models or help us heal our bonding wounds to develop more secure bonding capacities.
- ➤ 4 main styles of Adult Attachment or Bonding: Secure, Anxious-Preoccupied, Avoidant-Fearful, Avoidant-Dismissive
- ➤ Adult Attachment style impacts particular ways that we relate, connect & bond with others. It can offer insight into our own childhood bonding history & as adults it impacts how we relate in close relationships, select a romantic partner, our relationship progression tendencies, capacity for depth of connection & ability to trust others, how we attach to our own children, & our relationship template for how we navigate our connection needs & strategies for getting them met.
- ➤ Connection requires safety, both physical & emotional. Learning to experience other people as "friend", as supportive human beings, as opposed to dangerous threatening objects, can require some attachment healing, trauma desensitization and reprogramming with increasingly safe examples of healthy connection.
- ➤ Porges' Polyvagal theory emphasizes that potential protection systems involved in safety & connection are involuntarily operating beneath conscious control inducing a range of physiological indicators such as sweating hands, increased heart rate, voice inhibition, emotional numbness, facial stoicism, etc.

When we feel safe, we get access to the Social Engagement System of the integrated emotional expressivity of the face, eye contact and relaxed chest with an open heart via the relaxed front of the body and we get fuller access to emotion, vocal range, facial expression, and connection. The breath is the primary integrator of safety, relaxation, & social connection because it literally turns on and off the myelinated vagus nerve that relaxes the more primitive protection mechanisms in our nervous systems in the fight/flight and immobilization/dissociation systems.

➤ For some "it takes time to open up to people" which reflects their process of feeling emotionally safe enough to open. Others have so much emotional numbness & calcified protection over our heart that it may have been a long time since we have felt have the front of our chest & belly relaxed & open for connection. For others who have learned to open & close our connection aperture with ease, it takes merely an instant to lovingly open in welcoming connection.

➤ We have multiple channels of connection & closeness including attention, eye contact, physical touch, mental-verbal, emotional vulnerability, heart, sexual & transpersonal

COMMUNICATION

Do your co-workers, friends & loved-ones
appreciate how you communicate &
feel you are real & authentic most of the time?

Are you able to make direct requests, ask questions to clarify, express needs & ask for what you want?

Do you check for understanding when you are speaking? Can you sense your own inner world & how the other person's system is receiving it moment to moment with each packet of words, energy & emotion?

"To effectively communicate, we must realize that we are all different in the way we perceive the world & use this understanding as a guide to our communication with others."

- Tony Robbins -

WHAT IS **COMMUNICATION**
the capacity for dynamic reciprocal exchange of shared experience & information

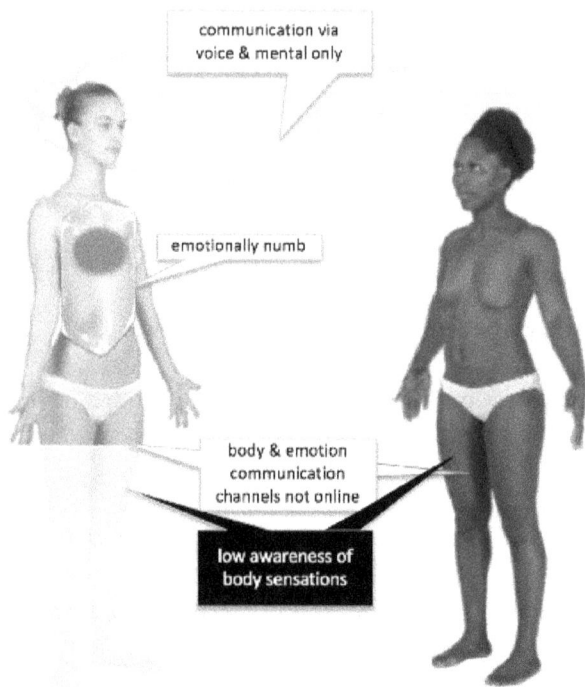

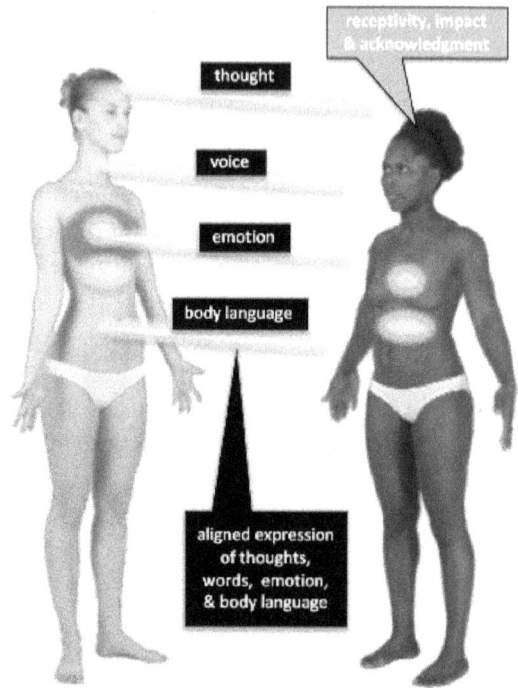

WHY **COMMUNICATION** MATTERS

Medium of Expression: a medium to share or express our unique self: to be felt, heard, understood, appreciated & seen by others

Shared Experience: a bridge to connection, rapport & shared experience

Getting Other's World: a vehicle to better get into someone else's world: to hear, understand, appreciate & see others

Empathy & Perspective-taking: enables feeling emotional resonance with others & understanding their perspectives

Transparent Communication: with emotional vulnerability, this is the essential doorway to closeness & connection

Conflict Resolution: the ability to have clearing conversations ultimately enhances openness & trust

Connection & Relationships: essential to develop, maintain & deepen connection & relating

Work: essential for effective conversation, correspondence, managing people, training & motivation in work

Clients: with & customers enables better service, understanding, sales & satisfaction

BARRIERS TO **COMMUNICATION**

EXPRESSION ISSUES:
Talking too fast: anxious or not embodied
Talking too long: self-absorbed, needing to be heard, wanting to power-over
Image Positioning: trying to say something smart or be seen in a certain way
Confusion: unclear, don't know what to say, believing you are
not smart
Hesitation or Withholding: fear of judgment or criticism, saying the wrong thing
Dishonesty or fear of feeling shame: or getting into trouble
Unworthy of having a Voice: shy, muted or struggle to say
what want to
Not Feeling Safe: doesn't feel safe to express myself
Superficiality: avoiding depth, afraid of intimacy or feeling
deeper emotions
Stoic: emotionally numb, closed, playing tough

TRANSMISSION ISSUES:
Different Communication Styles: gender, culture, personality
Different Comprehension Capacities: meaning-making
Inauthenticity: incongruence of mental words, emotions, &
body expressions
Not Checking for Understanding: lost in translation
Accuracy: direct versus diplomatic, beating around the bush

RECEIVING ISSUES:
Dissociation: not feeling & inhabiting your body due to trauma, defense or hyper-mental
Distracted: internally preoccupied by your own mental-emotion noise or externally by digital stimulation / environment
Confusion: unclear, don't know what to say, believe not smart
Hyper-Mental: excessive mental activity, overly theoretical, living in fantasy, lost in the past or future
Emotional Overwhelm: redirecting attention to own internal experience or easier to dissociate than stay in connection
Fear of Connection & Intimacy: fear of emotional closeness & connection
Poor Attention / Busy Mind: requires intimate attention to focus & sense one's own plus another's experience
Self-Absorption: overly focused on having your own needs met before being resourced enough to attend to someone else anxiously waiting for your turn to talk or not listening because you are thinking of what you want to say
Interrupting: talking over or always having to speak the last word
Ignoring: disregarding or pretending to not care as a power-play
Multitasking: task-switching while splitting attention between 2 or more things
Advice or Fixing: giving unrequested advice or trying to problem solve when the person simply wants you to listen
Self-Referencing: self-referencing from central column rather than others avoids losing self & getting lost in others

Over-listening: to others to avoid your own emotions or sharing your own experience
Bias: judgment, prejudice, filter, or fixating on first impression
Selective Perception: I can only hear what I want to hear
Judgmental: critical, negative, or condemning point of view about others or the world with fixed attention & closed heart limiting alternate perspective taking, empathy, compassion & connection

COMMUNICATION DEVELOPMENT SUCCESS STORY

With athleticism & strong physicality, you would imagine Devin was a pretty confident guy when he walked into a room. But inside he felt like he was constantly trying to avoid criticism & as a result had a strained communication style. When he spoke it seemed like he was looking inside of himself trying to formulate just the right thing to say while at the same time talking fast saying the same thing over & over again in different ways, attempting to get it just right & avoid criticism. Rewiring some old patterns, he learned to open his eyes, seeing & feeling others while speaking & feeling himself simultaneously. He started meditating, learning to breath more & pause more while communicating, slowing down his speech & increasing his senses. During the course of this rewiring, he was learning that presence in communication involves embodiment, connection & larger Awareness versus the very act of editing only inside of his own mental world, which decreases the connection with & trust from his listeners as well as the effectiveness of the communication exchange between both parties. No longer afraid of being criticized or subtly hiding, the way he communicated & expressed himself was not just about talking in conversation; it was symbolic of how he expressed himself in the world as well. Over the course of our work together, he has started a side business, in addition to his existing role as a Marketing Director, based on some greater clarity & extraordinary talents that now felt safer & had more room to express themselves. He finally feels like he is living on purpose and beginning to do professionally what he was born to do.

"Words are singularly the most powerful force available to humanity. We can choose to use this force constructively with words of encouragement, or destructively using words of despair. Words have energy and power with the ability to help, to heal, to hinder, to hurt, to harm, to humiliate and to humble."

- Yehuda Berg -

Communication is an exchange of information and experience between two or more parties through expressing and receiving using a shared system of symbols and signifiers. From a larger view, all living organisms, including animals, plants, fungi and even bacteria participate in the symphony of communication—through sending and receiving information, expression and listening—some for functional survival and others for shared experience and meaning-making. Human communication is unique for its extensive use of language, which enables a richer and more nuanced medium for shared human experience. As such, communication can be a bridge to connection via exchanging information through words, sounds, body language, gestures, facial expression, emotion, timing, and subtleties. It is derived from the Latin *commūnicātus*, meaning *"to impart, to share or make common"*. Whereas self-expression is a one-way channel, communication is a two-way channel comprised of expression or making one's experience known by broadcasting with the intent to share with others, the effectiveness of which is also dependent on the other end receiving the expresser's experience or through receptive listening. The desire to express is often to get it out, emote or feel heard, but the desire to communicate implies an intention to share one's experience with another—the extent to which the transmission is clearly sent and received is the degree of effectiveness of the communication. Just because one person is speaking does not mean the other person hears and understands what the first person intended to express.

There is an oft-quoted statistic that 93% of all human to human communication is nonverbal, which is based on research by Dr. Albert Mehrabian in which he cites that 7% of messages are conveyed through words, 38% via voice, and 55% through nonverbal components.[1]   In reality, because we humans are highly complex beings and each of us have different personalities, cultural conditionings, capacities, and styles of speaking, expressing, expressing, listening, learning and communication, so designing social experiments to effectively measure the range of human communication channels can have inherent limitations. Whatever the percentage is, let us agree that communication involves much more than merely speaking and translating words. Yet, communication is an area in which many of us lose presence. Sometimes we speak to express without attunement to and consideration of the unique listener or our audience, and in failing to do so, often do not check for understanding or do not formulate and translate our message so it can be effectively be received by others. Often, if the speaker can have barriers imbibing presence and effective communication and is not connected to the other person or persons through any of the connection channels or on occasion, only through the mental-verbal channel. It is not uncommon for us to have too much mental noise inside our own experience to clearly hear the multi-channeled expression of others. Or, at other times we only pay attention to the words someone is speaking and in doing so, lose awareness of other channels of connection and communication like emotion, body language, and other subtleties.

HOW COMMUNICATION DEVELOPS

We human adults tend to think of communication in mental-verbal means because this is the channel we perhaps subconsciously think is most important. However, nature shows us there are many other channels of communication between pairs and groups. In early infancy, before we have developed the ability to speak, our early communication occurs through the process of attunement to eye contact, facial expression, body language, emotion, and sound. Because we are unable to speak, these are our communication tools to ensure our survival needs for connection, nourishment, and safety are met. Research shows that very young infants can distinguish between different sounds, but cannot produce them until most start babbling around 6 months old.[2]   Interestingly, deaf babies also babble (although they begin later around 11 months), suggesting that babbling is not caused by babies imitating certain sounds they hear, but that it is actually a natural part of an innate impulse to express ourselves as well as the process of language development. Apparently around 11-12 months many babies can speak single words which become short phrases, by 17-months they can link meaning to words and by around 3 years, many can speak complete sentences and express needs with words.[3]   When meeting an unfamiliar word, kids and even we as adults use context and the other channels of communication to infer an approximate meaning.

As we grow, our vocabulary increases, but for most of us, our point of view stays inside our own skin, which we will learn more about in the *Empathy, Perspectives, Impact & Compassion section*. Some believe it is for their our own protection and for others, it is due to being self-absorbed, needing to be heard or not caring about others. In the first case, some people feel shy, muted or struggle to communicate what they want to say. Some people have beliefs that can limit the free expression of their voice. Some can feel afraid of being judged or criticized, be afraid of saying the wrong thing, feel like they don't know what to say, believe they are not smart or worthy of having a voice. An attempt to communicate with this type of person can feel strained as they struggle to express and participate in half the communication. In the second case of being more self-absorbed, some of us have a need to be heard which until fulfilled has us pay more attention to our own speech than to the objects of our expression. At times we find ourselves thinking of what to say while others are speaking or merely waiting for our turn to talk without fully experiencing the other person. Some peoples' own inner world is so over stimulated with sensations, emotions, and thoughts that they sometimes need to verbally vomit and or don't have any extra free attention to care about anyone else. Some have yet to open their own heart enough to genuinely care about others. Attempting to communicate with this type of self-consumed person can feel a lack of rapport and connection or at worst can be potentially draining.

COMMUNICATION EXPRESSION

Greater presence in communication always begins with the basics of more fully inhabiting our own experience of authentic expression, especially including grounding, breathing, body sensing, and emotion. These help us not only include all of these important parts of our expression but also helps us to slow down our nervous system and quiet our inner world enough so that our communication can be clearer and more connected to the recipient. If we aren't connected to our own body when we speak it is nearly impossible for us to feel connected to the listener. When we are not sensing our embodied experience while speaking it can result in talking too fast, talking too long, going off on tangents, not making sense, etc. Some people have never learned to take someone else's perspective, so for them, it is less about a mutual communication and more about a self-absorbed need to be heard, efforting, convincing, negotiating, or trying to be right. Sometimes superficiality can limit the range of our expression if we are avoiding depth, are afraid of intimacy or are trying to push down emotion. Communicating with greater presence includes all parts of us, the listener and life surrounding, which includes noticing if any emotions or body tensions are inhibiting freer expression such as a lump in our throat, a shield over our chest, or a knot of fear in our gut. Sometimes these bodily sensations can be clues to hidden potential. Some people have parts that do not feel safe to express for fear of not being accepted, worry we may be criticized for what we say or a feeling that we do not feel worthy of sharing our own opinions. In these cases, we may withhold or manipulate our expressions so as to be viewed a certain way.

SYNCHRONIZED AUTHENTICITY

Recalling from the *Connection section*, that there are various channels of connection: mental-verbal, touch, emotional, sexual, heart, transpersonal, etc. and all of these are factors in our communication. Each person has a unique voice expressed by the vibration of our vocal cords, combined with emotion and energy. When our system is most relaxed, so too is our face and voice, offering us both a greater range and a more natural, authentic expression. Stephen Porges notes that physiologically the muscles of that regulate facial expression, vocal tonality (larynx and pharynx), and listening (middle ear) are all linked to the heart.[4]   There are times that others can sense when our expression is inauthentic, which is a misalignment of mental content of words, emotions, and body language (energy). When this happens, our expression can feel fake, withheld, constricted, manipulative, confusing or untrustworthy. The expresser is sometimes more aware of only his or her mental activity and is therefore disconnected from their body, meaning not aware of or can't simultaneously feel body language and emotion while speaking. On the other end of the authentic alignment spectrum, when our mental words, emotions, and energy are more naturally synchronized, the listener's experience of our expression as resonating with a more authentic synchronized expression being communicated more clearly and a higher probability of effectively being received. As we become more and more embodied and synchronized in our authentic expression of thoughts, intentions, body, and emotion and energy, eventually our life becomes more and more authentic and aligned with our unique purpose.

OWNING YOUR OWN EXPERIENCE

Owning your own experience is part of **Authentic Relating**, which involves speaking in the first person and owning our own thoughts, beliefs, emotions, judgments, curiosities, underlying intentions, and noticings. This helps prevent projection of our experience onto others and allows others to authentically relate to the impact of our unique expression versus trying to defend against something being put into their side that they may or may not resonate with.

COMMUNICATION FROM IMMEDIACY

Expressing what we are feeling, what we are noticing, what we are curious about, etc. has our expression feel most alive in the present moment and thus speaking from immediacy is a potent doorway into deeper presence. When people express only the mental-verbal part of themselves it does not feel as enjoyable to listen to them. Likewise, sometimes we speak about the past or the future or some gossip, the news or regurgitating some cultural judgment—and when these are spoken only mentally, the farther from deep presence and engaging communication we stray. Sharing a past memory while feeling connected to our body, allowing the feelings and energy to be part of the expression while openly connecting to the listener—that is a more alive expression, even if it is a past story. Stories can be beautiful, inspiring, educational, vulnerable, humorous, etc. but the measure of presence with story-telling is, does both the expresser and the listener feel more open and connected during and after the exchange. In contrast, other people talk excessively and use a lot of stories disconnected from their bodies while talking so as to capture attention or fill the space. Exploring what the deeper intention is for telling that story can lead everyone into deeper presence, as can speaking from increasing degrees of immediacy—which is what is happening right now.

Can you feel your entire body and breath and connection to the other and spacious Awareness while speaking?

RHYTHM & TIMING, EXPRESSION & SILENCE

Every conversation has its own timing, a natural rhythm, and flow. Sometimes we talk too fast, disconnected from our body and breath, or trying to hurry over emotional content. Sometimes we talk too long when we have lost connection to our body or the listener. At other times we can also not give others a fair chance to speak—maybe we do all the talking, don't ask questions, try to speak over or cut others off. A great conversation has a rhythm to it, a natural flow. It might contain back and forth, ebbs and flows, fast-talking excitement and passion, slow intervals of confusion or clarifying *"ah ha's"*, waves of melodic words mixed with plenty of silence and space allowing pregnant pauses of emergent possibilities. The pauses allow deeper presence to emerge, emotions to be included, moments of intimacy, *"ah ha"* moments; pauses allow our systems to have space to open more. To stay in the flow, we need to stay attuned our own experience, our listeners and the overall moment. This attunement gives us information and when combined with discernment allows us to direct and flow with the natural rhythm of the conversation, sensing when to be direct vs. tactful, when to change the subject vs. stay and work through the tension, when to clarify a misunderstanding and when to move on, when to allow silence and when the moment could be enhanced by another wave of expression or when the natural conclusion of the conversation has arrived.

COMMUNICATION TRANSMISSION

ATTUNEMENT & TRANSLATION TO THE AUDIENCE

It is most common that when speaking, the majority of what we are aware of is our own mental activity, and the next step into deeper presence with communication is that we learn to be able to feel our breath, body, emotions, and feet on the ground as we speak. In addition to having our expression feel much more authentic, integrated, clear and enjoyable to receive, being more embodied also tends to slow down and quiet mental static. Once this happens more often, then we can make contact and feel a connection with the audience while expressing. So rather than a verbal vomit or speaking through a bullhorn unable to see who we are speaking at, being more embodied and connected allows us to empress a message more uniquely tailored to an effective communication transmission. It takes two to tango and communication is a two-way exchange. The expresser is responsible for owning our own experience and being attuned to the listener or audience to better ensure an effective transmission. In between the expression and the receiving is a space, in between the *Me-Map* and the *You-Map* is a *We-Map*, and it is in this We-Space that the communication transmission occurs.

We described above how exclusively mental-verbal expression, talking too long, talking too fast or inauthentic incongruence of mental words, emotions and body expressions can inhibit the effective receiving of speaker's expression. Another related transmission issue is degrees of accuracy; sometimes when an expression is relatively inaccurate we can either mentally discern this or sometimes we hear it mentally but at the body level of perception, something feels off about the expression. Either the expresser or listener can skillfully name this if they notice it and if they discern it would be useful to do so. We all come from unique genetic backgrounds, cultures, first languages, personalities, genders, traumas, value system/worldviews and life experiences which gives us all relatively unique filters through which we make meaning and interpret our experiences of the world, and in this case communication transmissions. Therefore, being attuned to our audience helps check for understanding.

CHECKING FOR UNDERSTANDING

In the experience of a communication exchange, words in the form of sounds may come out of our mouth, as well as our body expressing some degrees of movement, emotion, and energy. The art of communication is that in this transmission, there is an attempt to communicate our inner experience and have that be heard, seen, felt and understood in the listener's inner world. It is one thing if a foreigner comes to our country and is trying to communicate something to us, but if we have ever been the one trying to express ourselves in their world when they didn't speak our language, we probably either felt frustrated, we realized how much got lost in translation or had an increased appreciation for the multiple channels of communication in addition to the variety of words. Porges' Polyvgal research tells us that the intonation of our voice produces a field of vibration that is transmitted and potentially received through neuroception that allows our nervous system receptors to turn on and off defensive behaviors as well as receive the full-bodied communication expression of the other.   Whether we are conscious of whether or not our body is a sensing mechanism that gives off cues when the communication transmission is being received. But is our presence while speaking deep enough to check?

SIGNS WE COULD BE BETTER ABOUT CHECKING FOR UNDERSTANDING

Do you find yourself speaking for long periods without a breath or response from the other person?
Do you get feedback that you talk really fast?
Do you repeat the same points over or say the same thing over and over again?
Do you go too far in explaining yourself in a discussion?

High-level attunement in effective communication transmission is like a slowed down, multi-sensory experience; as the expression arises from our whole system (mental-words, emotions, body sensations, energy, etc.) you sense the authenticity internally and then as it is being transmitted, if we are connected and attuned to the other person we can sense each packet of communication and whether it is being effectively received. This way we can when the other person or our audience subtly loses attention, gets distracted, or didn't understand a word or concept, etc. In the transmission process, either side can have unconscious gaps in presence; we may have had an underlying intention that the listener noticed or that the expresser had a bundle of frustration underneath the last packet of communication/information that the listener named so we could feel, release and open into deeper freedom and presence. In communicating from deeper presence and connection, the speaker is responsible for attuning to the listener and checking for understanding via sensing a variety of system cues, and on the other end, the listener is responsible for naming when he or she lost attention, feels confused or didn't understand.

OPEN SYSTEM / CLOSED SYSTEM

In a two-person conversational exchange, is there mutual openness in both people's system? To what degree is mutual openness enough to effectively send and receive a communication transmission? Is the expresser open enough to reveal a fuller range of authentic expression and is the listener open enough to listen and receive what is being expressed? Remember effective communication is an embodied experience, not just a mental sport. We recall from the physiology science of polyvagal theory, that safety and relaxation are required for our ears, throat, heart, and breath to be open. We also know that reactive emotional triggers not only affect the degree the muscle relaxation of the front of the core of the body but also can hijack the limbic-emotional brain such that we lose access to our frontal human adult mental capacities to communicate and listen. In the other reptilian defense mechanism of Stephen Porges' theory, we can freeze up, get numb or quiet and shut down. We refer to this as a closed system, which protects us from being physically or emotionally hurt. But with this protective defense, we also close off connection and contract it in from the open spaciousness that is connected to the larger world, it also closes us off to sending and receiving effective communication. Our system is a receiving instrument of experience, in receiving to see, feel and know the world, and in expressing to connect and communicate with others as well as potentially express a unique message or purpose. When our system is open, the expressing and receiving channels are more open, and conversely the more closed we are the less we can express and receive from others and life. The more closed someone's system is the more continuing to communicate with them feels like an effort and can leave the expresser feeling uninterested, frustrated, or depleted. When we contract, we close our system, and clamp down on the flow of life through us – whether speech, emotion or subtle energies – it blocks communication and connection. Whereas during and after leaving a conversation with greater relative openness of both systems, however, the people can tend to feel more open, energized and connected.

Just as a musician tunes his or her instrument first by their our own ears and then in resonance with others we are playing with, so too with subtle attunement, we can refine our own expression until it is in greater resonance inside and in being received by listeners. Just as a discordant note played on an instrument sounds *"off"*, so too does an inaccurate or incongruent expression can feel off to a speaker and/or listener with a more refined subtle vantage Awareness (see the *Vantage section* for more information). Again this incongruence feels off because the mental words, emotion, and body language, are not being expressed in resonance. If we have ever had a hyper-mental professor who speaks in a monotonous tone and is boring to listen to, part of the reason is that in turning off and not including emotion and the energy of body language of his or her expression, the professor is clamping off their aliveness. If we have enough subtle sensitivity we can sense when something about a transmission feels off, when the resonance of the cord sounds off, in the case of an undisclosed intention, an unacknowledged emotion, an inaccuracy, a dishonesty, a manipulation, or a withhold. Even if the listener disagrees upon receiving the expression, there can still be a feeling of resonant authenticity of the speaker in the congruence of what they are expressing.

COMMUNICATION RECEIVING

This end of the communication exchange is essentially listening. Distracted attention, multitasking (task-switching), confusion, dissociation, preoccupied with excessive mental activity, feeling emotionally triggered or overwhelmed, or fear of emotional closeness and connection are all causes of poor attention related to communication receiving issues. Free and focused attention is the first requisite for listening and receiving a communication. The receiver must be able to focus their attention enough to receive the packet of expression from the sender.

Whether the receiver understands the communication is secondary if he or she can't focus attention enough to receive the packet. Biases, judgment, prejudices, and selective perception (only hearing what I want to hear) can all filter the listener's ability to cleanly receive the transmitted expression. Other receiving issues result when the listener has an agenda such as to trying to fix, give advice, feels a need to be heard, interrupts, tries to talk over the other, is busy thinking of what to say or is self-absorbed and overly focused on having his or her own needs met before being resourced enough to listen and receive.

If our attention is focused enough and our bias level is low enough and our agenda is minimal enough, then the transmission can at least get close enough to us to be received to some degree. The next factor though is the listener's level of depth of presence. In the most superficial level that we primarily hear the words and focus on what it means to "me"— taking just our own perspective. Sometimes our mind quickly jumps to conclusions or judgments to fit new experience into our existing mental maps; to avoid this bias and self-absorption requires slowing down and Awareness, because if we jump to conclusions too quickly the open flow of communication has been stifled. If we go a level deeper we are able to feel a sense of connection among two people with a *Me-Map* and a *You-Map* that enables a person to take at least two perspectives. At the next level of depth, the more both people's system is open the more multi-level transmission including body language, facial expression, vocal tonality, energy, emotion, and mental words becomes increasingly available. Even deeper listening allows picking up deeper subtleties, undisclosed intentions, unspoken information, deeper emotion, etc. As presence deepens and expands to greater Vantages, even more information can be received moment to moment in and as Awareness.

INTERPRETATION REPRESENTATION & MEANING MAKING

Words are essentially sounds that our brain interprets through symbol interpretation based on our mind's meaning-making function. We could get really mental here but it might not add sufficient value to go too deeply into this, so suffice it to say that we all have our own unique meaning-making filters through which any communication must be received. Later we will learn about *Stages of Worldview Development* and *Vantage* which are two significant, yet still evolving structures of human meaning-making. Suffice to say that as our capacity to take perspectives and worldviews expand, so too does our ability to receive more information in a communication exchange. Most notably, at a certain construct-aware-worldview stage the constructed nature of words, language and me meaning-making tends to have people stop over-emphasizing words and instead focus more and more on the fuller range of experience arising out of immediacy.

COMMUNICATION RESPONDING

The response is the volley that maintains the connection and communication. Many people could benefit from pausing and intentionally breathing a little more in their communication exchanges. Not only does pausing allow greater awareness of aspects of our inner experience and the other's experience and life surrounding, but slowing down and pausing also reduces unconscious reactive communication habits and increases opportunity for response flexibility. A silence is only awkward when someone does that mental disconnected withdrawal or when they believe a natural pause is awkward and actually they themselves inject their own anxiety into the connection. This anxiety is an added emotional interpretation unrelated to the essential silence of a pause. We can also mentally withdrawal, try to leave or change the subject to avoid uncomfortable emotion, closeness, or subjects of depth. There are of course times when changing the subject in a conversation is part of the natural flow of the conversation, or it may be skillfully appropriate or enable better timing of agenda, but it can also be due to avoidance. Responses may include repeating what the speaker said, authentically responding, empathizing, sharing impact, expressing appreciation, asking a curious question, or establishing a healthy boundary.

REPEAT: I heard you say _____
RESPOND: authentically respond
EMPATHIZE: I imagine you felt _____
IMPACT: Hearing that I felt _____
APPRECIATION: I appreciated that or when _____
CURIOSITY: Ask a question
BOUNDARY: "No", redirect, pause, stop

LEVELS OF DEPTH

There are relative limits to how much one's system can open in a conversation. The container, the context, the amount of grace and capacity for depth are all variables that can enhance the openness of one or more of the connection channels of the expresser or listener systems. In general, the system with the most relaxed and open presence via nervous system relaxation and Vantage openness sets the threshold of how deep the exchange can go. Said in a different way, if we feel more relaxed and heart open when speaking with a particular person, it is because his or her heart and nervous system can positively entrain with ours and we can experience a deeper relaxation and openness then we would normally be able to access on our own. ^6 However, the opposite is also true though that if one person's nervous system is stressed or distressed it can negatively influence, through a process called emotional contagion, and instigate a reaction in our system. This is where we have a powerful opportunity to practice presence, grounding down like an oak tree, using our breath to anchor in deeply relaxed unreactive presence, allowing our steady presence to provide a resource to help the other feel, release and restore. However, the person with the more closed system can still resist or reach a threshold of how open he or she is willing to go and feel. When they hit their limit the resistance may show up as resistance, distraction, discomfort that arises that he or she then suppress, wanting to change the subject or end the conversation. The listener can easily relax into whatever depth of Vantage he or she wants and sense into the essence of the person underneath the words, but a speaker can only go so far if the other person/listener is unwilling to receive. In such cases, the speaker's energy hits a wall that cannot open further—we still have some degree of free will and can contract in the face of infinity if the ego so chooses. When this happens, the best thing to do is to radically accept the other person exactly as they are, return the conversation to immediacy when possible and relax open as Awareness beyond as the One and including the two.

- Communication is a dynamic reciprocal exchange of shared experience that requires sending & receiving multi-channel information. Whereas pure self-expression is one-way, communication is a two-way channel comprised of an expression being broadcast with the intent to share our experience to be effectively received & understood by others & vice versa to curiously know others world.
- Communication can be a bridge to connection via exchanging information through words, sounds, body language, gestures, facial expression, emotion, timing & subtleties.
- Greater presence in communication always begins with the basics of more fully embodying (grounding, breathing, body sensing) & inhabiting our own experience of authentic expression which is the congruent synchronization of mental-verbal, emotion & body language.
- In addition to having our expression feel much more authentic, integrated, clear, & enjoyable to receive, being more embodied as we communicate also tends to slow down us down, increase connection & quiet mental static.
- Expressing what we are feeling, what we are noticing, what we are curious about, etc. has our expression feel most alive in the present moment & thus speaking from immediacy is a potent doorway into deeper presence.
- A great conversation has a rhythm to it, a natural flow. It might contain back and forth, ebbs and flows, fast-talking excitement and passion, slow intervals of confusion or clarifying "ah ha's", waves of melodic words mixed with plenty of silence & space allowing pregnant pauses of emergent possibilities.
- Attuned speaking & checking for understanding: as the speaker, if we are connected & attuned to the other person we can sense each packet of communication & whether it is being effectively received: sensing when the other(s) subtly loses attention, gets distracted, or didn't understand a word or concept, etc.
- Porges' Polyvgal research tells us that the intonation of our voice produces a field of vibration that is transmitted & potentially received through neuroception that allows our nervous system receptors to turn on & off defensive behaviors as well as receive the full-bodied communication expression of the other. Whether we are conscious of whether or not, our body is a sensing mechanism that gives off cues when the communication transmission is being received.
- Open/Closed System: When our system is open, the expressing & receiving channels are more open, & conversely the more closed we are the less we can express & receive from others & life. The more closed someone's system is the more continuing to communicate with them feels like an effort & can leave the expresser feeling uninterested, frustrated, or depleted. When we close our system in contraction, we clamp down on the flow of life through us – whether speech, emotion or subtle energies – blocking communication & connection.
- A silence is only awkward when someone does that mental disconnected withdrawal or when they believe a natural pause is awkward & actually they themselves inject their own anxiety into the connection. Otherwise, many people could benefit from pausing & intentionally breathing a little more in their communication exchanges. Not only does pausing allow greater awareness

of spaciousness & deeper aspects of our inner experiences, but slowing down & pausing also reduces unconscious reactive communication habits & increases opportunity for response flexibility & something novel to emerge from immediacy.

BOUNDARIES

Are you able to say "**NO**" when necessary? Are you able to set limits to maintain **healthy boundaries**?

Do you **emit healthy boundaries** & do people tend to treat you & speak to you with respect?

Are you always the one helping or over-tending
to others while **sacrificing yourself**?
Do you like to **merge** with others &
lose yourself in connection?

"Learning to set boundaries and sticking to them even when someone doesn't like it. You don't owe anyone an explanation for your boundaries. It's not mean to have them, it's healthy. It's only once we can love and assert ourselves and say, I will not tolerate, x,y,z, that we can be whole, healthy & not in bondage to someone but instead stand free in a relationship."

- Jennifer Gafford -

WHAT ARE **BOUNDARIES**

the capacity to set, maintain & emit physical, emotional & energetic limits for space, autonomy & self-respect by opening or closing your embodied system

Labels on left figure:
- he feels smothered & discombobulated
- unable to take her own POV (Me-Map) his POV (You-Map) & shared POV (We-Map)
- confusion of identity without healthy sense of self
- lacking sense of being centered in her own axis
- fear of loss of love & connection
- lack of healthy boundaries
- connection thru merging, nice during sex but not daily life
- ungrounded

Labels on right figure:
- meeting in heart connection with healthy individuation
- power axis of central channel
- Inhabiting physicality sovereignty & self-respect
- grounded, stable base

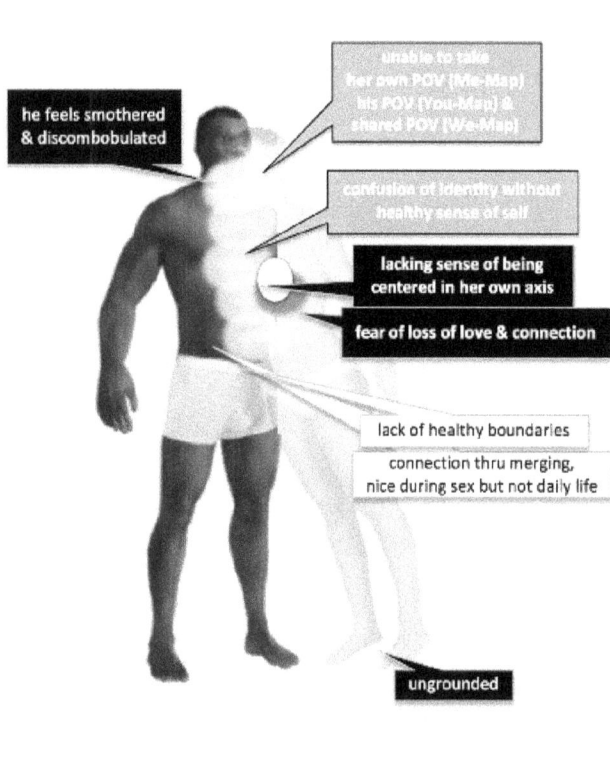

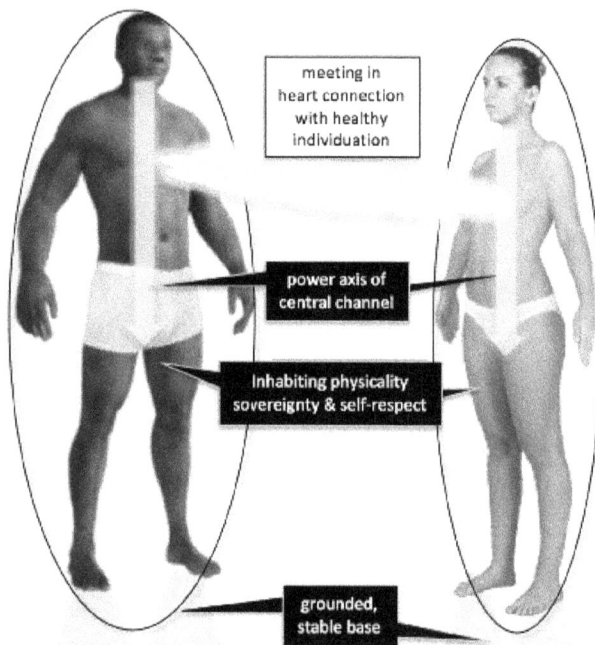

WHY **BOUNDARIES** MATTER

Protection: natural protection against physical or emotional harm & unwanted intrusion including people who are controlling, invasive, abusive, pushy, demanding, needy or smothering

Semi-Permeable Filter: capacity to set appropriate limits like the discerning filtration of a semi-permeable membrane, allowing some things in (to say "YES") & keeping some things out (to say "NO")

Setting Limits: shows others how they can treat you, first via words & agreements then advanced via emitted energetic boundaries

Self-Respect: not having healthy boundaries allows you to be taken advantage of, abused & disrespected

Personal Power: enough self-love, grounding, owning of personal space, integration of anger, self-respect & able to say "NO"

Healthy Relating: a healthy relationship depends on enough energetic & emotional space for two individuated beings to have their own unique experiences provided/protected by healthy personal boundaries

Connected & Individuated: able to be connected in relation AND to maintain healthy individuation; boundaries are required for healthy connection between 2 people, otherwise, it becomes merging or co-dependency

Freedom to Express: your own feelings, perspective or independence without guilt or fear

BARRIERS TO **BOUNDARIES**

Dissociation: not feeling & inhabiting your body due to trauma, defense or hyper-mental

Self-Referencing: part of healthy boundaries, the ability to self-reference from central column rather than others

Anxious Heart: fear or worry about losing closeness & connection

Collapse: contraction not owning your personal space & power

Anger: disowning of anger due to your past unconscious expression or how it was aggressively expressed at you

Trauma / Abuse: past emotional, physical, mental or sexual abuse

Saying "No": unable to say "no", believing it is rude or jeopardizes the relationship or threatens loss of love

Pleasing: compromising your authentic expression in order to be liked, belong or validated, being too nice or too acquiescing; fear of disapproval, fear of conflict, or fear of loss of love

Self-Sacrifice / Self-Neglect: lack of self-consideration or self-care, feeling undeserving of having needs of your own self-care sometimes as codependency, self-sacrificing your own feelings & needs to please others or earn worth

Codependency: over-tending to others, worth through being the helper, rescuer, consummate caretaker

Merging: Lack of individuation & healthy boundaries can lead to merging rather than meeting in connection

Self-respect / Worthiness: feeling unworthy or undeserving of self-respect & boundaries; you may not believe you have any rights of your own that are respected or don't defend your own dignity

Stifled Development of healthy Autonomy: overbearing or overprotective parents

Invasive Parents: overprotective, overbearing, controlling, smothering, or stifling parents

Poor Boundaried Parents: too nice, too permissive, or inconsistently disciplining parents

Fear / Terror: believing "the world is not safe", "it is not safe to be me", "it is not safe to be in my body"

BOUNDARIES DEVELOPMENT SUCCESS STORY

Reggie was a visionary Chief Executive Officer in the technology industry, with too much on his plate especially after having recently separated from his wife. He was gifted a connection whether in cyber connectivity or human rapport. In the boundaries department, however, he was not yet as skilled, yet. It's easy to get distracted by the tip of the iceberg above the surface, but there's usually a lot more underneath the water. Upon deeper investigation, this visionary businessman was primarily stressed by spreading himself in too many directions on the work front. Clarifying in & aligning with his deeper purpose he implemented systems that helped to align his highest leverage projects and priorities which allowed him to delegate better and more easily say no to tasks not aligned with his highest-leverage direction. Better boundaries and more potency at work plus with self-care (hydration, sleep, movement, better food quality) substantially decreased his baseline stress levels. While he was a powerhouse in the boardroom and a master of creating rapport with new people, yet socially he felt trapped by his own social persona. He made friends with his inner pleaser, fear of not being liked, integrated his ability to end a one-on-one conversation, learned to say "NO", & maintain his energetic boundaries without merging. Instead of having to isolate himself to create space, now he can create space and connection while respecting himself & others.

"Daring to set boundaries is about having the courage to love ourselves even when we risk disappointing others."

- Brene Brown -

Every living creature has its own territory in which it lives and in nature, organisms naturally protect themselves from physical harm and unwanted intrusion for the sake of survival. Humans have the additional social, sexual and emotional dynamics of relating which complicates boundaries. As children, between the ages of 1.5-3 years, we begin exploring our independence, developing a personal will and sense of autonomy by testing limits and learning to say *"NO"*.

Overprotective or controlling parents can contribute to rebelliousness. A parent(s) with weak boundaries—in confusing their own identity, need fulfillment and roles with their child—can collapse their child's boundaries. As discussed previously in the *Attunement section*, some parents use their child to fulfill their own unmet needs, which can stifle the child's developing autonomy, capacity for self-direction, and even create a role reversal, in which the child must parent and tend to the adult's unmet needs and emotional imbalance. In addition, therapist John Bradshaw also described a dynamic whereby a parent(s) dysfunctionally makes their child—usually of the opposite sex—a surrogate spouse for the parent's emotional intimacy needs. Any of these scenarios can negatively impact the developing boundaries of the child. Furthermore, inconsistent parental discipline can lead to confusion, self-doubt, and hesitancy, all of which can stifle the development of a child's own self of will, decision-making, authentic expression, and boundaries.

Whereas we were more merged in identity and emotion in the earlier stages of child development, as we are developing increasing individuality, we are still very dependent little beings and trying to develop a semi-permeable membrane of healthy boundaries—as we might remember from biology that living cells have. Our cells need to have barrier integrity (healthy boundaries), but in a partially porous way such that they can still allow in nutrients and out toxins or waste. Similarly, we humans need to have our own individuated nucleus and emotional experience, while also being open to connection and receptive to sensing and feeling others and the world around us. While there is a natural process of developing boundaries that inherently wants to happen, it is a process that must be learned from our caregivers and environment. If we have ever noticed that we share similar postures, gestures, movements or mannerisms as our parents or siblings, it may be because of what some childhood development researchers attribute to the body-based learning stored in our implicit memory. Our nervous systems absorb a lot from our environment and especially as children when we are developing and learning how to be in our bodies and the world. In that vein, our parents, caregivers and older siblings can indirectly teach us through their ways of being and maintaining their own boundaries as well as how they hold their own energetic boundaries and self-respect. We also directly learn boundaries by how respectfully they treat us in allowing us to be in our *"terrible two's"*, resisting seemingly everything, say *"NO"* as our favorite word, etc. but still maintaining the boundary and being the parent. On one extreme is the overprotective, overbearing, smothering, or stifling parent and on the other end of lacking healthy boundaries is the too nice, too permissive, or inconsistently disciplining parent afraid of not being loved. Parenting can be such a challenging, delicate and skill-requiring process.

PHYSICAL BOUNDARIES

The initial foundation of developing healthy boundaries starts on the physical level with being grounded, embodied and owning our physical space. It is like an imaginary line or subtle field that each of us can emit to varying degrees depending on the health of our boundary function. Personal boundaries operate in two directions, affecting interactions both the incoming from others and outgoing to others.

EMOTIONAL BOUNDARIES

Healthy external boundaries require clear internal boundaries – knowing our own emotions vs. others feelings as well as our responsibilities to ourselves vs. others. Emotional boundaries allow two or more people to meet in the connection of shared resonance as two autonomous beings while still having their own emotional experiences when relating. Without the functionality of healthy boundaries, we might tend to merge in connection and confuse emotions, energy, and identity with each other, which might lead to codependency. Or, it may result in the need to periodically withdraw and isolate to create our own space to breathe, because we haven't learned to have healthy boundaries, while simultaneously being connected. When semi-permeable boundaries are activated, then we can receive some inputs while filtering others. The semi-permeability part is that when we are connected and related that we can feel emotional impact without being emotionally manipulated. This can get complicated at times and requires practice for us to be able to own our own emotional experience and be able to openly feel compassion and empathy; to feel impact without being made responsible for someone else's emotional process. It might involve that we learn to not take other's words or actions less personally, while at other times being able to vulnerably show the hurt or impact on us and to make request that honor our boundaries. It could include learning to not feel guilty for someone else's negative feelings but to apologize and clean up the situation when our actions have had a negative impact on someone else.

Again semi-permeability is the key when we can say *"YES"* or *"NO"*, that we can maintain two open, yet individuated people meeting in connection that can selectively allow some things in and others not. Some people are too emotionally closed and boundaried while others are too open. The end goal would be that our healthy functioning boundaries would be more metaphorically like a dimmable light switch rather than having the lights always turned on (letting everything in) or always turned off (keeping everything out). If our lights are always turned off, and our system is always guarded, closed and numbed to others, then the consequence is not feeling connected to others of life.

IDENTITY BOUNDARIES

It is our birthright to protect ourselves from harm and when healthy boundaries are online, there is an inherent human drive to maintain our dignity. We should have the right to say *"YES"* or *"NO"*, to be treated with respect, to conserve energy, to ask for help, or to decline to answer something. The ability to set, maintain and emit a boundary depends partially on self-respect and self-love.

Where is the limit of what you are willing to tolerate?
Where is the boundary of your dignity and self-respect?
How do you know when you are over-stepping others' boundaries and potentially taking advantage of them?
Can you care about someone, feel compassion for and possibly support them in a healthy agreed upon way if they ask, without being overly-responsible for or overly-worrying about their problems to the sacrifice or detriment of yourself?
Can you care about another person without trying to change, fix or control them? Do you give unsolicited advice?

The ability to take responsibility for our own actions without inaccurately blaming others and on the other side hard to respect our own boundaries and skillfully communicate about something that might be a boundary violation for us. The more empowered and accountable we are for our own feelings, actions and life, the less we tend to blame others. If someone accurately calls us out for something we can humbly and undefensively acknowledge the truth, and perhaps even feel a small healthy degree of guilt or shame. However, if inaccurately blamed for something we are not responsible for, instead of inauthentically apologizing or aggressively defending, we could stay in our own center and not take responsibility for their process.

LEARNING TO SET, MAINTAIN & EMIT HEALTHY BOUNDARIES

Healthy boundaries need to be learned and embodied—hopefully, this section has allowed us to assess to some degree how that process functions for us in our relationships and life. As mentioned above, the first step is learning to be more grounded and embodied in our own space—how can we expect to protect our home when we are not inhabiting it? It can also be useful to effectively desensitize previous traumatic or disempowering boundary related experiences. Cultivating greater self-respect and self-love can be a lifelong process for some, but we need just enough to feel we deserve to be treated with respect and that we are still loved even if we sometimes say *"NO"* or set a limit. Part of honoring our own boundary is acknowledging that our own needs are equally as important as our partner's. Part of this self-love process for some people involves rewiring, that instead of our energy and self-worth coming from the other person, that we increasingly learn to self-source energy and worth so we are full and whole as an individual, thus able to meet another partner in healthy adult individuated connection. We can notice patterns of pleasing, being overly concerned about being liked, which either leads to selling ourselves out or secretly feeling resentful later. Fear of not being loved is not real love, either for our self or from another.

Having healthy boundaries also requires consciously integrating anger—one essential function of which is enforcing health boundaries and self-respect. For many people, anger is either disowned or comes out unconsciously as aggression distinguishes anger versus physical or verbal aggression. But anger in it's pure form, if it can be felt with sufficient emotional presence and awareness enables:

BENEFITS OF HEALTHY ANGER

1) **healthy boundaries** & *self-respect* & the ability to say *"NO"*
2) **healthy determination** instead of victimhood or collapse
3) **illumination of injustice or unconsciousness** that can use the light of awareness shined on it

Acknowledging and honoring the boundaries for ourselves and our partner helps guide the relationship toward more mutual respect and healthy connection. Initially, as we are learning to set healthy limits, we might do so with anger. We might notice that if it's done in anger, frustration or by nagging, it is not usually received as well, but sometimes that is what needed. Sometimes consequences need to be expressed to encourage compliance and respect. Of course, boundaries tend to be communicated more effectively when we're centered, calm, clear and firm, but it can be a process to get to this place, so keep practicing. Setting boundaries is a learned skill and is an art until it becomes more effortless when it is energetically embodied. Weaker-boundaried people tend to be codependent, merge or get taken advantage of, while rigid boundaried people might be so closed with fearful protection that they don't allow love and connection in. People with healthy boundaries are somewhere in between like a flexible semi-permeable filter—with the capacity for modulating between both healthy self-respect and open vulnerability. If they need to move toward one polarity, they can do so with conscious intentionality with ever greater clarity of what comes in as a *"YES"* and what goes out as a *"NO"*, and people subconsciously feel the self-respect they feel for themselves and treat us accordingly. We will not as easily be psychologically taken advantage of or emotionally manipulated. The way we carry ourselves subtlety pings people about how to communicate, respect and treat us.

Integral psychotherapist, Robert Augustus Masters, who has worked with thousands of couples over the past 3 decades, has mapped out several stages individuals go through in his book *Transformations thru Intimacy*.[2] In his extensive clinical experience in the trenches working with couples over many years he notes at least 4 main stages couples evolve through: 1) **Selfish**, 2) **Co-dependent**, 3) **Inter-dependent**, 4) **Awakening Being**. In his second stage is where healthy boundaries tend to be learned. As Dan Siegel says it takes two open, yet individuated *"ME's"* to be available for a healthy connected

"WE". Speaking to Augustus Master's 4th stage of Awakening Being, and hearing people talk about "no boundaries" this refers to a transpersonal stage that transcends AND includes the personal sense of self, having a felt sense of becoming part of an expanded identity larger than even our interpersonal relationships. We can read more about this in the *Vantage section* but for now work on cultivating healthy boundaries, and perhaps even greater self-love, before we worry too much about transcending. Dan Siegel sums up the spectrum of boundaries here:

> *"if we don't know where I end in the other begins we will have a difficult time establishing healthy connections. Those of us with weakly formed boundaries will be easily manipulated and influenced, often confusing our partner's feelings for own. Those of us with firm boundaries will have a hard time opening our hearts to love. Our walls are simply too firm to penetrate. People with healthy boundaries tend to live somewhere in between. They have the capacity for vulnerability and self-protection at all times. When they do move toward one polarity, they do so with intentionality. In all cases, their sense of self remains intact."*[3]

BOUNDARY SUMMARY & KEY TAKEAWAYS

➤ Healthy boundaries are like semi-permeable filters that enable us to set, maintain & emit physical, emotional & energetic limits for space, autonomy & self-respect

➤ Boundaries can function on the levels of physical, emotional, mental & identity.

➤ Healthy Relating & Connection: requires enough energetic & emotional space for two individuated beings to have their own unique experiences so they can meet in connection otherwise, it becomes merging or co-dependency.

➤ There is a natural process of developing boundaries that inherently wants to happen, but it is a process that must be learned to filter interactions both the incoming from others & outgoing to others; we need to have our own individuated nucleus & emotional experience, while also being open to connection & receptive to sensing and feeling others & the world around us.

➤ Having healthy boundaries also requires consciously integrating anger versus disowning it or unconsciously acting out aggressively

➤ Weaker-boundaried people tend to be codependent, merge or get taken advantage of, while rigid boundaried people might be so closed with protection that they don't allow love and connection in. Healthy boundaries are somewhere in between like a flexible semi-permeable filter—with the capacity for modulating between both healthy self-respect & open vulnerability.

➤ Integral psychotherapist, Robert Augustus Masters has identified 4 Stages of Relationship Development for couples: 1) Selfish, 2) Co-dependent, 3) Inter-dependent, 4) Awakening Being

VULNERABILITY: TRANSPARENCY & OPENNESS

Are you able to be **open & transparent** allowing others to know you, see you, feel you & connect with you?

Are you afraid of emotional closeness & connection,
letting others in, or allowing others to know
your beauty & struggles?

Do you stay guarded, fear being judged or
use humor, clichés & superficiality to avoid real depth?

———————————

"The intention and outcome of vulnerability is trust, intimacy and connection." …"Belonging starts with self-acceptance. Your level of belonging, in fact, can never be greater than your level of self-acceptance, because believing that you're enough is what gives you the courage to be authentic, vulnerable & imperfect"

- Brene Brown -

———————————

WHAT IS IT **VULNERABILITY**

the capacity to transparently open yourself in relationships to allow your unique self to be seen, heard, felt & known either in the simplicity of being or vulnerably expressing deeper feelings, opinions, desires & struggles

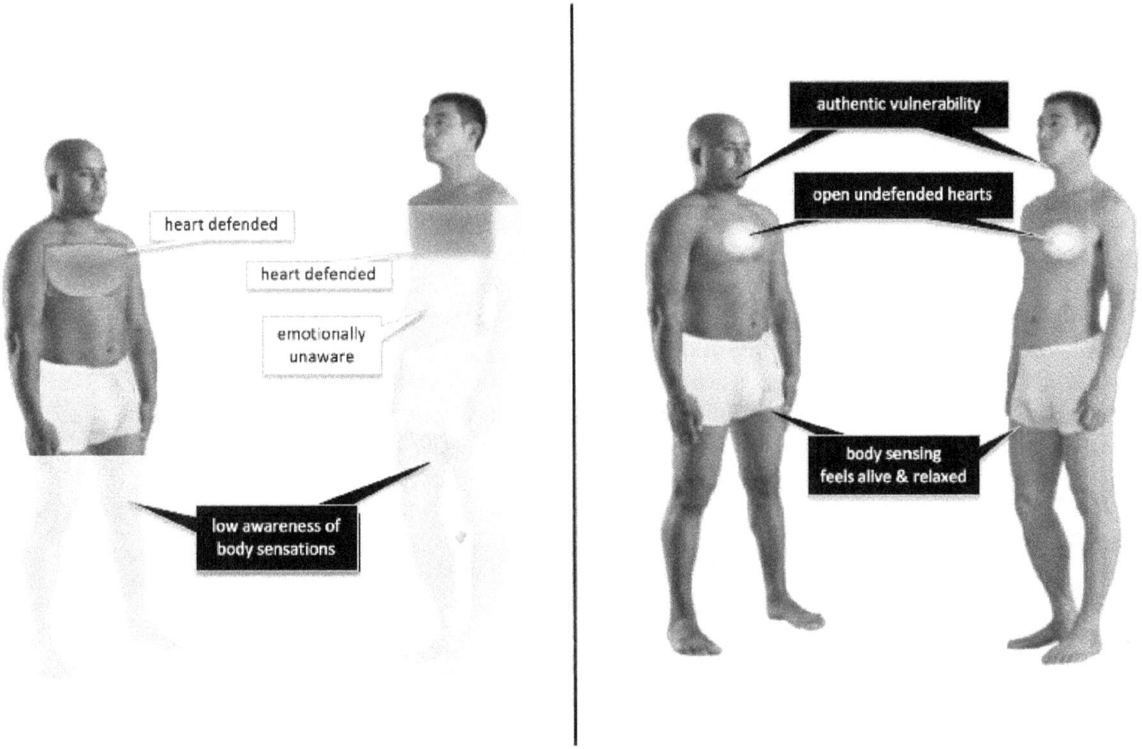
heart defended
heart defended
emotionally unaware
low awareness of body sensations
authentic vulnerability
open undefended hearts
body sensing feels alive & relaxed

WHY **VULNERABILITY** MATTERS

Connection & Closeness: transparent openness through with emotional vulnerability is the doorway to closeness & connection
Transparency in communication increases as you relax your protective guard and is a gauge of your self-acceptance

Opening: allows us to be known, seen, heard & feel connected to ourselves, others & life

Closure: allows us to protect or defend but can leave us disconnected; the ability to open & close is required for healthy boundaries

Mutual Responsiveness: closeness & connection deepens as you both allow yourselves be open in connecting with each other & while you both respond in a way that makes each other feel safe, understood, & supported

Courage: vulnerability isn't weakness; it requires self-acceptance & courage to openly allow ourselves to be seen, felt & known

Free & Real Expression: safety & vulnerability allows freedom to express deeper feelings, opinions, desires & struggles so that others can know & connect with you

Acceptance & Connection: we all want to be feel acceptance, belonging & connection while authentically expressing ourselves

BARRIERS TO **VULNERABILITY**

Fear of Connection & Intimacy or Avoidant Attachment: fear of emotional closeness & connection
Image Positioning: hiding something or trying to say something to be seen in a certain way or meet expectation
Hesitation or Withholding: guarded, hiding, fear of being judged or criticized, fear of saying the wrong thing
Fear of being Seen: hiding or blocking real expression to avoid criticism, disapproval or rejection
Shame: fear of being seen; unreleased shame related to past experiences of feeling not good enough
Superficiality: avoiding depth, afraid of intimacy or feeling deeper emotions
Avoidant Humor: laugh or use humor to avoid deeper conversation, emotion & connection
Hyper-Mental: excessive mental activity, overly theoretical, living in fantasy, lost in the past or future
Gender Stereotype: believing or associating emotionality with a certain gender which could threaten identity
Confused Belief that vulnerability = weakness: believe being vulnerable a weakness
Hyper-Positive: disowning any thoughts or emotions other than positivity
Stoic / Rigid: closed, defended, emotionally numb, playing tough or using power games
Emotionally Guarded: you do not like to reveal anything personal, talk about yourself or share deeper feelings, not feeling emotionally safe (judgment, rejection, hurt), not feeling belonging, or only feeling safe with a few trusted people with whom you are sometimes able to open up & share personal things
Clogged Heart: unreleased sadness, hurt, anger & resentment from the past, unfelt & unexpressed emotions emotions can create closure & stagnation in your system
Betrayal Experiences: unreleased charge on past experiences of trust being betrayed or negative impact of over-sharing
Power-over: underlying intentions to dominate or take advantage of rather than mutually empowered connection
Inexperience: have never experienced openness or real presence, listening, attunement & empathy from someone

VULNERABILITY DEVELOPMENT SUCCESS STORY

Andy was a captain in his fire department, tall, blue-eyed, healthy, fit, husband & father of two little ones. If you saw him down the street, you would probably think he was a cool, confident and collected leader. While this was generally true, criticism was his undoing. He had a strong inner critic & according to him, he spent too much energy worrying about avoiding criticism by others which had him keep up a protective shield against it. This subtle protective guard prevented anyone from seeing inside or getting to know him more deeply. Again from an outsider perspective, you might think "What a cool guy with a great life!" but inside that was not his felt experience. He said he wanted to learn to stop beating himself up, reduce anxiety, and feel more connected to people and that he felt isolated even amongst his friends at work and his wife at home. First, we desensitize some of his relevant past charged experiences, then helped him learn to ground, breath & more confidently inhabit his body especially in social relating. Next, we developed a more peaceful alliance with his inner critic. Finally, then he felt safe to soften his protective shield against vulnerability and it was through this transparency & openness that he was able to let people into know him, see him and connect with him. Now, with all the anxiety & protection turned down, he walks around much more relaxed, confident, open & smiling. "Oh, presence and connection. It seems so simple now that I can feel in my body how to do it."

"If there is any need that is perpetually unmet on this planet, it is the need to feel seen. To feel seen in our humanity, in our vulnerability, in our beautiful imperfection. When we are held safe in that, a key turns inside of our hearts, freeing us from our isolation, transforming our inner world. If there is anything we can offer each other, it is the gift of sight. "I see you"-perhaps the most important words we can utter to another. I see you..."

--- Jeff Brown ---

HOW VULNERABILITY DEVELOPS

We come into the world as newborn infants fused with our environments, unprotected in the big world, and completely dependent on our adult caregivers for nourishment, love, and protection. We are also very sensitive little beings, especially to the emotional world around us, to what we are feeling and to what our primary caregivers are feeling can get blurry. We are naturally open to give and receive love, but also have survival and emotional needs. The essential heart nutrients of emotional attunement and connection help our systems stay open and transparent. As we grew through childhood, we learned how to be social and connected human beings through safety, acceptance, and attunement. Other children were at times loving and playful, as well as hurtful. Similarly, our teachers or mentors were at times inspiring and other times critical and shaming. These patterns seem to continue throughout our adult lives and based on a combination of past wounding, conditioning, and capacity, each of us having varying abilities to open our hearts, be real and transparent to allow others to see us, feel us, know us, and be connected.

As we are learning to navigate through life and balancing our need for transparent authentic expression with the social connection of belonging, most of us have probably asked ourselves some of these questions:

Am I loved and received for being me?
Is it emotionally safe: "If I am open and undefended will I be emotionally accepted?"
Is it physically safe: "will I be bullied or abused by kids at school, older siblings, or adults?"
Am I good enough and loveable?
How do I avoid being judged or criticized?
As I am learning how to express emotional discomfort in my body, will I still be accepted?
As I am learning how to communicate, will I still be accepted?

Brene Brown, Ph.D—a research professor at the *University of Houston Graduate College of Social Work*—is an expert on the subject of human vulnerability, having spent the first five years of her social psychology research studying human connection.[1] When she asked people about love, most shared stories of heartbreak; when she asked about belonging, they shared stories of being excluded; when she asked people about connection, they told stories of the pain of disconnection. Surprised, she stepped back and realized that fear and shame were a common thread running through all these people' stories. Interviewing thousands of people from various cultures, she recognized that these are universal emotions that we all experience, yet as they relate to transparency, they can have us feel the need to hide, shield and protect the deeper more authentic and tender parts of ourselves. However, while protecting our emotional vulnerability we also close off the very pathway through which we experience closeness and connection. We cannot taste the dynamism of life by staying locked in our room, nor can we experience the depth of intimacy with a guarded heart. It is often fear and shame that prevents us from feeling safe enough to be transparent and open our hearts and emotional worlds to allow others to see us, feel us, know us and connect with us. However, paradoxically it is also this same open-hearted transparency that allows people to see inside and connect to each other. It is often the fear of hurt, rejection, judgment, disapproval, and abandonment based on a combination of *past emotional experiences* and *beliefs* that perpetuate the feelings of unworthiness which fuel further isolation, loneliness, disconnection and avoidance of true intimacy. Most of us protectively guard ourselves against this open vulnerability after emotional wounds suffered as children or adults. It is from this place of transparency that we allow others to see inside us; however, this requires us feeling safe enough and accepting enough of ourselves as we are to be authentically honest and transparently show the innermost aspects of ourselves. Thus, is it takes great courage and perhaps some inner work to realize greater wholeness, self-acceptance and *"engaging in our lives from a place of worthiness"*—as Brene Brown calls it—to ultimately allow us to be more able to experience the most fulfilling *"wholehearted"* lives of openness possible.

Our system's capacity to be transparent starts with our connection to ourselves. Are we able to honestly look at ourselves? If we aren't willing to allow parts to even be seen by ourselves, how can others be allowed in? Our opening and closing are like barrier membranes to life or *"openness"* to be seen, known and connected with others and by life surrounding. Our tendency to be open or to close up is like a barrier membrane to life—it determines if we are willing to be seen, to be known and connected with others. This is often associated with the *"heart"* in the center of the chest, although psychologically, this transparency could be equated with emotional vulnerability, which is intimately related physiologically to the relaxation and subtle softness in the front of the chest and belly. With that said, every quality exists on a spectrum with a polar opposite, in this case, *"open"* and *"closed."* However, openness is not a static thing but rather a dynamic process, so opening and closing are more accurate descriptions of this relative process. We each tend to have a baseline degree of openness, although many of us go through our daily life more on the closed guarded protected side of the spectrum. However, after developing a greater flexibility in learning to open or close our system more volitionally, our aperture of openness tends to fluctuate, subtly opening or closing moment to moment.

Some people think that they *"should"* be more open all of the time. The first caution to be aware of is that if our system has disowned its capacity to close then we can't possibly have healthy boundaries, self-respect against being taken advantage of, and the ability to say *"NO"*, etc. Secondly, in relating, emotional vulnerability is the doorway to the openness of connection and the closeness of intimacy. So, while it certainly feels better to feel more openness and connection in ourselves and those we are relating with, sometimes emotional trigger and closure does happen. Let us not overly pressure ourselves with the impossible belief our system should be open all the time because if we do then a layer of self-judgment can complicate things even more and take even longer to reopen. Instead, let us focus more on recovery time and reopening into emotional vulnerability by returning to a deeper presence in our body, attuning to our own breath, sensations, and emotions. On this level, we play with the relative openness of our personal system within the interpersonal domain of relating with others.

OVER-SHARING

There is also such a thing as being too transparent and over-sharing. Brene Brown offers a potent reminder: *"The intention and outcome of vulnerability is trust, intimacy, and connection. The outcome of over-sharing is distrust, disconnection and usually a little judgment."* Let us not think the shield of protection for transparency and openness should be eliminated—remember transcend and include. This guardian can be very useful in moments of aggression or attack when we truly need to protect our heart. However, when our heart is congested from the past, we are holding onto past shame, or afraid and we are unable to open our hearts and allow others to see inside and connect with us, it profoundly limits our openness to our own authentic expression, connection with others and openness to life. For most of us, greater openness and transparency is a process of releasing, healing, forgiving, trusting and having the courage to increasingly open our hearts. We increase our capacity for open transparency as we become more emotionally free from our past by releasing the emotional charge on previous experiences, especially in the case of vulnerability, shame-related past experiences and events with associated rejection or hurt. As we increasingly develop a healthier relationship with shame by releasing our past resulting in feeling like we have nothing to be ashamed of and increasing our present ability to feel small amounts of healthy shame in the moment so we no longer are afraid of feeling shame. While at the same time, feeling a greater sense of worthiness and self-acceptance, it becomes increasingly easier to be vulnerable, real, open-hearted, and connected, while simultaneously giving permission to others to do the same. Emotional closeness and intimacy grow deeper each time we allow ourselves to be vulnerable, open and connected with another person and they respond in a way that makes us feel safe, understood, and supported. Conversely, mutual intimacy is also cultivated when the other person is vulnerable with us and we respond in a safe and supportive way. It is through our open transparency of our hearts that we experience intimacy, love, joy, and appreciate beauty, feel wonder, savor stillness and silence, and feel deeply connected to others. Ultimately this becomes a moment-to-moment courageous choice, to be transparently open personally with ourselves, with others and with Life. As we deepen in Presence, the polarity of human safety and insecurity relaxes into the vulnerability of profound Openness.

OPENNESS WITH LIFE

Eventually, as our system continues to evolve, our openness is in relation to Life surrounding. In advanced stages of adult human development, the transparent openness membrane of a system transcends and includes concerns about safety, acceptance, and self-absorption, in focusing more on the allowing of expression and availability to the totality of the moment, which is felt to be an inseparable part of Life. At previous stages of the personal self-identify (see *Stages of Worldview Development section*), the openness of expression via voice and movement tends to be either efforting to position itself to be seen in a certain way and/or inhibiting itself out of fear of being seen or judged. *"I want you to see me as all of these qualities but I don't want you to see these parts."* Here the personal identity's self-protective and projective efforts are increasingly seen to compete with greater transparent openness. We might ask ourselves, *"Is part of me capturing others' attention to be seen as this* and not seen as that or relaxing into the transparent openness of Awareness itself, allow the moment to express or not as inspired. Because again every quality exists on a spectrum within the totality of Awareness— in other words, everything is contained within the boundlessness of Awareness—we couldn't be "open" without the possibility of also being relatively *"closed"*, nor could we be transparent without its polar opposite guardedness. As many people evolve and continue to experience more and more openness, one place some get tripped up is in identifying with always being open, because for the individual system this *"state"* of openness seems to be the bridge to feeling connected with all. Rather from a greater view, opening and closing of a unique system, both happen within Awareness. So, while of course from the relative self it feels better to be open, the view from the Awareness of Presence is *already* wide open. As relative presence and Absolute Presence simultaneously co-arise, so too we practice our human transparency allowing our relative system to be more and more open from within the greater *Vantage* of ever-present Presence.

VULNERABILITY SUMMARY & KEY TAKEAWAYS

➤ Vulnerability is to transparently open yourself in relationships to allow your unique self to be seen, heard, felt & known either in the simplicity of being or vulnerably expressing deeper feelings, opinions, desires & struggles.

➤ Transparent openness through with emotional vulnerability is the doorway to closeness & connection.

➤ Vulnerability isn't weakness; it requires self-acceptance & courage to openly allow ourselves to be seen, felt & known.

➤ Safety & vulnerability allows freedom to express deeper feelings, opinions, desires & struggles so that others can know & connect with us.

➤ Mutual Responsiveness: as each person undefendedly opens in vulnerability & the other responds in an accepting way that has us feel safe, understood, & supported, it permissions more & more transparent opening, closeness & connection.

➤ When Brene Brown, an expert on vulnerability, realized that fear & shame were universal emotions that had thousands of people she interviewed hiding & protecting their authentic vulnerability, yet our emotional vulnerability is the doorway to connection, these heart shieldings were also inhibiting our experience of closeness & connection.

➤ It is often the fear of hurt, rejection, judgment, disapproval, and abandonment based on a combination of past emotional experiences and beliefs that perpetuate the feelings of danger or unworthiness which fuel further isolation, loneliness, disconnection & avoidance of true vulnerable human intimacy & connection.

➤ "The intention & outcome of vulnerability is trust, intimacy, & connection. The outcome of over-sharing is distrust, disconnection & usually a little judgment." – Brene Brown

GENDER ESSENCE & SEXUAL POLARITY

Are you more oriented to freedom, purpose & initiation? Or more oriented to love, flow & receptivity?

Are you more inspired to grow thru through competition & challenge or are you more inspired by beauty & feel like you grow through praise & support?

Do you know your gender essence & can you
create magnetic sexual polarity & attraction
in your romantic relationship?

———————

MASCULINE *"When you feel sexual lust or desire for any woman, breathe deeply and allow the feeling of desire to magnify. And allow it to magnify more. Don't let the energy become lodged in your head or genitals, but circulate it throughout your body. Using your breath as the instrument of circulation, bathe every cell in the stimulated energy. Inhale it into your heart, and then feel outward from your heart, feeling the world as if it were your lover. With an exhale, move into the world and penetrate it, skillfully and spontaneously, opening it into love."*

– David Deida –

FEMININE *"Sexually and in everyday life, when your lover can feel your energy and skillfully guide you to deeper and more passionate flow, your body relaxes. You can trust him, and surrender to the depth of his loving command. When he seems unable to feel you, then you naturally withdraw your trust, take control, and do your best to lead yourself."*

– David Deida –

———————

WHAT IS **GENDER ESSENCE & SEXUAL POLARITY**
the capacity to embody your gender essence (on the spectrum of masculine or feminine energies) in life & create sexual polarity in romantic relation while integrating some degree of its opposite

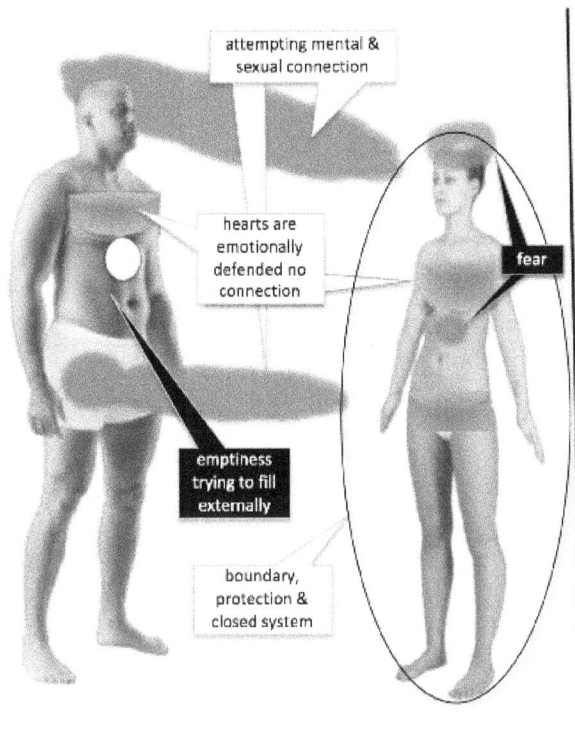

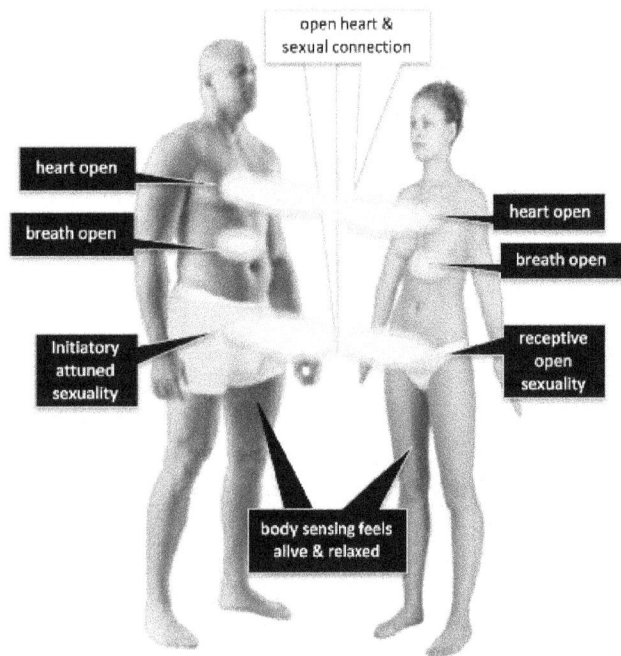

WHY **GENDER ESSENCE & SEXUAL POLARITY** MATTERS

Distinction: to clarify gender distinctions between biology male & female, mentally & socially constructed identity (man & woman, heterosexual/homosexual/gender fluid), & energetics masculine & feminine

Sexual-Spiritual Drive Essence: to better understand more fully live into your essential energetic drives toward freedom & purpose or love & relationship

Masculine: aware of, appreciating & living drives of directive, decisive, seeking freedom & purpose, living on the edge, growing thru challenge,

Feminine: aware of, appreciating & living drives of receptivity, seeking Love, intimacy, connection, radiance, beauty, caring, flowing, growing thru praise

Dynamic Range: to more fully embody your gender energetic essence & integrate to some degree its polar opposite

Polarity & Paradox: to be more aware of the dance of energetic opposites in your body, relating & in life

Passionate Sexual Attraction: sexual attraction in romantic relationship comes from the magnetic charge of masculine & feminine polarity

BARRIERS TO **SEXUAL GENDER POLARITY**

Fear of Connection & Intimacy: fear of emotional closeness & connection

Abuse/Trauma: can lead to closing down sexually or becoming hyper-sexual

Repression: family, culture or religion can have a repressed & shaming attitude toward sexuality

Shame: worth, shame & sexuality can become entangled

Porn Addiction: can have similar underlying avoidance causes as other addictions

Impotence: poor health & circulation

Immaturity: stunted psychological & sexual development

Stress / Life Imbalance: can drain life force or leading to disowned sexuality

Dissociation & Avoidant Attachment: can be afraid of their body, emotional intimacy & sexuality

Soft New Age Guys & Hardened Career Women: confused as to their essence, some get stuck in the process of integrating the opposite energy

Merging: lack of individuation & healthy boundaries can lead to merging rather than meeting in connection; you can't have a sexual polarity between two when you have a single merged blob

SEXUAL GENDER POLARITY DEVELOPMENT SUCCESS STORY

James & Elle had a great life by many accounts: work, home, family, travel, finances, health, fitness, etc. but their connection & passion were off. With 2 young children, careers and busy lifestyles, their lives were full & thriving but their relationship was off. Upon closer examination, we discovered that when Elle got stressed she went into a more masculine-bull-in-a-china-shop-mode. It was not easy for her to work, be a mother & a wife. When she got stressed she got tense & intense, taking charge in some moments and chaotically malfunctioning in other. First, we improved communication and delegation, supplemented this with some outside support. Next, she learned how to relax more in the engagement of her day and how to calm her nervous system before it started to get too hyper-stressed. Feeling calmer and safer we reestablished connection and bonding between James & Elle. Then finally we introduced masculine & feminine energetics through car driving metaphors and dancing practices. A couple months later their life is still great and now so too is their connection, passion & sexual polarity!

"If the masculine partner's presence wavers, then the feminine partner loses trust, guards herself emotionally, and can't enjoy the bliss of opening her body and heart fully as the flow of feminine love. If the feminine partner's radiance diminishes--so that body and heart close, ripples of pleasure decrease, and emotional expression becomes muted--then the masculine partner is stuck in the realm of head and tail, bereft of full-bodied, heart-given sensual energy, unattracted beyond his own self-controlled detachment or selfish stimulation."

– David Deida –

Gender can be either very confusing or a very charged issue for some people. Part of the confusion lies in our assumption that the other gender is like us combined with a lack of curiosity to get the other's world. Gender expert, Allison Armstrong best-selling author and event facilitator on the subject says:

> *"99% of the confusion and frustration between men and women is because we assume we're versions of each other. It goes both ways, although men are a little bit more forgiving. They allow for the mystery of women. But honestly, when men look at women they see a softer, more lovely, multitasking, emotionally-indulgent man. And they interact with us as if we're men! Realizing that we're not versions of each other meant that I needed to pay much closer attention."*

In the latter case, we are referencing the emotional triggering that some people experience related to the gender topic—and whether this is due to trauma, confusion or social neutering—ironically, it is the magnetic charge of essential polar opposites that creates sexual attraction among humans. As we will discover, these polar forces are an inherent part of our world and they animate our fundamental drives in life and provide the magnetism of epic relational passion. Just like with the electromagnetic polarity of metal prongs of an electrical cord conducting electricity from an electrical outlet, of the magnetism between the Earths north and south poles, sexual polarity also requires the magnetic energy created by the attraction of two polarized energies: masculine and feminine. Before we continue further, let us draw some distinctions:

BIOLOGY (male & female): based on anatomy, genetics, & hormone levels

IDENTITY (man & woman): ways of being based on beliefs, meaning-making & socially constructed concepts

ENERGETIC POLARITY (masculine & feminine): magnetic attraction created by two polarizing energies

BIOLOGY: MALE & FEMALE

Biologically most of us are born with either male or female sex organs—except in very rare cases of true hermaphroditism, in which an individual is born with ovarian and testicular tissue, known as *ovotesticular disorder of sex development*.[2] Besides these exceptions, the majority of humans have varying hormone levels of testosterone and estrogen which tend to correspond with biology (male & female) but are significantly affected by diet and lifestyle. Now as science and medicine are increasingly understanding the dynamic range of human hormonal systems, males or females who chose to have a biological sex change operation can use hormones to enhance the biological changes. Nonetheless, there are distinct biological differences in male and female—in this regard we are equal yet different.

IDENTITY: MAN & WOMAN

Identity is the aspect of gender dynamics that is perhaps the most controversial and requires extra caution and clarity because it is the most enculturated and mentally constructed (i.e. made up). What it means to be a *"man"* or *"woman"* is made up based on cultural stereotypes of tendencies. For example, to say that a man can't wear pink or boys don't cry, are not biological facts of life, but rather social beliefs that are made up. A male or female can wear whatever color they want and both genders feel emotion and can cry as a method of release although neurologically the female brain is wired to experience greater emotional intensity. So, on the subject of emotionality, we have to be very clear and distinguish science from stereotype and cultural norms. Yes, the female brain experiences emotion with more intensity, but both genders are biologically (male and female) wired as humans to experience emotions. To further emphasize the influence of cultural beliefs and unspoken rules, compare the allowable emotionality of someone from a Latin culture (male or female) to someone from an Asian culture (male or female).

ENERGETIC POLARITY: MASCULINE & FEMININE

With this energetic aspect of gender, both males and females carry the potential for both masculine and feminine energies. In other words, a male has the capacity to inhabit both masculine and feminine energies and a female the capacity to inhabit both masculine and feminine energies. David Deida is perhaps the foremost expert on Sexual Polarity and he describes it as people having unique percentages of masculine and feminine energies on top of a foundation of their true sexual essence.   In Deida's decades of working with people in workshop and couples coaching, he believes that around 10% of people are more androgynous or have a more neutral 50%/50% sexual essence and tend to be more balanced in their orientation to life and relationship, in the latter case, most prefer relationships that are more friendly loving and are not interested in the passionate

MASCULINE	FEMININE

attraction of sexually polarized partnerships. Otherwise, the remaining 90% of us tend to have a primary sexual essence in the way we orient to life and relationship that lies somewhere on either side of the middle of the sexual energy spectrum.

In other words, each of us lives somewhere on this spectrum and one of these energies tends to instinctively animate us more of the time. As a general example, a male could have 80% masculine / 20% feminine sexual essence, while another male could have a 40% masculine / 60% feminine sexual essence. This sexual essence, although it is usually closely related to gender, is technically not the same because a male could have a more feminine essence or vice versa a female could have a more masculine core energy. Gay males and lesbian female illustrate this very clearly because, as we will get into attraction later, even in a homosexual relationship, one partner usually animates the initiatory masculine energy while the other inhabits the more receptive feminine pole if in the relationship, there is passion via polarity regardless of gender biology. The following chart illustrates some of the essential masculine and feminine human qualities:

MASCULINE – ESSENTIAL QUALITIES	FEMININE – ESSENTIAL QUALITIES
Initiatory	Receptive
Seeking Freedom	Seeking Love
Sense of Purpose (desire to complete missions)	the Sense of Connection (desire for intimacy)
Competitive (grow through challenge)	Radiance & Beauty (grow through praise & support)
Evolving (living on the edge)	Caring (nurturing life)
Decisive & Directive	Flowing & Unpredictable

An interesting experiment related to gender is to put a group of males of different ages and cultures together in a room with no instructions and observe what happens. And likewise to put a group of diverse females in a room together. Obviously personalities, ages, generations, culture, socio-economic class, etc. all combine to influence ways of being, but there is still an essential difference—a distinct energetic difference arises in the two separate rooms. Then when the two groups return to the larger room while staying on their respective sides and the arch of polar attraction between the pairs of opposites ensues. The masculine energy that gets concentrated in the males regardless of age or culture tend to maintain more freedom and autonomy, decides to work towards a goal or organizing principle and if they are playful they tend to do so competitively, engaging either their intellects in discussion or physicality in movement or sport. In contrast, the feminine energy that gets concentrated in the females usually ends up orienting to connection and touch perhaps in caring, grooming, massaging, and snuggling with each other or as a spontaneous expression of flowing movement, dancing, singing, etc. These females were more likely to be flowing and connecting than organized hierarchically or directed to a purpose or intended agenda. Their dialogue tended to be more about love, relationships, connection, beauty, care, etc. whether about themselves, their families, communities or the world. I have been a participant in this on several occasions, as well as facilitated this experiment several times and the scenario allows the essential masculine and feminine energetic qualities beyond biology, identity, or beliefs to concentrate and amplify in isolation together. So as it relates to presence, this experiment enables us to pay more attention to how the direct masculine and feminine energetics tend to express themselves in as momentary exchange other than the mentally or socially constructed concepts of what it means to be a man or woman.

SEXUAL ESSENCE & ESSENTIAL DRIVES

Some consider sexual energy to be our life force energy and to that end, we can be animated in a more directive, empty and free way, or a receptive, full and loving way. The following chart compares the two essential drives.

MASCULINE – ESSENTIAL DRIVES	FEMININE – ESSENTIAL DRIVES
more often would rather:	*more often would rather:*
-be concerned with FREEDOM: no limitations or constraints	- be concerned with LOVE: giving, receiving & being filled with love
- thrive on COMPETITION, challenged, & overcoming obstacles	- yearn to be SEEN & feel LOVED
- feel EMPTY, free, clear, unbothered, undistracted	- feel FULL of life, love, food, chocolate, conversation, adornments, etc.
- feeling of emptiness of RELEASE just after orgasm	- feeling of FULLNESS & ALIVENESS just after orgasm
- enjoy moments of ZONING OUT in front of the TV or drinking feel DIRECTED & on PURPOSE, completing a mission	- like the FULLNESS of life: parties, connection, eating, surrounded by joy
- watch sports or a movie about war, freedom or challenge	- feel FLOWING, CONNECTION & CLOSENESS
	- watch a romance movie

David Deida powerfully and poetically elucidates these concepts in his book *The Way of the Superior Man*:

"Your sexual essence is your sexual core. If you have a more masculine sexual essence, you would, of course, enjoy staying home and playing with the kids, but, deep down, you are driven by a sense of mission. You may not know your mission, but unless you discover this deep purpose and live it fully, your life will feel empty at its core, even if your intimate relationship and family life are full of love. If you have a more feminine sexual essence, your professional life may be incredibly successful, but your core won't be fulfilled unless love is flowing fully in your family or intimate life. The "mission" or the search for freedom is the priority of the masculine, whereas the search for love is the priority of the feminine. This is why people with masculine essences would rather watch a football game or boxing match on TV than a love story. Sports are all about achieving freedom, such as by breaking free of your opponent's tackle or a barrage of punches, and about succeeding at your mission, by carrying the ball into the end zone or remaining standing after 10 rounds. For the masculine, mission, competition, and putting it all on the line (indeed, facing death), are all forms of ecstasy. Witness the masculine popularity of war stories, dangerous heroism, and sports playoffs. But, for the feminine, the search for love touches the core. Whether on soap operas, in love stories, or talking with friends about relationships, the desire for love is what appears in feminine forms of entertainment. The feminine wants to be filled with love, and if the bliss of real love is not forthcoming, chocolate and ice cream—or a good romantic drama—will do. The masculine wants to feel the bliss of a life lived at the edge, and if he doesn't have the balls to do it himself, he'll watch it on TV, in sporting events and cop shows. Even happy and fulfilled men and women find it enjoyable to watch sports and eat ice cream, of course. I am just trying to make a point: even though all people have both masculine and feminine qualities that they could use in any moment—to kick corporate ass or nurture children, for

instance—most men and women also have a more masculine or feminine core. And this shows up in their regularly chosen entertainments, as much as in their preferred sexual play." [4]

SEXUAL ATTRACTION COMES FROM POLARITY

Attraction occurs with the energetic charge from the polarity of opposites. So not only are these masculine and feminine energies essential life energies to be expressed and experienced in the world, but also sexual polarity is the main energetic force that ignites the passionate flow of sexual attraction that arcs between the masculine and feminine poles in a romantic relationship. In the electricity example, the electrical charge of energy is conducted when the *"masculine"* pronged plug is inserted into the *"feminine"* receptive outlet. Two masculine plugs can hang out together but they don't create sexual polarity and most of the time we would probably find them engaging in the masculine drives. Gender essence alone does not create polarized sexual attraction because that requires reciprocal opposite polar energy. However, being aware of where our essence rests on the spectrum helps us understand just one important dimension of our "attraction" to others. (Shadow Attraction of disowned qualities is another major, yet hidden attraction dynamic to be discussed elsewhere—see *Behavioral Flexibility & Shadow section* for more on this topic).

The open-hearted love and connection in a relationship (whether romantic, friendship or familial) is distinct from the polarizing sexual energy of attraction. The sexual polarity often gets dampened in longer-term relationships, primarily due to lack of Awareness amongst the couple of the energetic polarity dynamic, as well as how to cultivate and turn it on. The open-hearted love may be strong and the couple may play house well together, but if they want a dynamic thriving relationship it is important to be aware of and cultivate the arc of sexual attraction created by masculine and feminine polarities. (Of course, there are numerous other factors including closed hearts, low emotional intimacy, unresolved transgressions or resentments, as well as avoidance of true closeness and connection, etc.). The take-home message is that two polarizing opposite energies, in addition to a loving heart connection and emotional intimacy, are needed to create the passionate energy of sexual attraction in any romantic relationship.

STAGES OF SEXUAL DEVELOPMENT
revised & reprinted with permission from Martin Ucik [5]

1. REPRESSED SEXUALITY
In this lowest stage, the body and sex are viewed with suspicion as something negative and dirty. Usually driven by shame, guilt and fear that originate from childhood trauma and abuse, adults at this level either avoid sexual activities altogether perform out of duty in a dissociated way (with eyes closed, under the sheets, in the dark or develop forms of obsessive-compulsive disorders around their sexuality that can lead to sexual addiction or other abusive behaviors. Oral sex or similarly playful sensual activities are usually out of the question for people at this stage, remind them of abuse or confusing it with shame.

2. FUCKING

In the fucking stage, sexuality is instinctual, self-serving and limited to physical hedonistic pleasures of the body. Sex partners tend to objectify the other without seeking a deeper personal connection. They want to have fun, get off and don't care about their partner's emotional needs feelings or sexual desires. There is no shame or guilt and everything goes, which can be confused with the higher unrestrained forms of transcendent sexuality. In this stage, males often dominate and manipulate females into having intercourse and to engage in hurtful practices. In the fucking stage, everything is seen as OK as long as the partners cooperate or at least do not call the police. Rarely is there a prior conversation about consent sexual preferences sexual history STDs, no-no's, expectations for commitment or possible consequences such as emotional and sexual dependency or pregnancy. Women at this stage often have an unspoken expectation of their male partners to make an exclusive commitment after intercourse and feel used and abused if he moves on. They may also become intentionally pregnant without the man's consent to hook him and/or to collect child support payments. Once the excitement of the newness wears off couples it in the stage often lose interest in sex with each other and stop having sex or seek a new fuck buddy.

3. HAVING SEX

Sex becomes a conscious choice between a couple that has a mutual understanding and agreement about the implications and consequences of being sexual. Having sex is seen as a beautiful and important activity which brings two people together and provides many physical and emotional health benefits. There is usually an agreement for monogamy or openness about multiple lovers, and partners try to find the time and energy to be sexual with each other. Sex partners in this stage go beyond the purely physical aspects (fucking) and see each other as conscious subjects. They focus on pleasing the other within the context of individual boundaries rather than trying to openly express and meet their own sexual needs, desires, and fantasies. This leads to sexuality at the lowest common denominator that often leaves both partners unfulfilled overtime. Over time, relationship difficulties such as power struggles or emotional withdrawal tend to be carried into the bedroom, but don't get resolved there. Instead of working on deeper issues to improve their sexual relationship, couples in this stage sometimes try new positions or locations, engage in role-playing, apply sex toys, watch porn movies, or join swinger clubs to keep their sex life interesting. Unless they evolve to the next higher stage of sexual development, merely having sex will eventually turn stale, die completely, or become so difficult that their partnership ends when one of them falls in lust with a new sex partner.

4. LOVE MAKING

In the lovemaking stage, a couples sexuality becomes the expression of their genuine love, mutual acceptance, deep emotional intimacy, and the joy of being together. Body mind and heart are integrated into lovemaking which is no longer just *"a thing that couples do"*, but an expression of who they are as sexual human beings. No special effort to find the time or energy to be sexual needs to be made by them. Their lovemaking is the life-giving and rejuvenating affirmation of their bond and the depth of their connection. They're open to talking about their desires and exploring all forms of healthy sexual play that bring deeper pleasure into their relating. They naturally stay in verbal and nonverbal communication with more presence and eye contact with each other during their lovemaking. Sex at this level is not used to cover a conflict, to keep score, or to manipulate each other. Instead, sexual and emotional blocks that may arise are worked out between them, and therapeutic help is sought if they can't resolve the problems that they face on their own.

5. TRANSCENDENT SEX
This stage represents all advanced sacred or tantric practices that lead to spiritual state experiences through sexual union, that transcend the lovers' sense of separation from each other and the universe. This kind of sexuality emerges as a stage between partners that either share a deep soul connection or who might also embody higher levels of physical vitality, emotional openness, and relational skill, combined with access to advanced spiritual states (see *Vantage section*) with the ability for potent presence and flowing surrender. Spiritual practices such as meditation, partner yoga, and ecstatic dance are often interwoven in this form of lovemaking. Partners who consciously engage in transcendent sexuality allocate ample quality time for their lovemaking instead of waiting until they're in the mood. They may need nothing special to open as freedom and love itself or they may create sacred space with rituals with special decoration, bedding, lighting, music, tastes, smells, oils, breathing, eye gazing, chanting, dancing, etc. Love making is likely a dynamic alternating between a variety of giving and receiving states of pleasure, positions, and speeds from deep slow and connected to ravishing fucking (that may be falsely interpreted as a form of rape). Due to profound state access and heightened subtle energetics, deeper emotional blocks and limiting patterns embedded in the body can be revealed and released through this depth of sexuality. Often men have cultivated the ability to have deeply open breathing and multiple orgasms without ejaculation and women also have cultivated the ability to have multiple organisms via clitoris, g-spot or deep cervix although this type of sex usually focuses more on open-hearted loving connection, subtle energetics, and radical openness/union than merely a goal to release and ejaculate.

SEXUAL RECIPROCAL
So, Sexual Polarity requires a magnetic spark of attraction between two polar opposites—the greater the polarization, the greater the attraction and passion. According to this theory, we are sexually attracted to our sexual energy reciprocal. If someone is a male with an 80% masculine essence, that person would likely be attracted to a woman with a stronger feminine essence, while most likely not feeling as sexually attracted to a woman whose sexual energy balanced 50%/50% in her essential drives toward life. Thus the ultra-masculine male often tends to be in a sexual romantic relationship with the super feminine female—if there relationship is a romantic one and they have the attraction of sexual polarity between them—while a more masculine female would tend to sexually attract a more extra sensitive feminine male. In either of these examples, the couple can still be sexually polarized but when both the male and female are more sexually neutral 50%/50% then the flow of polarized sexual energy is turned off and they can be safe friends. Remember, even the homosexual community appreciates polarity regardless of gender biology (male with male, female with female) thus gay couples of the same biology still tend to have one partner who animates the more masculine and the other who animates the more feminine pole if they want to have sexual polarity in their relationship. If they are content playing too nice, friendly brother and sister or simply running a household together and they do not care about passionate attraction, then polarity will not be of interest to them.

Note that the flow of sexual energy is a healthy, natural part of life, especially when it is accompanied with Awareness and open-hearted connection. Furthermore, as described above, not only is our sexual essence the flame of sexual passion in our romantic relationship that needs to be consciously embraced, tended and enhanced for thriving in love and life, *but it is our essential drive toward life*. So while there is perhaps much healing needed between males and females for much historical trauma and oppression, and while racial and gender equality as essential human birthrights need to be further integrated across cultures on our planet, let us not confuse *biology* with *energetic sexual essence*, lest we neuter the energetic complimentary differences between masculine and feminine.

males and females are EQUALS	masculine and feminine are COMPLIMENTARY OPPOSITES

APPRECIATING YOUR COMPLIMENTARY SEXUAL OPPOSITE

If we find ourselves judging a quality in the opposite gender, saying *"I just don't understand men"*, or we get uncomfortable when she expresses emotion and wish she would *"be more like a guy"*, then these are clues pointing us towards for our shadow reclamation. Or in other words, opportunities for us to examine more closely that specific quality that bothers us and find where it also lives in us. First, those competitive, directive masculine tendencies or the flowing, shifting moods of the feminine are essential complementary yin and yang energies in the world and our partner—those which magnetize the dynamism of life (north and south poles) and romance (passionate attraction). So the next time we are irritated by or judge a quality in the opposite gender energy, remember that that polarity animates the planet we live on and offers the spark of sexual attraction in our romantic relationship. Further, let us be extra careful not to try to force our partner to suppress their own sexual-spiritual essence or we will not only kill the sexual attraction in our relationship, but more devastatingly confuse and disrupt their essential drive and orientation toward life. Secondly, that irritation or judgment is a call for us to take the perspective, empathize or get the world of our partner or that other person and deeply explore a potentially disowned shadow aspect inside ourselves.

STAGES OF INTEGRATING YOUR SEXUAL OPPOSITE

Now with the above shadow aspect mentioned, understand that our greatest potential beckons that we eventually move to integrate our polar opposite, in other words, a male will always be a male unless he has a sex change operation, but every human has both masculine and feminine energy potentials inside, and even though a male probably has a masculine sexual essence most oriented to mission and freedom, in his highest expression the way he shows up and *"penetrates the world with his work and his woman"* is sourced by both radical freedom AND love.

In our less developed versions, many MEN either have shame around or limit their identity based on what they have come to believe or what their culture says it means *"to be a man."*[6] Mental conceptions about man or woman are the greatest limiters to our greater potential. But as we will learn and understand more in the *Behavioral Flexibility & Shadow section*, any quality that is not able to be felt and known inside of us is a disowned potential. This doesn't mean that a male needs to cry at a commercial or regularly cross-dress to prove his feminine side, but it does suggest that he would not be afraid of animating any more feminine quality on command, and likewise a female does not have to train for MMA to prove her masculinity, although she could if she wanted to, but it does mean that she would be able to acknowledge the light artful and dark violent sides of competition in the world. Furthermore, this also means that he or she can increasingly get the other perspective and for the sake of an experiential challenge he or she could allow their body to temporarily animate the opposite energy as a sign of his or her developed integration. Perhaps at the highest level, even subject and object merge into the unspeakable seamless unity of the moment, transcending and including identity and concept, gender and sexual energy, but this profound openness contains the radical aliveness everything and infinite empty nothingness. These advanced frontiers are not for everyone so if you feel or didn't mentally understand this last sentence, worry not. Until this is experientially known, let us continue to develop and strengthen our healthy sexual essence, while eventually integrating its opposite to even a small degree.

Martin Ucik, the author of Integral Relationships[7] , outlined Masculine in relation to Feminine and vice versa; in other words, the degree to which a person has integrated the opposite gender inside of herself or himself without seeking or avoiding the apparent other. This incorporates the anima/animus complex advanced by Carl Jung. (Note that for simplicity this stage conception limits its domain to interpreting gender integration development to heterosexual relationships although it does not assume anything beyond that.)
revised & reprinted with permission from Martin Ucik (for more information see Integral Relationships p58-66.)

MASCULINE ANIMA (developmental progression of a Male relating to & embodying his gender opposite)
1. Women as Mother — image of mother
- mama's boy; needs mommy to care for him; provider of nourishment, security, love
- prey for exploitation & control by her; limited sexual desire or impotence
TRANSITION: healing mother wounds, "growing up", embracing masculinity

2. Women as Sex Object — he desires her to make him feel good
- sees all women as sex objects; uses women as objects for personal pleasure & does not respect them
- female anima represents the collective sexual image rather than a unique human being: Porn Star, Playboy Playmate, etc.
- repeated sex adventures or sex addiction
TRANSITION: learning respect for women

3. Women as Wife — he wants her loyalty & support as wife
- man is ready to care for wife & devoted to family
- wants her to be a supportive, understanding, caring, faithful wife, available sex partner, & mother
- sexuality usually integrated into a relationship rather than autonomous driving force
- can differentiate between love (partnership) & lust (sex object) which allows the possible creation of a lasting partnership
TRANSITION: beginning inner exploration

4. Women as Inspiration — she inspires him to explore his inner world, creativity, purpose & best self
- he seeks other sources of aliveness, passion, joy, purpose, peace, love

- the quest for purpose & spirituality: "Who am I?" "Why am I here" "What should I do?" "What is the meaning of life?"
- the liberating process of awakening to authenticity, purpose, passion, love capacity (independent of a woman)
- polyamory, commitment phobic
TRANSITION: Awareness of purpose and autonomous identity

5. **Women as Equal Partner** — he meets her as an opposite & equal partner
- he has found his own purposeful identity that does not rely on her love, inspiration, approval
- he shows empathy, care, support when she is unhappy but doesn't feel responsibility, insecurity, or shame
- feels confident, secure, comfortable to express his masculine sexual essence while he embraces his feminine aspect; allows him to invite differing views from a partner without denigrating her or feeling threatened
- accepts that conflicts & ambivalence are inherent to human relationships though resolution contributes to ongoing healing, personal growth, & spiritual realization
- he neither clings nor pushes away but opens to fully embrace her at all levels of his being when together while staying content & fulfilled when apart

---

 FEMININE ANIMUS (developmental progression of a Female relating to & embodying her gender opposite)
1. Men as Alien Outsider — she fears-hates-loves him (denies & suppresses animus as alien inside & outside herself)
- she trusts females & distrusts, hates, fears men countered by strange curiosity she cannot differentiate
- seduce & withhold syndrome: she seduces then when he gets close she withdraws, then she approaches to ask for more when he becomes distant
- the domain is household, family, female-oriented work (can seem confident in that domain) but leaves anything outside of that to men & mature women
TRANSITION: heal previous male transgressions; often there was a childhood abuse or abandonment by a man

2. Men as Father/God/King — she wants his approval: her self-esteem directly linked to response from men
- needs to be seen as most attractive female; monitors her value by internalized judgment & thru externalized male reflection
- personality split: a. imitates male behavior to be liked by them (success, tomboy, wit, teasing, competing for challenging) b. presents as sexually seductive femme fatale to be desired (beautiful appearance, graceful charm)
- gravitates toward men she perceives as more attractive, intelligent, successful than she could be
- the effort to live up to men: dietary restriction, intense exercise, adaptive intellectual interests, new talents, or sexual availability as the perfect mate
- depression when beauty & sexual attractiveness wane; isolation from intimacy; psychosomatic illness
TRANSITION: needs support to find worth, passions, & identity independent of male approval

3. Men as Hero — she wants him to take care of her
- views man as a protector & provider w/ strength, courage & ability: he can meet her needs, cherish her, marry her
- he is her ideal often unrealistic image of a knight in shining armor who fulfills expectations for good looks,
    intelligence, reputation, financial stability, generosity, loyalty, kindness, care, integrity, faithfulness, etc.
- she bargains with appearance, health, fitness, & male notions of success (career, education, social justice)
- she may function well in a competitive male world, share responsibilities, contribute as an equal
- she wants to marry up to fulfill expectations for social status; her devotion & self-sacrificing to support his success
    can lead to feelings of resentment for denying her own potential
TRANSITION: may enter an inward journey once become aware of her transitory physical attractiveness, ability to
    succeed with men, and limitations of finding acceptance in the male world

4. Men as Independent Beings — she wants her independence & feminine authority
- makes an active choice for her self-interest & self-fulfillment independent of partner/husband
- can break from conventional roles of caring mother, can show tough love, or feel fulfilled outside partnership with a man
- realization she has constructed her own experiences in relation to men & now wants her own identity
- stops trying to be perfect in all things to please a partner (who was her heroic father figure)
- she becomes emotionally free from his approval & support having discovered her own worthiness & foundation:
    may feel free from evaluation & needs of men for first time in her life
- challenges men to care less about male needs, seeks financial independence, refuses responsibility for relationship
    sustenance
- financial independence (career success, divorcing well, alimony, generous lovers, parental support, Social Security
    benefits
- highly independent, impossible to please, commitment phobic
- complains about a lack of good men: can become men-hating diehard singles, "friends with benefits", or serial monogamists
- can look down upon women at stages 2 or 3 as still dependent on a man & don't understand stage 5 women
- can still feel a deeper fear of abandonment or diminishment of skill as well as secret longing for stability & support
    of partnership during times of stress, fatigue, loneliness, or desire for sex that leads to ambivalence
TRANSITION: realize attempt to go it alone is limited; we are always in relation; we have human needs (economic,
    physical, sexual, emotional)
NOTE to MALES: nothing you can do: care for self emotionally, protect assets, support her with love & compassion
    in her transition

5. Men as Equal Partners — she wants him as an opposite & equal partner
- having fully claimed her own authority after transcending animus complex, no longer sees men as foreign, superior,
    inferior, or independent

- realization balanced personality develops in a self-other conception, never thru discovery of independent self
- desires synergy (spiritual, material, sexual, emotional, mental, physical, etc.) created when met by opposite & equal
    man
- accepts that conflicts & ambivalence are inherent to human relationships though resolution contributes to ongoing healing, personal growth, and spiritual realization

---

HEALING PROTECTIVE SHELLS

David Deida in his years of working with thousands of males and females in the experiential trenches of coaching and workshops discovered that some people developed protective shells on top of their sexual essence.[8] For some, they adopted protective ways of being to secure parental love, as a result of trauma, familial patterns, cultural patterns, etc.

Statistically, women under 30 years old in the United States are earning more money in the same jobs, have a higher rate of acceptance in law school and medical school. Yes, females have masculine and feminine energies and the masculine energy is oriented to a sense of purpose and offering it to the world. Increasing numbers of females are integrating their masculine energy into their lives which is part of the healthy developmental process. Some females who are expressing more masculine aspects of themselves might be doing so because they have a masculine essence, or because they are in a developmental phase of integrating more masculine aspects, or because they have a protective layer or shell over their essence.

SAFETY, SEXUAL HEALING & OPENNESS

Sexuality is the source of fertility, creativity, and passion as well as much trauma, frustration and confusion on our planet. Before we can deeply open sexually it is essential that we feel safe. Much repair work needs to be done in our world, our communities and families to heal, in order to reopen and mature sexual energy in our bodies, relationships and lives. Again, our sexual energy is our life force, and some also associate with our playfulness, spontaneity, healthy desire, pleasure, passion, and creativity amongst other things. Yet, if we have experienced trauma or chosen to close down our sexual energy, not only are we cutting off our sexuality, but also aspects of our enjoyment and passion for life. So, we can imagine how unsafe someone must have felt at one point if they chose to shut down their sexual life force in order to protect themselves. For some who have experienced on-going sexual abuse, single incident sexual assault, had to navigate inappropriate attention, or even learned sexual closure from their parents, specific trauma desensitization and somatic-oriented sexual healing sessions might be needed before their system feels safe enough to reopen sexually.

ULTIMATELY

Recall the previous spectrum depiction and the theory that each unique being has a natural sexual essence that lies somewhere on the spectrum. Underneath compensated layers of protection, trauma, or developmental integration phases, how does the unique sexual-spiritual essence want to live through us and orient to life? Deida reminds us of the importance of living true to our sexual essence:

"when you deny your true core you deny the possibility of true and real love. Love is openness, through and through. And true spirituality is the practice of love, the practice of openness. A person who denies their own essence and hides their true desires is divided and unable to relax into the full openness of love. Their spirit becomes cramped and kinked. Unable to feel the natural ease and unconstrained power of their own core, they feel threatened and however frightened. This fear is the texture of their inability to open fully in love. Such a person is spiritually handicapped, obstructed at heart, even though they may have achieved a safe relationship and a successful career." [9]

We can safely say "the masculine energy" (whether being expressed in a male or female) tends to express these qualities listed next.

Classically Masculine Energetic Qualities: initiatory, seeking freedom, sense of purpose (desire to complete missions), competitive (grow through challenge), evolving (living on the edge), decisive & directive.

For some that ultimate concern is more towards love and fullness, for others more towards purpose and freedom, and for a smaller percentage, their essence is naturally more androgynously balanced. Wherever our essential orientation to life lies on the spectrum, ultimately life beckons us to integrate the opposite. To be unified with everything includes the spacious emptiness and stillness of Freedom AND the radical fullness and movement of Love itself. How does life want to passionately express itself to Itself, through this living uniqueness upon the great vast canvas of Life?

GENDER ESSENCE & SEXUAL POLARITY SUMMARY & KEY TAKEAWAYS
➤ Masculine & Feminine animate our fundamental drives in life (Gender Essence) & when polarized these energies also create the magnetic charge of sexual attraction & passion among humans.
➤ Definitions & Distinctions of Gender Terminology
   BIOLOGY (male & female): based on anatomy, genetics, & hormone levels
   IDENTITY (man & woman): ways of being based on beliefs, meaning-making & socially constructed concepts
   ENERGIES (masculine & feminine): magnetic attraction created by two polarizing energies (Males & females are equals, masculine & feminine energies are complimentary opposites, but man or woman are mentally made up & socially constructed. We are greatly limiting ourselves & stuck in mental concepts when we say "this is what it 'means' to be a man",
➤ Classically Feminine Energetic Qualities: receptive, seeking love, sense of connection (desire for

intimacy), radiance & beauty (grow through praise & support), caring (nurturing life), flowing & responsive

- The open-hearted love & connection in a relationship (whether romantic, friendship or familial) is distinct from the polarizing sexual energy of attraction between masculine & feminine energies.
- Stages of Sexual Development by Martin Ucik 1) Repressed Sexuality 2) Fucking 3) Having Sex 4) Love Making 5) Transcendent Sex
- Sexual Energy Reciprocal: sexual Polarity requires a magnetic spark of attraction between two polar opposites—the greater the polarization, the greater the attraction & passion. Thus the ultra-masculine male often tends to be more attracted in sexual romantic relationship with the super feminine female, while a more masculine female would tend to sexually attract a more extra sensitive feminine male, whereas more balanced 50%/50% males or females tend to experience less magnetic polarity & thus less romance & passionate attraction.
- Stages of Integrating Your Sexual Opposite
- MALES: 1) Women as Mother 2) Women as Sex Object 3) Women as Wife 4) Women as Inspiration 5) Women as Equal Partner
- FEMALES: 1) Men as Alien Outsider 2)Men as Father/God/King 3) Men as Hero 4) Independent Beings 5) Men as Equal Partners
- Sexuality is the source of fertility, creativity, & passion as well as much trauma, frustration & confusion on our planet. Before we can deeply open sexually it is essential that we feel safe. Much repair work needs to be done in our world, our communities & families to heal, in order to reopen & mature sexual energy in our bodies, relationships & lives.

CONFLICT

Is your tendency in conflict to avoid & withdrawal, please others & compromise yourself,
or aggressively overpower?

Are you able to openly receive constructive feedback without shutting down or getting defensive? Are you able to give
constructive feedback in a skillful way?

Are you better able to navigate conflict & tension in real time, be emotionally vulnerable & relax defenses, take
responsibility & apologize when necessary & recover more quickly in restoring open connection?

*"Peace requires something far more difficult than revenge or merely turning the other cheek; it requires empathizing with the
fears and unmet needs that provide the impetus for people to attack each other. Being aware of these feelings and needs, people
lose their desire to attack back because they can see the human ignorance leading to these attacks; instead, their goal becomes
providing the empathic connection and education that will enable them to transcend their violence and engage in cooperative
relationships."*

- Marshall Rosenberg -

WHAT IS PRESENCE IN **CONFLICT**

the capacity to maintain awareness of ourselves and other(s) in the midst of conflict by
1) owning our own embodied experience (thoughts, emotions, sensations) with emotionally vulnerable communication
while still being able to simultaneously
2) acknowledge and sense the inner experience of the other(s)

WHY PRESENCE IN **CONFLICT** MATTERS

Growth & Development: disruption of status quo, awareness of harmful pattern, something that is not working or needs to evolve

Diversity: fostering awareness of the variety & range of life, human experience & ways of being

Creative Solutions: stirring-up passion & enlivening energy for new insights & actions

More authentic & intimate Communication & Relationships: expressing & liberating; withholds, resentments, confusion

Perspective-taking & Mutual Understanding: can allow us to see things from different views whether they be partial or we agree

Acceptance: meeting life as it shows up rather than our expectations

Responsive Flexibility: learning to listen, see different perspectives, examine our assumptions,

Skillful Relational Navigation: responding more skillfully relating with moods, reactivity, close-mindedness vs. unconscious reacting

Sustained Engagement: being able to embody, connect & engage in conflict rather than having to leave, escape, withdrawal

Feedback: being able to receive feedback openly rather than shutting down emotionally or reacting

Healthy Boundaries: being able to say no without fear or doubt; being able to agree to disagree while still staying in relation

BARRIERS TO PRESENCE IN **CONFLICT**

Dissociation: not feeling & inhabiting your body due to trauma, defense or hyper-mental

Collapse: contraction not owning your personal space & power

Anger: disowning of anger due to your past unconsciously expression or how it was aggressively expressed at you

Trauma / Abuse: past emotional, physical, mental or sexual abuse

Saying "NO": unable to say "NO", believing it is rude or jeopardizes the relationship or threatens loss of love

Pleasing: compromising your authentic expression in order to be liked, belong or validated, being too nice or too acquiescing; fear of disapproval, fear of conflict, or fear of loss of love

Childhood Familial / Environmental Conditioning: accommodating, aggressive, abusive or manipulative modeling

Spiritual Bypassing: using spiritual practices & beliefs to avoid your emotions, body, life & participation in the world

Emotional Numbness: numbing your emotional sensing due to past trauma or emotional overwhelm to avoid feeling pain

Emotionally Unsafe: not feeling safe as a child or in some past relations to feel & express your emotion

Fear of Connection, Intimacy or Emotional intensity: fear of emotional closeness & connection

Superficiality: avoiding depth, afraid of intimacy or feeling deeper emotions

Unworthy of having a Voice: shy, muted or struggle to communicate what you want to say

"Relational conflict including violence and war is one of our evolutionary assignment, along with addressing other big-ticket items such as economic justice, basic human rights & environmental sustainability. We have much to learn about how to curb the frequent outbreaks of violence and war that have been so devastating in our collective history. We need to learn how to reliably transform our conflicts into opportunity and creativity and to develop solid methods for helping people around the world get along. Personal conflict resolution practice is one of the best ways to contribute to this collective goal... "But rather than relying on a thin, idealized hope that we will all one day just get along, we can approach conflict resolution as an art form that we are privileged to develop and hone. We can except the challenge, becoming adept in transforming our personal struggles, and contribute to the unfolding of new ways of being for humanity"
- Diane Hamilton -

Many people probably associate presence more with peace than they do conflict. However, true Presence contains everything including the full spectrum of peace and harmony to diversity and conflict. This section is titled *Presence in Conflict* because it describes our capacity for presence in the midst of conflict which involves our ability to stay embodied, in connected relation with others, and open with expanded Awareness.

In early infancy, we are completely dependent on our caregivers for survival and as we get a little older our will starts to develop, commonly expressing itself as resistance and our favorite phrase being *"NO"*. Sometimes our infant impulses and resistance may not necessarily be aligned with our parents' agendas, but a parents' ability to navigate this *"NO"* phase while staying embodied (grounded, heart open, breathing, emotionally aware), related and aware is both an example of presence in conflict as well as important for the healthy development of our young, developing will function. As we continue to grow and are exposed to a wider span of social engagement, we experience a variety of ways of relating to conflict. Some of us probably tend towards avoiding conflict (**ignorance**), others towards pleasing compromise or charming manipulation (**passion**) and others towards power and dominance (**aggression**). Diane Hamilton is a master of this theme and much of this section is inspired by participation in her Integral Facilitator training and her book *Everything is Workable: a Zen Approach to Conflict Resolution.*[1]   Hamilton describes these three conflict styles previously mentioned: ignorance, passion and aggression as 3 basic ways we protect ourselves when faced with challenges from others and life.

AVOIDANCE - move away, avoid, deny, withdrawal, disappear, escape, pretend nothing happened, or become stubborn with too much pressure

ACCOMMODATION - move towards, overly-accommodating, grasping, fearfully holding on, neediness, charming manipulation, or inauthentically compromising ourselves to get what we want

AGGRESSIVE - move against, power-oriented confrontational, aggressive, excessively competitive, willful assertiveness pushing over or away, making boundaries (setting limits, saying *"NO"*) or boundary invading

EMOTIONAL PRESENCE IN CONFLICT

Differing opinions and perspectives are but one aspect of conflict; usually, it is the most challenging for us to stay embodied, related and aware, in the midst of the emotional intensity of conflict. Sometimes the emotional intensity overwhelms us and we can use variations on any of the three strategies previously mentioned; especially *avoidance* (emotional shut-down or withdrawal) or *aggression*.

NOTICING & NAMING STATE CHANGES & REACTIVITY

We may have had the experience of being engaged in a normal conversation one minute and then all of the sudden the mood shifted—either to *avoidance of connection, accommodation or aggression*. With greater Awareness comes the ability to notice that something has shifted either in the quality of the connection or the emotional intensity and then secondarily in the ability to name what we are sensing. When we are emotionally triggered from a body and brain perspective, it is very challenging to be open, connected and to really listen to others' perspective. Remember the polyvagal system discussed in the *Body Sensing, Heart* and *Vulnerability sections* is the body correlated to our feelings of embodied safety and connection.[2] When our faces go flat or blank it is because we lose muscle tone and a protector of vulnerability is now mobilized into defense. Not only has our tone of voice changed but so too the nervous system connected to our ears and our hearing function has also shifted so our ability to listen is turned down and in the midst of emotional reactivity our blood flow and brain activity that could be in the more rational front regions of our brain can get hijacked into the limbic-emotional brain, which inhibits our reasonable thinking. In simple terms, it is not a good time to use a lot of words or try to have a logical conversation. Instead, the focus should be on de-escalating emotional intensity in the body and using the emotional vulnerability of naming each other's present state to restore safety and connection. While perspective taking is the imperative bridge to mediation and conflict resolution it usually can't physiologically happen in the midst of excessive emotional reactivity because of the physiological inhibitions just mentioned. So first we have to come back into greater presence by safely calming our nervous systems and restoring connection.

SAFETY & RELAXATION

Conflict can threaten our physical safety, emotional well-being, social belonging, relational bond, or sense of identity, beliefs, and self-esteem.[3] This shows up in our bodies—particularly the front of the face, chest, and belly—the part of our nervous system that scans for cues of safety and connection, can very quickly turn down our functioning and immobilize us or turn up our defenses in coordination with limbic reactive structures. Fast-talking or mental talking usually doesn't always calm people down, but relaxed embodied listening or speaking in slow resonant voice with attuned intonation can feel soothing to our core nervous system in a primal way. Steven Porges describes field experiments he has observed in watching toddlers screaming with their irritated, unattuned father whose body gets tenser and whose voice gets louder and monotone which is a trigger of defense; whereas then the youngsters quickly calms with the loving attuned presence of the mother, as she receives her child relaxed, breathing, making eye contact, using few soothing words in a soft tone of voice.[4] The important takeaway here is when a conflict occurs, to practice maintaining greater awareness while relaxing our body and breath, so we can make moves to reconnect with each other in emotional vulnerability versus fighting like arguing lawyers. Would we rather drain our relational passion in too frequent verbal arguments or channel our healthy aggression into passionate heart-connected aggressive ravishment in the bedroom? There is certainly a beauty to a perspective enhancing debate or the enlivening and boundary protecting of healthy anger but often these happen as unconscious disconnected reactivity. There is a time and a place for all things within the light of Awareness, but our brains and bodies are not as receptive to listening and integrating discussion in the higher brain function hijacking of the emotional reactivity and defensiveness of conflict.

EMOTIONAL VULNERABILITY IS THE DOORWAY TO RECONNECTION

The first doorway back into presence and connection is naming the quality of emotional presence. This may initially involve owning our withdrawal and secondarily the underlying emotions our withdrawal or emotional numbness strategy is helping to protect such as fear, hurt or the shame we want to hide. In this case, usually more distress or discomfort arises than we may want to feel so we numb or disconnect by pulling away to escape the intensity. This starts by naming the noticing of the change of state into withdrawal or reactivity:

"It seems to me like something shifted...what do you notice?"
"I feel triggered"
"What are you feeling in the core of your body right now?"
"I notice I just shut-down"

Dishonesty, rigid posturing and pretending to be fine when we are really triggered is also a form of withdrawing from intimacy because this is in a way hiding the deeper truth. When we feel triggered or shut-down, real transparency is needed in authentically name what is really going on underneath the hoods of persona or protection. Not only is this a move toward greater closeness, but also builds trust and is an opportunity for deeper presence. The state change of conflict is an invitation for greater undefended curiosity and to vulnerably reveal more of our authentic self.

Or it might mean naming the anger before it turns into verbal or physical aggression, feeling and breathing into that until it can be metabolized and released, revealing the next, more vulnerable level. Anger in its virtue can help us to healthfully respect our boundaries or it can be an aggression-turned defense protecting a bruised ego or more vulnerable parts. The aggressive defense tends to shield the tender heart and mobilize its mental-verbal arsenal of attacks.

Diane Hamilton says *"in the context of a conflict resolution practice, the moments in which our ego is offended are golden. They provide the perfect opportunity to see our self-protective mechanisms at work and learn to unwind them. We can take responsibility for ourselves instead of the usual blaming and finger-pointing."*[5] Ideally, if one partner can maintain a greater presence and stay resourced it can really help to de-escalate emotional intensity and restore connection faster. When both people get reactive it can require even more skill to return to embodied presence, connection and awareness.

Past emotional trauma and reactive patterns are stored in our body[6] and can get triggered during conflict. This might show up as looking like the other person's words, behavior or energy is that of a younger child or teenager. If one person notices that the other seems to have regressed into a younger pattern, whether as a shut-down/freeze/numb state or a younger aggressive reactivity, the most skillful way for the more resourced partner to navigate the conflict without re-traumatizing the pattern is to name the change of state, as mentioned earlier, and meet the pattern with an open spacious presence. It is so easy to get entangled in the reactive pattern but the evolutionary move is if one person can stay relatively more resourced in presence and allow the pattern to be seen, felt, released and re-patterned. It is very important not to become each others' healing therapist or savior and while often regressive moments with healing opportunity do happen in bonding relationships and it is useful for both partners to learn how to maintain presence during conflict, there are times when a couple or friends in conflict would be better served by working with a third-party who can maintain a neutral perspective. Otherwise, even with the best of intentions to resolve it, many couples can stay in the same looping conflict pattern for a long time. In this case, it can be really important and useful to bring in an outside, neutral perspective in the form of a trained emotional presence or somatic-oriented therapist or coach. Over-processing drains or burns-out too much of the relationship energy and romantic passion, not to mention the negative impact on both individuals lives when the relational bond on the home-front is destabilized. Additionally, the recurring situation can become a habit in relating, further reinforcing the same pattern over and over. Emotionally Focused Couples Therapy (EFT-C), is the most scientifically validated effective couples therapy and the only one to actually increase secure bonding (see Attachment portion of the *Connection section*).[7] EFT-C was initially developed in the 1980's by psychotherapist Sue Johnson who found that couples in conflict were caught in a negative dance of interactions--she calls *demon dialogues* that kept them stuck and unable to resolve their conflicts. Using attachment theory and prioritizing the restoring of connection, she developed a treatment to help these couples in distress to restore connection, increase body awareness to decrease the emotional intensity and learn more attuned communication skills. Today, EFT-C is the most empirically validated type of couples therapy.[8] Research over more than 20 years has shown that 90% of couples show significant improvements and 70–75% of couples move from distress to recovery, as compared to the unimpressive results of most conventional couples therapies which focus more on analyzing the past or mental negotiation.[9]

What we do, say and be in moments of disconnection is crucial to our sense of connection, safety, belonging, acceptance and secure bonding. Johnson and colleagues research shows that with a secure base, less emotional triggers, arguments are calmer and end quicker. If both parties go unconscious, become fully identified with the conflict and get sucked into the reactive level of content, then it can take longer to return to presence. Awareness contains everything including the content of conflict, and while it is easier to sense the spacious quality of Awareness when the moment seems more quiet and peaceful, the advanced practice is our ability to feel embodied emotional vulnerability from a greater Vantage of Presence, in the midst of a conflict. With heightened clarity of perception and emotional vulnerability would ideally be the moment when something shifted in us or the other person and the possibility of undefended connection was restored before escalation or entanglement happened—the moment just as one person closed and withdrew from closeness and connection or began to become reactive.

Otherwise, if the distance of disconnection or emotional intensity has already escalated, then hopefully one person can maintain a greater presence. If one person can stay resourced in their body and with a wider perspective or witnessing Awareness, then it can positively affect the triggered person's process and more safely and quickly invite them back into presence and connection. After de-escalating our emotional intensity and restoring connection, perspective taking is the imperative bridge to mediation and conflict resolution. For some, this involves learning to take other perspectives in addition to their own, while for other people it involves learning to be aware of and express their own perspective including their own opinions, preferences, desires, and needs.

CLEANING-UP THE PAST & RESTORING CLOSENESS

Have we ever been the transgressor or recipient of a conflict that seemed to come out of nowhere and upon deeper investigation, ended up being the result of a past, completely unrelated transgression? Or have we ever pulled away or had the other person retract due to a past unresolved conflict? Uncleared (felt, expressed, released, apologized, and forgiven) conflicts lead to scarring or disconnection. Even small unresolved infractions can cumulatively add up and create chronic distance in intimacy and connection.

DISCERNMENT

Life contains a whole spectrum of ways of being and the ultimate presence includes everything from peace to conflict. So presence is not always about staying perfectly peaceful at all times in a conflict; sometimes skillfulness requires silence and listening; other times expressing our perspective or the increased intensity of anger in respecting our own boundaries or the humility of vulnerably owning our impact combined with a sincere apology. Discerning Awareness enables us to know when to engage and when went to take a break and when to walk away.

Not everyone wants to resolve a conflict, especially the aggressive types and sometimes we are too triggered and unwilling to downshift. Even accommodators can have their subtle ways of manipulation to sneakily achieve their agenda and if they are unwilling to relate on even ground, should not be engaged. There are times when protective anger, saying a strong *"NO"*, taking a time-out or walking away is the most skillful action that can be taken in a conflict. And at other times, it is enlivening and refreshing to have a good wrestle, but good competitors always make eye contact and shake hands after a good challenge. Diane Hamilton reminds us *"the idea is not to eliminate conflicts...the aim is to transform it...if we had no disagreements with the world we would have a little reason to grow and less opportunity to become more compassionate, wakeful human beings."*[10]

Learning to pause, slow down, notice reactivity or withdrawal, sense our breath and body, and vulnerably name deeper emotions, in order to reconnect and calm emotional reactivity so that we can openly listen to others, empathize, and consider their perspectives, be more aware of our underlying assumptions, beliefs, and intentions, all while being humbly willing to open, connect and evolve are perhaps the real skills of presence in conflict. In this vein our markers or improved presence in connection can be:

less often (stronger bond, better communication)
less intense (better ability to turn down emotional intensity)
less violence (low blows, name calling, hurting)
faster recovery (reconnection & repair)
more presence (including body, emotion, connection, perspectives, Awareness)
more openness (clearing the past, apologizing, forgiveness, communication)

"Relational conflict including violence and war is one of our evolutionary assignment, along with addressing other big-ticket items such as economic justice, basic human rights & environmental sustainability. We have much to learn about how to curb the frequent outbreaks of violence and war that of been so devastating in our collective history. We need to learn how to reliably transform are conflicts into opportunity and creativity and to develop solid methods for helping people around the world get along. Personal conflict resolution practice is one of the best ways to contribute to this collective goal... "But rather than relying on a thin, idealized hope that we will all one day just get along, we can approach conflict resolution as an art form that we are privileged to develop and hone. We can except the challenge, becoming adept in transforming our personal struggles, and contribute to the unfolding of new ways of being for humanity" [11] - *Diane Hamilton*

CONFLICT SUMMARY & KEY TAKEAWAYS

➤ Presence more often associated with peace than conflict, however, true Presence contains everything including the full spectrum of peace & harmony to diversity & conflict.

➤ While conflict is a challenging aspect of being human & one of the most difficult situations to maintain presence, it is also essential for growth, including diversity, creative solutions, divergent perspectives, feedback & healthy 'boundaries.

➤ Diane Hamilton identifies 3 main ways of relating to conflict: 1) avoiding conflict (ignorance), 2) pleasing compromise or charming manipulation (passion) 3) power & dominance (aggression).

➤ Conflict can threaten our physical safety, emotional well-being, social belonging, relational bond, or sense of identity, beliefs, & self-esteem.

➤ While perspective taking & empathy are ultimately the imperative bridges to mediation & conflict resolution, they usually can't physiologically happen in the midst of excessive emotional reactivity. When our chest is tight & heart is guarded, the nerves connected from heart to ears decrease our hearing function & our ability to listen is turned down plus in the midst of emotional reactivity our blood flow & brain activity gets hijacked away from the more rational front regions of our brain & into the limbic-emotional brain, which inhibits our reasonable thinking. In simple terms, it is not a good time to use a lot of words or try to have a logical conversation when one or more persons are emotionally triggered. Instead, the focus should be on de-escalating emotional intensity in the body & using the emotional vulnerability of naming each other's present state to restore safety & connection. The fastest doorway back into presence & connection is vulnerably naming the quality of emotion in our bodies.

➤ "In the context of a conflict resolution practice, the moments in which our ego is offended are golden. They provide the perfect opportunity to see our self-protective mechanisms at work and learn to unwind them. We can take responsibility for ourselves instead of the usual blaming and finger-pointing." — Diane Hamilton

➢ Past emotional trauma & reactive patterns are stored in our body & can get triggered during conflict. This might show up as looking like the other person's words, behavior or energy is that of a younger child or teenager which could range from reactivity & aggression or a shut-down/freeze/numb state. The most skillful way for the more resourced person to navigate the conflict without re-traumatizing the pattern is to name the change of state, & meet the pattern with an open spacious presence.

➢ It is so easy to get entangled in the reactive pattern of another person, but ideally the evolutionary move is if one person can stay relatively more resourced in presence & allow the other person's pattern to be seen, felt, released & re-patterned.

➢ It is very important not to become each others' healing therapist or savior & while often regressive moments with healing opportunity do happen in bonding relationships & while it is useful for both partners to learn how to maintain presence during conflict, there are times when a couple or friends in conflict would be better served by working with a third-party who can maintain a neutral perspective. Otherwise, even with the best of intentions to resolve it, many couples can stay in the same looping conflict pattern for a long time or waste their relationship life force on fighting and/or healing.

➢ Emotionally Focused Couples Therapy (EFT-C), is the most scientifically validated effective couples therapy (based on whole-body emotional presence & connection rather than purely mental approaches) & the only researched approach to actually increase secure bonding.

➢ Learning to pause, slow down, notice reactivity or withdrawal, sense our breath & body, & vulnerably name deeper emotions, in order to reconnect & calm emotional reactivity so that we can openly listen to others, empathize & consider their perspectives, be more aware of our underlying assumptions, beliefs & intentions, all while being humbly willing to open, connect & evolve are perhaps the real skills of presence in conflict.

➢ Because conflict is an important part of our growth & diversity, instead of focusing on being scared of or never having any conflict, instead better presence in conflict skill markers are: less often (stronger bond, better communication) less intense (better ability to turn down emotional intensity), less violence (low blows, name calling, hurting), faster recovery (reconnection & repair), more presence (including body, emotion, connection, perspectives, Awareness)

ATTENTION

Would your friends & loved-ones say you tend to
zone out, be distracted, have wandering eyes or pay more attention to your phone while they are speaking?

Do you often feel scattered, overwhelmed, over-committed, find yourself multitasking
or lacking focus on priorities?

Can you focus attention on your breath to quiet mental activity or intimately focus attention on another while listening
with deep presence & connection?

———————•———————

"Control of conscious attention determines the quality of life." ... "If one has failed to develop curiosity & interest in the early years, it is a good idea to acquire them now, before it is too late to improve the quality of life. To do so is fairly easy in principle, but more difficult in practice. Yet it is sure worth trying. The first step is to develop the habit of doing whatever needs to be done with concentrated attention, with skill rather than inertia. Even the most routine tasks, like washing dishes, dressing, or mowing the lawn become more rewarding if we approach them with the care it would take to make a work of art. The next step is to transfer some psychic energy each day from tasks that we don't like doing, or from passive leisure, into something we never did before, or something we enjoy doing but don't do often enough because it seems too much trouble. There are literally millions of potentially interesting things in the world to see, to do, to learn about. But they don't become actually interesting until we devote attention to them."

--- Mihaly Csikszentmihalyi ---

———————•———————

WHAT IS **ATTENTION**

the capacity to intentionally sustain focus in the present moment in a state of "effortless absorption" on an object or in the engagement of activity while selectively ignoring irrelevant information

WHY **ATTENTION** MATTERS

Concentration: selective narrowing of focus on object or activity
Selective Disregard: selectively ignoring irrelevant information
Quieting Mental Chatter: focusing attention is essential for quieting mental chatter
Work Productivity: focusing, avoiding distraction, procrastination, task completion, goal achievement
Connection & Intimacy: both require focusing of intimate attention for connection
Flow States: effortless present moment full engagement in an activity for creativity, learning, optimal performance, or intrinsic enjoyment

ATTENTION BARRIERS

Dissociation: not feeling & inhabiting your body due to trauma, defense or hyper-mental
Distracted: internally by your own mental-emotional noise or externally by digital stimulation or the environment
Emotional Overwhelm: redirecting attention to own internal experience or easier to dissociate than stay in connection
Hyper-Mental: excessive mental activity, overly theoretical, living in fantasy, lost in the past or future
Emotional Overwhelm: inability to feel & release emotions, resulting in strategies like numbing & dissociation to reduce overwhelm
Confusion: unclear, clouded, frozen, unclear
Multitasking: task-switching while splitting attention between 2 or more things
Brain Dysfunction: brain chemistry imbalance or brain-activity dysregulation
Boredom: lack of interest or under-challenged
Anxiety: ungrounded, over-stimulated, over-challenged, trauma, anxious-attachment, stress, etc.
Nutritional Deficiencies: nutrients, fatty acids
Food Disruptors: food intolerance, excess sugar & food additives
Heavy Metal Toxicity: air pollution, dental amalgam mercury fillings, eating excess mercury-toxic fish, mother-child transfer in the womb, mercury-containing vaccines
Inflammation: brain, gut or systemic body inflammation

ATTENTION DEVELOPMENT SUCCESS STORY

Dane was a smooth-talking, surfer, guys guy who worked in sales & was skeptical of anything development related. His wife, however, was a successful persona in the personal development field so he got a wake-up call when his relationship came to a breaking point—partially due to his lack of attention on his own interior development & also because he was externally scattering attention toward other women. Plus, he was tired of ignoring the voice inside him yearning to do something more with his life. From all his younger years in rugby, surfing & beer-related shenanigans, he had the physicality & power of presence, but he needed to train his attention so he could stay in presence with communication, emotion, intimacy & relational conflict instead of checking out, avoiding or becoming defensively aggressive. We approached meditation as attention training like he would learn a new skill in a sport. We explained how the first stage of meditation involved the training of his attention & how important that was for his own happiness, thriving relationship & even his success at work in his ability to focus & sell. Training his attention help to quiet down, which helped him too. As he trained his attention, the mental chatter quieted, he learned to relax & open his heart while relaxing more deeply into himself & feeling more comfortable in his own skin. People felt safer around him. As he relaxes his previously protective defenses & intimidation relaxed, his presence became magnetic instead of repulsive, which revealed a big-hearted man who wanted to love & be loved. As he became better at training his attention, so too did his presence & connection with himself, customers, friends & his beautiful bride.

"Meditation (training of attention) is a lifelong process. Give it a try. As you get deeper and more disciplined into the process, you'll get deeper and more disciplined in your mind and life."

- Brendon Burchard -

WHY DOES ATTENTION MATTER

Attention is the cognitive and behavioral process of selectively focusing on a distinct aspect of experience, while ignoring other information. Attention is currently a major area of investigation in psychology, neuroscience and education, with applications ranging from learning to mental health and the nature of consciousness to artificial intelligence, but that is not a new area of human investigation. It has also been a primary curiosity of the perennial philosophical exploration throughout the ages. The ability or inability to concentrate attention in the heightened sensory stimulated world of the information age has recently become even more of an interest and concern. Distraction is the dividing of attention from the intended object of attention to an internal or external source of diversion. It is caused by a lack of interest in the object of attention, a greater attractiveness of something else, avoidance, procrastination or often a brain hardware issue or neurophysiological inability to focus. Almost continually distracted by impulses, recurrent thoughts, and external digital stimuli, we struggle to focus and lack peace of mind.

- the average U.S. adult attention span is around 8 seconds (Microsoft study)
- the average U.S. office worker checked their email inbox 30 times per hour (Radicati Group research)
- 38% of employees habitually check work email at the dinner table, 50% while still in bed & 69% won't go to bed without first checking work email (Good Technology study)

Multitasking is really possible and is actually task-switching, alternating attention back and forth between two or more objects or tasks. Although a few professions like air-traffic controller require this skill of task-switching, research demonstrates it is actually less effective, less productive and less enjoyable for people in most other professions. Most significantly in terms of our subjective experience, constant task-switching inhibits us from experiencing the absorbed attention of full-engagement in *Flow States*. Whereas Mindfulness involves a more wide angle open Awareness, concentrating attention is more like the focus of a zoom lens. Let us define *Flow* then as "a state of effortlessly absorbed attention in the engagement of the present moment activity" with such focused selectivity that even awareness of self, others and surroundings dissolves. Sufficient interest combined with sufficient skill and self-efficacy support the selective focusing of attention and full engagement in activity. A person's subjective experience of absorbed attention is one of interesting challenge, full engagement and absorption of attention in an activity and an intrinsically enjoyable experience in and of itself regardless of outcomes. Research shows that those who are actively engaged in their work with sufficient challenge and skill, enjoy it more than passive leisure activities, such as watching television. Our work is a powerful opportunity to practice absorbing our attention and entering *Flow*, as are our relational interactions.

Distraction or multitasking can also really impair the quality of relationships and connection. Presence, eye contact, connectedness, authenticity and open-hearted intimate engagement are some of the most desired and important qualities in healthy relationships and friendships. Our bodies may be physically in attendance but our attention, a key to presence, maybe elsewhere and resulting in our presence not being available. When we are multitasking with fractionated attention, whether partially engaged with mobile devices, computers or television, they become barriers to trust, empathy, and closeness. If we justify our *"multitasking"* as a way to have more time for our relationships, let us be really honest with ourselves and know that our attention and deeper presence is what is really most desired. Fantasy, dissociation, distracted by technology or being lost in thought exist on the lesser end of the presence spectrum while progressively learning to regulate and direct attention is one of the most liberating, enjoyable and essential human skills.

DEVELOPING THE BRAIN FOR ATTENTION (HARDWARE)

Our capacity for attention actually begins to develop in our mother's womb with the growing fetal brain. Our parents' state of health at the time of conception, our mother's diet during pregnancy and breastfeeding, and our early childhood diet are all important nutrient developmental factors in our your developing brains. Although all vitamins and minerals are important for a myriad of biological functions, Omega 3 essential fatty acids (EPA & DHA) are especially important in brain development—especially considering that around 60% of the brain is composed of DHA.[4]   Later as children continue to grow into an adulthood, there are certain essential nutrients our brains need to properly develop and function[5]; and there are certain inflammatory and toxic inputs that can on the other end of the spectrum disrupt brain function and attention.[6]

Research has linked hyperactivity, ADD & ADHD to:
Deficiencies: nutrients, fatty acids & exercise
Disruptors: food intolerance, excess sugar, food additives, heavy metals & inflammation

Some the of the most significant nutrient influencers on attention are deficiencies in magnesium and B6[7] and especially Omega 3 fatty acids.[8]   Because the brain and nervous system are very dependent on these healthy fats to function—called essential because the body does not manufacture them and we must consume them in our diet or through supplementation—scientifically-controlled studies have demonstrated that giving fish oil to children with these kinds of problems improves attention, spelling, reading, and behavior in school.[9]   As far as the attention disruptors are concerned, **high sugar consumption** has been linked with hyperactivity, anxiety, learning difficulties and lower IQ.[10]   **Artificial food colorings** has also been shown to disrupt attention and stimulate hyperactivity.[11]   Research shows trans fats (fried food, hydrogenated oils, margarine) increase inflammation, damage brain cells and disrupt normal brain function in kids with ADHD.[12]   **Food allergies** can also inflame the brain and disrupt many other bodily systems.[13]   Research has linked food allergies to many symptoms, but in the context of attention, the results include: hyperactivity, learning disabilities, lack of motivation, brain fog, slowed thought processes, irritability, depression, and fatigue.[14]   According to studies in two of the most prestigious medical journals gluten intolerance is linked to 55 diseases (New England Journal of Medicine—NEJM)[15] and 30% of people of European descent carry gluten intolerance genes (Lancet).[16]   Although once thought to be primarily a disorder of the intestines only 1 in 8 has digestive symptoms and research now shows that gluten primarily attacks are thought to be on the neurological system[17] , which can result in a range of neurological manifestations especially attention.[18]   If we wonder why a book on presence is going into detail on nutrient deficiencies and neuro toxicity it is because it's really difficult to focus our attention with presence when our brain is toxically assaulted, inflamed or deficient in nutrients for normal function.

Movement and **exercise** can also be thought of as another essential nutrient for our brain's attention focus, although it is not food related. Mark Hyman MD, Functional Medicine pioneer and author of the *UltraMind Solution: Fix Your Broken Brain by Healing Your Body First* cites a plethora of research demonstrating that exercise builds new neural connections, rewires our brains for better attention, better mood and faster, smoother, more efficient processing and states that "exercise can give us the same neurotransmitter and mental benefits as Ritalin and Zyprexa (attention drugs) without the risk or side effects."[19] Research out of Harvard demonstrates that exercise is so essential for normal brain health that not exercising is actually a depressant. Indeed, research shows that exercise beats or equals *Prozac* or psychotherapy as an anti-depressant in head-to-head studies.[20]

Although not a conventionally considered factor, research has shown excessive levels of heavy metals such as lead and mercury have significant detrimental effects on our brains, behavior, and attention. **Lead toxicity** has been clearly linked to ADHD and behavioral problems in children.[21][22]   In one 11-year long-term effect study [23][24] published in the top two most prominent medical journals JAMA and NEJM, Dr. Herbert Needleman studied the impact of lead on 2146 children in 1st and 2nd grade by examining the lead in the teeth, which gives a more accurate total storage level than the bloodstream. Children with the highest lead levels not only had the lowest IQ's but were more hyperactive, impulsive, distractible, disorganized, and had difficulty following directions. Recent lead toxicity research shows the greatest decline in IQ scores occurs between a level of 1-10 micrograms per deciliter, which is not very much.[25]

However, **mercury toxicity** is even worse and has been correlated with ADHD symptoms[26] as well as many other more severe neurological issues. It is the second most toxic substance known to human biology next to plutonium and the literary reference to the mad hatter is due to mercury exposure in the 19th-century hat making process.[27] As far as current human exposure threats are concerned, mercury can come from dental fillings, pregnant mothers in the womb, eating fish with high levels, air pollution, and vaccines. Mercury levels in bodily tissues—especially the brain—have been shown to be directly correlated with the amount of mercury in dental fillings in the mouth.[28] It is ironic that the Environmental Protection Agency EPA www.epa.gov/mercury//healthcare.htm, considers these mercury fillings hazardous toxic waste material that requires high regulation and careful removal from dental offices, yet we still put these in peoples' mouths.[29] As for air pollution, mercury is discharged from coal-burning industrial facilities at a rate of over 6,000,000 lbs. per year[30] which also gets into our oceans and rivers, accumulating most of the largest fish which live longest and eat the most over their lifetimes like tuna, swordfish, shark, most river fish. One study showed 25% of New Yorkers have toxic blood levels of mercury due to eating too much fish and sushi.[31] Even more alarming, 15% of 4 million children (600,000) born annually in the U.S. are exposed to toxic levels of mercury in the womb.[32] Autopsy studies on human brains reveal damage in only a few areas for adults—particularly those responsible for dementia and depression, but for children when mercury exposure occurred in the womb or early years, it was deposited in the entire developing brain which disrupted normal brain development and function.[33] Fortunately, Functional Medicine Doctors have developed successful protocols using DMSA, DMPS, EDTA, and other chelators to help people detoxify accumulated heavy metals from their body and brains.[34][35]

Automatic Negative Thoughts (ANTS) can also significantly disrupt our attentional focus. Mark George, MD and his colleagues at the *National Institutes of Health* conducted research showing that difficulty focusing and negative thoughts correlated with inflamed brain areas often involved with anxiety and depression, while a quieter mind with more positive thoughts reflected a generalized calming effect in the brain. So yes, our thoughts do matter AND so does the health of your brain. The question is what comes first *"the chicken or the egg"*? Do ANTs craft our brain physiology or does our brain psychology generate ANTs? The answer appears to be both: our thoughts have a real effect on the body, while our body has a real effect on the quality of our mind:

> *"Counseling, therapy, coaching, cognitive behavioral therapy, and even psychoanalysis can be essential components of an overall plan for mental health. But if you are mercury poisoned, deficient in folic acid, have low thyroid function, drink 12 cups of coffee daily, eat a half pound of sugar daily (the amount consumed by the average American), or have an inflamed brain from eating gluten, it is very difficult to talk or meditate your way out of suffering"*[36]

Many people try to improve attention by taking adding pharmaceutical drugs, yet the above-mentioned factors are fundamental to building and maintaining a healthy brain and attention hardware. Now with this foundation attended to, let us return to the developmental journey of attention from a behavioral psychology angle—the software side—and how the engagement of our attention relates to presence.

DEVELOPING THE PSYCHOLOGY OF ATTENTION (SOFTWARE)

Living in the information age, we are exposed to unprecedented amounts of sensory stimuli and information. As a result, many children, as well as adults, frequently use their attention for multitasking—the attempt to perform two or more tasks simultaneously. Interestingly, as noted earlier neuroscience reveals that multitasking is really task switching or unfocused fractionated attention. According to research at Vanderbilt University, when people attempted to do two tasks simultaneously, they were only actually doing one task at a time and were instead just switching back and forth, which created a bottleneck in the brain's information processing area. Although multitasking is necessary for some professions, such as the aforementioned air traffic controller, for most other tasks, the consensus conclusion is that the brain cannot as effectively do two things at once. Multitasking is actually dividing attention which diminishes presence. Additionally, multitasking does not save time, but rather the task switchers actually work more slowly and tend to make more mistakes due to the extra cognitive load, as the brain must continually reorient and adjust to the second task while remembering where it paused with the first task. Often, what we believe are memory problems are actually a lack of focused attention. We cannot remember later what we do not pay attention to now. When attention is scattered and brain circuits are overloaded with stimuli, it impairs focus, prioritization, and organization. Poor concentration, divided attention and lack of presence limits work effectiveness and interpersonal relating. Another study at the University of Utah found that people multitask not because they have the ability or are *"good at it"*, but rather because they are less able to focus on a single task while blocking out distractions.[37] In other words, those of us that have not trained our brains to focus our attention tend to *"multitask"*, which is actually fractionating our attention, and thus making us less productive and the process less enjoyable than it would be with focused engagement. With Awareness, we can notice when we are distracted or not focused on one thing and practice training our attention for dramatically increased presence and thereby enhanced productivity, creativity, work quality, Istates and enjoyment of life.

Again, if the average U.S. adult attention span is about 8 seconds, then what is above average attention? At the opposite end of the spectrum of distraction, fractionated attention and multitasking is effortlessly absorbed attention or what is referred to in psychology as *Flow* states. Mihaly Csikszentmihalyi, a Hungarian born psychologist, researcher and professor, is the leading expect of **Flow** who coined the term in his fascination with artists, especially painters, and their astonishing capacity for attention and getting lost in their work for hours and days, even sometimes to the extent of neglecting all else including their own self-care (food, water, and sleep).[38] Csikszentmihalyi began studying the people that were happy and enjoyed their work or hobbies across various domains. His research included athletes, dancers, rock climbers, artists, authors, chess players, and factory workers among others. He defined *Flow as "a state in which the individual's focus, or attention, is completely absorbed in the present moment activity at the expense of all else, including oneself."* [39]

Although being in a *Flow* state is commonly associated with optimal performance and can have many benefits beyond the pure enjoyment of absorbed attention in an activity for its own sake, there are some potential dark sides of hyper-focus. While it is precisely the capacity to selectively limit attention to the pure engagement of the activity that effectively enables one to experience the effortless absorption in an activity, yet it occurs via minimizing awareness of self, others, or the environment. Csikszentmihalyi recognizes some of these downsides in that losing Awareness of a larger field of the moment, can occur to the exclusion of the needs of one's self, others and the environment. Additionally, his research found that moral discernment is not a natural element of *Flow*, as people can be in a Flow state in the midst of destructive activity in one's surroundings and to others Research on *Flow* and optimal experience has continued in the past few decades particularly in the fields of psychology, education, business, athletics, and the arts, yet functioning in states of absorbed attention has been experienced and written about throughout recorded history across cultures—especially in the East. The following appear to be essential features of absorbed attention and while we can engage each quality independently, they all seem to be present in a *Flow state*:

- **selective narrowing of focus** on object or activity
- high level of interest in the activity
- clear goals with **immediate feedback**
- the sense of **competence, self-efficacy & agency**
- **loss of awareness** of time, needs, or self-consciousness
- experience is intrinsically rewarding & enjoyable for its own sake
- **effortless engagement**: merging of action & Awareness

Initially, Csikszentmihalyi and *Flow* researchers thought a person had to have sufficient interest to engage in the activity combined with a match between skill level and degree of difficulty of the activity—if it was too easy or not enough challenging enough it led to feels of boredom, while on the other end of the spectrum the activity was too challenging then it could cause anxiety. Either extremes of boredom or over-challenging anxiety were barriers to entering a *Flow* state. However, after continued research the theory was refined by realizing that both the competence or skill level or the person and the relative level of challenge has to be at above average levels in order to capture the person's full attention and facilitate the effortless engagement of absorbed attention in a *Flow* State; a person's level of interest and enjoyment related to the activity must be high enough. Wanting to be somewhere else or do something else can create a subtle or not-so-subtle misalignment of engagement that not only hijacks enjoyment and engagement in the activity but also effectively blocks the possibility of being animated by a *Flow* state. A sense of belief in one's abilities and previous skillfulness in an activity that enhances self-efficacy and promotes continued reengagement of interest and attention especially after errors. Once the interest of an individual with sufficient skill and self-efficacy is engaged, *Flow* states are ripe to arise through the process of selective attention as she or he allows awareness of everything else to drop away and becomes immersed in the activity. A *Flow* state is a full alignment of intentions, feelings, actions, and skills that it allows full attention to be so engrossed and engaged in the experience of the activity in the present moment that awareness of all else falls away.

While there are certainly physical disruptors, inflammatory influences, and deficiencies that can compromise our ability to focus attention, our modern world is also full of other people wanting to capture our attention, whether in proximity or through digital mediums or social media. We have an almost unlimited number of options and channels to switch back and forth between. The challenge level in the game of presence has been increased. Below are some tips for enhancing our attention both in terms of brain health and our intentional capacity to focus our attention and optimally enter *Flow* states of complete attentional absorption.

ATTENTION HARDWARE ESSENTIALS

Remove Disruptors: food allergens & intolerance, excess sugar, food additives, heavy metals & inflammation
Attention Enhancers: food (high quality, nutrient dense, whole foods & supplements) & movement/exercise

ATTENTION SOFTWARE ESSENTIALS

Ingredients for Flow (interest, skill, ability to concentrate)
Hindrances to Flow (under-challenge = boredom / over-challenge = anxiety)
Entering of Flow (relaxation, selective focusing, present moment engagement in the activity for its own sake)
Staying in Flow (clear short-term goals, immediate feedback, capacity for growth & learning)
Benefits of Flow (effortless engagement, creativity, learning, optimal performance, intrinsic enjoyment)

- Meditation, while ultimately Vantage of Awareness expanding method, it is initially about concentration or attention training.
- Attention Hardware Essentials
  - Remove Disruptors: food allergens & intolerance, excess sugar, food additives, heavy metals & inflammation
  - Attention Enhancers: food (high quality, nutrient dense, whole foods & supplements) & movement/exercise
- Attention Software Essentials
  - Ingredients for Flow (interest, skill, ability to concentrate)
  - Hindrances to Flow (under-challenge = boredom / over-challenge = anxiety)
  - Entering of Flow (relaxation, selective focusing, present moment engagement in the activity for its own sake)
  - Staying in Flow (clear short-term goals, immediate feedback, capacity for growth & learning)
  - Benefits of Flow (effortless engagement, creativity, learning, optimal performance, intrinsic enjoyment)

EMPATHY, PERSPECTIVES, IMPACT & COMPASSION

Do you tend to focus more on your own beliefs, opinions & point of view (POV)? Or do you tend to lose your sense of self & overly-tending to others? Or can you take your own perspective & that of another simultaneously?

Are you able to sense what others are feeling? Can you **empathize** & emotionally resonate with another's state?

Are you able to feel open-hearted **compassion** for the struggles of others & are you living your life as an instrument of service for the alleviation of suffering, the evolution of humanity & awakening?

"Three quarters of the miseries and misunderstandings in the world would finish if people were to put on the shoes of their adversaries and understood their points of view"

- Mahatma Gandhi -

The brain is so relational that our nervous system is actually "constructed to be captured by the nervous systems of others, so that we can experience others as if from within their skin, as well as from within our own."

- Dan Stern University of Geneva -

WHAT IS **EMPATHY, PERSPECTIVES, IMPACT & COMPASSION**

Perspectives: the capacity to mentally imagine & take multiple points of view
Empathy: the capacity to emotionally resonate with & share the feelings of another
Impact: the capacity to preemptively or retroactively imagine or sense the effect of words & actions on others & the world
Compassion: the capacity to feel a heartfelt awareness of others' struggles that inspires a desire to radiate loving-kindness or take action & be of service to alleviate suffering

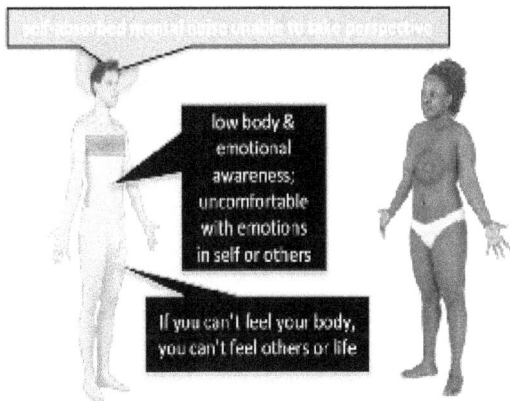

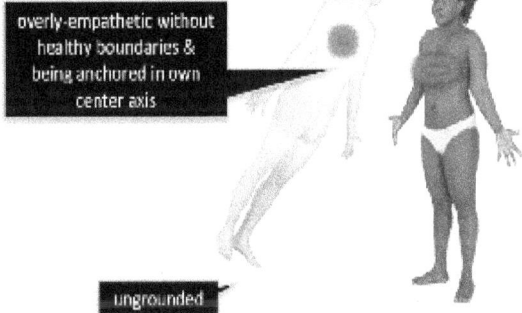

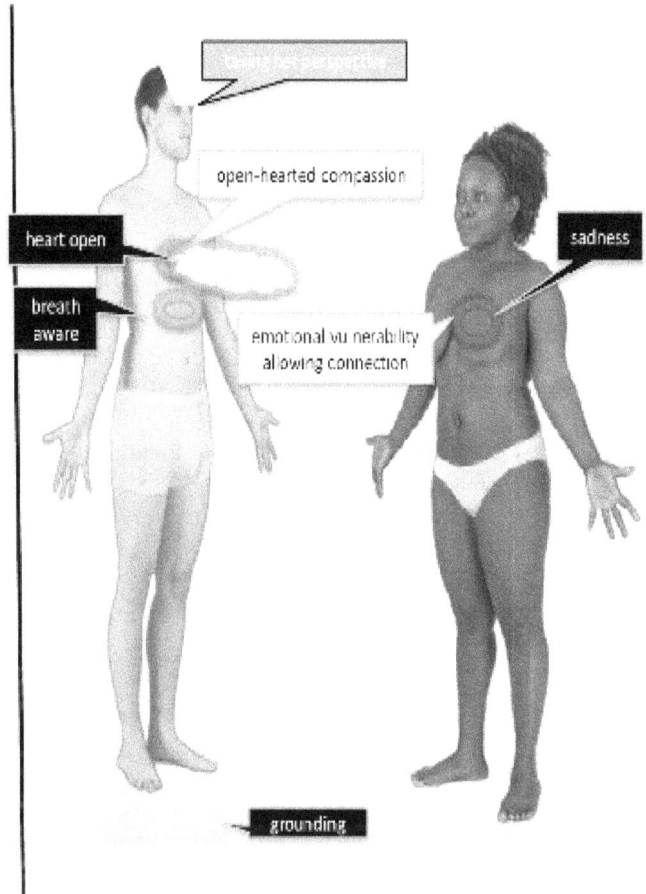

WHY **EMPATHY, PERSPECTIVES, IMPACT & COMPASSION** MATTERS

Understanding: perspective taking allows us to understand ourselves, others & the world from new points of view

Learning: perspective taking supports learning, evolving & engaging in new actions & ways of being

Transcending Bias: allows us to envision evolutionary ideals beyond cultural norms, inequality, racism, gender, etc.

Connection: perspective taking allows others feel seen, heard & understood, empathy allows others to feel felt in shared resonance, impact awareness is required for treating others with respect & consideration as well as sincere apologizing

Alleviating Pain: empathy & impact awareness can sometimes enable another to feel, soothe & release emotional pain

Apologizing: empathy & impact awareness are essentials in an effective apology between two parties, bridging connection, enabling the other to get that you now feel the impact your words or actions had on them & with that there is less chance of you doing it again

Less Harmful: consideration of the impact of our speech & actions on ourselves, others & the environment; without impact awareness we can be impulsive, disempowering & harmful to ourselves, others & our world

Accountability: impact allows for taking greater self-responsibility & accountability for our words & actions Best Action in Service: discerning best action for now with all things considered in the most resourceful way to relate to & work to alleviate the suffering in the world

Universal Human Justice & Care: allows us to question breeches in universal human rights & transform injustices & social systems

Span of Awareness: impact awareness & compassion widen our span of Awareness & shared humanity

EMPATHY, PERSPECTIVES, IMPACT & COMPASSION BARRIERS

Dissociation: not feeling & inhabiting your body allows taking perspectives but unable to feel empathy or impact

Self-Absorption: if your attention is occupied with fulfilling your own needs, it limits your span of awareness of others, must first be able to take another perspective to empathize, feel impact or compassion

Lack of Boundaries: losing awareness of yourself & your perspective via merging, getting lost in their world & taking on their state

Safety, Survival & Self-Esteem Needs: when our attention is prioritized to your own base needs, there is less availability for larger perspective, impact or compassion

Emotionally Shutdown: can't sense others, empathize or feel impact, when your own sensing system is shut down, closed or numb

Guilt & Shame: if you are unable to feel healthy shame you can't be aware of impact if you hurt another

Blame: a way to discharge discomfort that has an inverse relationship to taking responsibility for the impact of your words & actions

Insufficient Emotional Self-Awareness & Literacy: in order to be able to empathetically resonate with what another is feeling you must be aware of & allow yourself to feel that emotion in yourself first

Emotionally Triggered: emotions create static, prioritize attention to your own internal experience & limit points of view or empathy

Advice or Fixing: giving unrequested advice or trying to problem solve your agenda onto another's experience

Hyper-Mental: excessive mental activity, overly theoretical allows perspectives but unable to feel empathy or impact

Judgmental: critical, negative, or condemning point of view about others or the world with fixed attention & closed heart limiting alternate perspective taking, empathy, compassion & connection

Distress Tolerance: low ability to tolerate distress or suffering, turn away, deny, avoid, numb

"We are dangerous when we are not conscious of our responsibility for how we behave, think, and feel."
– Marshall Rosenberg –

"A human being is a part of the whole called by us universe, a part limited in time and space. He experiences himself, his thoughts and feeling as something separated from the rest, a kind of optical delusion of his consciousness. This delusion is a kind of prison for us, restricting us to our personal desires and to affection for a few persons nearest to us. Our task must be to free ourselves from this prison by widening our circle of compassion to embrace all living creatures and the whole of nature in its beauty."
– Albert Einstein –

WHAT ARE **EMPATHY, PERSPECTIVE, IMPACT & COMPASSION**

Empathy: the capacity to emotionally resonate & share the feelings of another
Perspectives: the capacity to mentally imagine & take multiple points of view
Impact: the capacity to preemptively or retroactively imagine or sense the effect of words or actions on others & the
world
Compassion: the capacity to feel a heartfelt awareness of others' struggles that inspires a desire to take action & be
of service

DEVELOPMENT

Modern scientific psychological and socio-biological researchers have presented persuasive evidence that some degree
of empathy and compassion exists even in groups of primates which they use as evidence that the potential for these
qualities are inherent in human behavior. Pioneer in this field, Frans de Waal, a primatologist at Emory University,
has comprehensively demonstrated through more than thirty years of research using examples throughout the animal
kingdom, suggesting that certain behaviors may have evolved from animals to humans.[1][2]   de Waal cites cases of whales
and dolphins that risk their lives to save injured companions, chimpanzees that come to the aid of victims of aggression,
elephants that attempt to revive slain comrades and then refuse to leave them. Examples of cross-species rescue and
adoption in the animal kingdom, further demonstrate our deep evolutionary compassionate roots. However, de Waal does
not maintain that animals are moral, only that some animals engage in actions, express emotions, and possess psychological
behaviors similar to those defined in human morality such that perhaps some degree all humans have the nervous system
wiring for moral expressions like empathy and compassion.

Nature and the animal kingdom certainly have their survivalist, hedonistic and harsher sides too though, as do we humans.
Whether we adults are self-absorbed in "looking out for #1" in order to survive in a harsh world or get our self-esteem
needs met or whether we are impulsive and want to be free to do what we want when we want without consideration of
or care about the consequences, we have not always extended our span of consideration to others. Because as we shall see
this EPIC moral bundle of Empathy, Perspective, Impact and Compassion are skills that can be learned in a developmental
process.

As infant bundles of love and depended needs, we are unable to self-regulate our nervous systems or emotions and need to
have our core needs be attuned to and met by our caregivers. Unable to speak in words our changing emotional states are
attempts at connection and best attempts to express our needs. Drooling, peeing and pooing all over ourselves, beckons
our care-givers patient attention and compassion or frustrated burden and awareness of the impact of that poop smell
if it doesn't get cleaned up. Attuned empathetic connection from our caregivers helps infants get needs met, regulate
emotional states, develop their nervous system, but also to get feedback & learn about themselves through the outside
empathetic perspectives of others. Emotional resonance is one of the easiest access points to human connection and it is
through this caring attunement and empathetic resonance that we feel love and connection as infants.

In some cases, our caregivers lacked certain capacities for secure connection and empathic attunement that supports healthy infant development. We humans begin as precious babies completely dependent on external nurturance and support, undifferentiated from others or our environment and thus our immature perspective-taking and empathy functions are unable to differentiate what we are feeling, what mom is feeling, the unspoken emotional tensions in the home or culture, etc. The first quality of this bundle of empathy, perspective, impact, and compassion that can develop is what psychologists call emotional contagion—the beginnings of empathy in our nervous system's ability to sense and be affected by emotions in others or a room. Although we can't verbalize it, we are sensitive little sponges, which is why it is even more important for our parents to be as resourced and emotionally free as possible when they are attuning to their infant. It is through this empathetic attunement from our caregivers that they not only try to sense and meet our needs but also through eye contact, touch, and emotional resonance (empathy) that we not only bond in connection but this process is literally wiring the hardware of our brains and continues from infancy into childhood and beyond. Our systems are becoming hard-wired to read the faces of others and resonate with their felt experience—unless this process is stunted as a youth or shut down due to trauma. One parental responsibility is, through the process of empathically resonating with our states in connection is to help the developing child to become aware of, feel, name & express their emotions. Ideally the parents are relaxed, open & emotionally free to attune to and empathetically reflect the child's emotional state and help him or her to more clearly know and name their inner states and regulate their own inner landscape of experience.

Universally, we humans broadcast emotion through tone of voice, facial expressions, body language, and other subtleties. Paul Ekman's cross-cultural research demonstrates the universal nature of human emotions across cultures from people in industrialized cities to people in indigenous tribes being able to read and name specific emotions through facial expressions in still photos without ever even meeting. He has also shown that humans born blind, express the same emotions through the same facial expressions.[3] Neuroscientist at the University of Geneva, Dan Stern states that the human brain and nervous system is so relational, that it is actually "constructed to be captured by the nervous systems of others, so that we can experience others as if from within their skin, as well as from within our own." Sue Johnson, in her book Love Sense notes that if we are emotionally literate enough of others, we can detect these emotional fluctuations in milliseconds: 1 millisecond to register changes in facial expression and if our empathy neural networks are developed enough, just 300 milliseconds to feel in our own body what they are feeling in theirs.[4]

Brain researchers suggest a mirror neuron system is responsible for our empathy capacities. In 1995, Italian researcher, Iaccomo Rizzolati discovered that when a monkey reached for food, a similar brain region fired when the monkey observed a person doing the same movement as when the monkey itself picked up the food. Much research has been done since then related to these fascinating findings on the mirror neuron systems in both monkeys and humans, and evidence from functional MRI demonstrates that humans have similar yet more complex mirror neurons systems that respond during both action and the observation of action. In an article entitled *Mirror Neurons and imitation learning as the driving force behind "the great leap forward" in human evolution*, visionary UCSD neuroscientist V.S. Ramachandran suggests "that the emergence of a sophisticated mirror neuron system set the stage for the emergence, in early hominids, of a number of uniquely human abilities such as...language, empathy, 'theory of other minds', and the ability to 'adopt another's point of view (POV)'.[5] Today the mirror neuron system is thought to be the basis of empathy, language learning, POV perspective taking, skill learning via imitation, and even the ability to sense underlying intentions. Similar capacities that enable us to imitate words in language learning and movement patterns in athletic skill development, also enable us to activate our own emotional brain areas when we observe emotions in others. Research neuroscientist Marco Iacoboni notes that the amount of activation is slightly less for the "mirrored experience" in others than when the same emotion is experienced on our own initiation. He emphasizes that a healthy mirror neuron system is essential for normal social development and "If you have 'broken mirrors,' or deficits in mirror neurons, you likely end up having social problems, as patients with autism do".[6]

So, we all potentially have the nervous circuitry to be able to empathetically sense and resonate with what others are feeling. Yet, while male socialization in many cultures conditions men to limit emotional expression, research shows that there is no gender difference in the ability recognize emotions in others.[7]   However, a lack of emotional literacy and empathy could stem from either a lack of development since childhood, a shutting down of the function at some point, a lack of emotional presence with certain emotions such that we could empathize with others, or damaging of associated brain functions as in the case of autism spectrum disorder.

It is important to understand that empathy has a body basis: our awareness of another person's state depends on how well we know our own inner landscape emotions, body sensations and perspectives. Dan Siegel, an interpersonal neurobiology expert and head of psychiatry at UCLA, notes that we feel others feelings by actually feeling our own body's nervous system and mental perspective mapping circuitry, which is the reason why people who are more aware of their bodies have been found to be more empathic because the same fundamental pathways for sensing our own internal state and resonating with others are related.[8]   However, as we will learn more about later in this section, in the developmental process of learning empathy, perspective-taking, impact awareness and compassion, we must learn to meet in connection with simultaneous embodied awareness as two individuated human beings as opposed to being self-absorbed, merging or losing self-referencing in relating. For those of us who have not yet embodied the ability to meet as two nervous systems in connection, the boundaries, emotions and identities can sometimes get blurry and confusing.

So in a relational interaction, how do we know if an emotion is mine or yours? Researchers also theorize that there are super mirror neurons that fire more rapidly for our own experiences and more slowly for the experiences of others, which can also inhibit imitating inappropriate actions and also help us distinguish the sense of self-reference from other-reference.[9] Not only does our mirror neuron system enable us to emotionally resonate with another's experience to help us know their inner world as a beautiful bridge to connection, but one of the more fascinating aspects of the mirror neuron system, known to date, is the way it allows us to potentially sense people's underlying intentions. Iacoboni reported that mirror neurons enabled distinguishing if another person who was picking up a cup of tea planned to drink from it versus clear it from the table.[10]   Perhaps our mirror neuron system is also a scientifically explainable medium for intuition and other extrasensory perceptions. Is it possible that some people have nervous systems that have been developed with more nuanced sensory awarenesses, utilizing latent human potentials?

PERSPECTIVE-TAKING
While part of our human empathy capacities involves emotionally resonating with another, there is another important

part of the process that involves mental perspective taking—which Dan Siegel compares to a metaphor of mental maps. In his book *Mindsight*, describes how empathy includes resonating with someone's emotional experience and how we can also make mental images or maps as we imagine another's inner experience—which in the context of this book, we will call perspective-taking. In addition to emotionally resonant attunement of another's state, we can make complex perceptual maps imagining another point of view, intentions, and meaning-making lenses, which Siegel delineates as Me-Maps, You-Maps and We-Maps. (Although we have been primarily using *"our"*, *"us"* and *"we"* for pronouns referring to our shared humanity, but for this section we will also be using *me*, *my* and *you* to be more clear in referring to specific perspectives). He cautions, however, that without a Me-Map (being able to take my own perspective and having an inner self-reference via our central axis and breath) one can be spun out in thoughts, flooded by emotions, or get lost in a You-Map, which is the root of merging and co-dependency. Whereas on the other end of the spectrum, if all a person can take a perspective on is their own Me-Map, he or she will tend to be self-absorbed or narcissistic. Healthy human connection requires that two individuated people, me and you, are both able to have our own Me-Maps, a separate You-Map of the other person and a third We-Map meeting in connection.

Let us make these Map references more practical in our daily lives. It is difficult to listen with presence to another person, if your own Me-Map is so distracted by mental noise or emotional chaos. Through your own inner regulation, you must be resourced enough and able to calm your own mental and emotional static to even be able to be available to take the other's perspectives. Next, with regards to empathy, you must be emotionally literate enough to read your own landscape of emotion, in order to be able to read another's. Finally, you must be able to stay in your own center and maintain your own individuated Me-Map while simultaneously attuned to another's individuated Map in order for healthy empathy to happen. It is important to understand this progression, because again, some people either get stuck in self-absorption—either shutting down parts of themselves (often body and emotions) and mostly aware of their own mental activity—which limits their ability to resonate in body and emotions with another person in connection, rapport or empathy. Also common in self-absorption is the person prioritizing trying to get *their* needs met or regulate *their* own emotions first—in which case this person can learn to take others perspective better and to feel more connected to others. By contrast, others can get hijacked by losing their own center by either abandoning themselves and going over into the other person or by merging. Siegel has a clever reminder that it takes a "Me and a Me to make a We," otherwise the interaction becomes a merged blob. He says "when resonance literally becomes merging, when we confuse me with you, then objectivity is lost. Resonance requires that we maintain differentiation—that we know who we each are—while also becoming linked. We let our internal states be influenced by, but not become identical with those of the other person."[12]

If you are self-absorbed, you cannot feel connection, empathy or impact, and if you are over-empathetic without maintaining our own perspective, central axis and healthy boundaries, then you will become a merged blob instead of a *Me* and *You* connecting as a *We*. Ideally, it takes two separate, yet open and receptive, individuals to find a reliable felt-sensory connection with each other—the combination of some degree of felt bodily resonance combined with two distinct Me-Maps and then in this connection, a mutually arising We-Map also gets created. If when you are relating, can you can take your own Me-perceptive while simultaneously being aware of the You-perspective of the other person, then a third shared We-perspective arises in this emerging shared We-Space. When you are talking to another person can you feel your own breath, body, heart and perspective while simultaneously being attuned to the other person's breath, body, heart and perspective?

When our resonance circuits are not developed, when we have high levels of unmet needs running us or are hijacked in heightened emotional intensity, we can lose awareness and a felt sense of others as fellow human beings and instead relate to others as objects. If I am self-absorbed only in my own Me-Map experience and I cannot feel you or take your You-Map perceptive, then I will tend to relate to you as a physical object to serve my needs and agendas without sensing your subjective inner experience as an equally unique human being with feelings, perspectives, hopes, fears, etc.
In a real-world example, you might only see another person as an object for your own worth validation, sexual gratification, social-status or self-esteem needs. As science studies and understands the brain to increasing degrees, we know that our human nervous system has to be relaxed and quiet enough for the higher order brain functions of empathy, impact awareness and compassion to be able to function. Otherwise in fight or flight responses of fear or anger, one might revert to lower order survival reactivity or selfishness. This is an explanation for our history of physical and sexual violence as a human species; if you cannot relate to others as a living being with an inner experience and you cannot feel the impact of that your actions on your own inner experience and that of others, then there is not much inhibiting you from harming others beyond societal laws and associated punishments.

Technically, empathy is an emotional resonance based process in the feeling capacity to share a similar emotional state with someone. Thus within the skill of emotional resonance, "empathy", there is also mental perspective-taking POV. Sometimes, in popular culture, empathy is often incorrectly attributed to the purely cognitive process of mental perspective-taking. Development of empathy as a skill actually requires sufficient cognitive intelligence in having the ability to take multiple perspectives, to be emotionally intelligent in the ability to be aware of, name, and feel an emotion in yourself and others, as well as interpersonal intelligence enough for resonant rapport and connection. Here in lies a dangerous potential for manipulation and false promises when someone has the ability to mentally take another's perspective and has learned to say the "right things," but if he or she hasn't developed sufficient emotional empathy and impact awareness to be able to feel the impact that his or her words and actions have on others. Therefore, the emotional resonance aspect is essential for getting and feeling the moral impact of words or actions on others. If I can't actually feel what you feel then it does not prevent me from taking advantage of you or acting in a way that might impact you to feel distress or harm.

IMPACT
What is the best action for now, with consideration of the impact on self, others and the world? Societal and existential questions of morality have occupied philosophers, religious leaders, rulers, policymakers, and lay people alike for thousands of years. From Hammurabi's code to royalty and governance, to the ancient Greeks and other great world philosophers, from the scriptures of all major religions to the ethics of scientific technology, leaders in all epochs, cultures and fields have questioned and legislated how they believed we should best live. Indeed, morality and ethics have been codified and mandated by cultural authorities for millennia, although historically not all governing bodies have been in the highest potential of their own impact awareness.

Like all qualities, empathy, perspective taking and impact awareness must be developed in our nervous systems so they can embody through our lives in our relations and in the world. Yet, reading the recorded human history it seems we have long struggled with ego-centrism and impulsivity—which we will learn more about why in the *Stages of Worldview section*. The more your brain is absorbed with *You*, the less you can feel the impact you are having or could have and in so the more you relate other humans is an object, enemy, or feared foreigner. In the midst of impulsivity, survival, power struggles, and inclinations to fulfill self-esteem needs, without the moral discernment of impact awareness online, the more likely harm, chaos and social anarchy are to ensue. For many, the only thing that stops us is not getting caught and avoiding punishment, although some do not even care about that. Some people who see the world from a more fundamentalist good and bad perspective, follow the rules commanded by their trusted institution—usually with a religious or nationalistic afflation—designed as a way to influence followers' behavior towards positive actions by trying suppress impulses by "being good" now to avoid sin and punishment in favor of future reward (in the afterlife, heaven and hell; salvation and damnation; final *Judgment Day*) in the absence of inner impact awareness. For some of us, the extent of our impact awareness with ourselves is in either impulsivity, I want to do whatever I feel like or I try to curb my impulses and "be good."

As impact awareness evolves it develops more perspective-taking ability for self and others now and in the future, including more healthy impulse control and rational brain function than in previous stages, but moral choices are still more related to following social convention, maintaining social order, social status and self-esteem. As impact awareness continues to mature, some people realize the relativity of our world and with a greater emphasis on honoring all perspectives and wanting everyone to be free tend to deny any objectively and want to get rid of all rules since they now think nothing is inherently right or wrong. Some people naïvely take this moral relativism and the desire to be free toward anarchy or an idealized hippie utopia. However, with some degree of freewill, people can choose to ignore the welfare of others, while pursuing self-interests above all else. Radhakrishnan, in explaining this apparent contradiction, remarked that "laws and regulations are necessary for the humans who do not naturally conform to the dictates of conscience. But, for those who have risen above their selfish egos, morality becomes the very condition of their being and the law fulfilled in love."[13]   This is precisely why it is important for a society with members that are not self-actualized moral agents to still have guiding ethical principles. At this next stage, impact awareness develops any even wider span to include me, you and all of us. Thus we now have an inner felt sense of our shared responsibility to come together as a collective whole and all participate in collective governance with awareness of our individual and collective impacts on each other and the world.

Ultimately, the highest expression of moral impact awareness honoring the collective values of universal justice and care were epitomized by great social change leaders like Martin Luther King, Jr., Rosa Parks, Gandhi, Nelson Mandela, etc. These epic leaders leveraged in their revolutionary campaigns toward greater equality, inspired by a sense of universal ideals beyond cultural norms or racism or gender inequality. At this level comes a greater awareness of intent and a larger span of impact awareness embracing interconnectivity and interdependence based on universally applicable principals such as the Golden Rule, the equality of human rights, respect for the dignity of each human being rather than on concrete rules. At this level of impact awareness, we can openly consider the existing laws, their relativity of justice and care, and discern the right action. Unjust laws could in theory be broken if they conflicted with truer universal moral principles and impact in the highest good for all. In 1948, the United Nations General Assembly outlined their views on the human rights that they believed were inherently guaranteed to all people as a birthright. Just a few years after World War II, recognizing that some nations were more humanistic than others, the *Universal Declaration of Human Rights* (UDHR) adopted by the U.N. was intended to serve as a universal standard of realization for all nations and peoples of the human family offering progressive measures—nationally and internationally—to ensure the effective acknowledgment and maintenance of the dignity, equality and inalienable rights inherent to all humanity. Most of us humans are not yet to the moral development of the great saints, sages and visionary revolutionaries let alone our spouse or "stranger" standing next to us. Many of us can become more aware of the impact on our fellow humans, applying the Golden Rule to our neighbors and more consciously considering how the impact of each decision will affect self, family, neighbors, local community, culture, nation, animals, plants, microorganisms, and all other matter in the universe. Hopefully in the future alongside of the continued emergence of an interconnected global community, mutual moral impact consideration will develop between individuals and the corporation, culture, and global community, in which all parties will think feel, act, live, and work for the humanism, ethical consumerism, ecological concern, and the universal compassion for all of creation. May I, you and We continue to developer greater internal impact awareness creating greater universal justice and care in *our* world.

COMPASSION

In English, the noun compassion--the root of which comes from Latin—means "to love together with."[14] In transcending our own ego-centric concerns, it is one of the highest human virtues in many philosophies and spiritual traditions related to the *ethic of reciprocity* also known as *the Golden Rule*: treat others as you want to be treated. This has been said similarly by various historic greats: "do unto others as you would have them do unto you" and "love thy neighbor as thyself" (Jesus), "he loves for his brother what he loves for himself" (Muhammad); "do naught unto others which would cause you pain if done to you" (Hinduism), "cultivate true love for all creation" and "may all beings be happy, loved & free from suffering" (Buddha). All of these wise reminders espouse an interconnected loving kindness, recalling from the Vantage section as living from a felt vantage of feeling unified Life.

Compassion is not just a mental concept, but an embodied state with an associated activated brain region and a warmth in the center of a relaxed open heart feeling touched by the struggles of others who we relate to as human just like us and so passionately moved to take action to be of service to others and the world. While feeling compassion requires the capacity for some combination of mental perspective-taking to imagine what it looks like to see through his or her eyes and emotionally resonant empathy to feel what it feels like to live in his or her skin, compassion then takes it to the next level with the passionate desire to positively contribute to the world and be of service and to others. Compassion is a positive emotional state somewhere on the emotional spectrum, perhaps including a mixture of love, concern, and a twinge of sadness. It requires a shared humanity of connection, identifying the person as a fellow living being, and being able to feel that we share the same desires and struggles, like me, this other being is part of this living world that is not always easy.

The importance of relating with others as a felt sense of "safe friend", as fellow humans is an essential feature of compassion. A fascinating University of Virginia Study used fMRI brain scans on participants while giving or potentially giving electrical shocks to the participant a close friend or a stranger.[15]   The results demonstrated that the brain regions responsible for threat response became active when the participant or their friend could potentially be shocked but not a "stranger". Whether in murder, rape, slavery, colonization, or genocide, and other atrocities, one common deficiency is that we lack the feeling of shared humanity, of "fellow humans". On the larger societal level, the importance of empathy, perspective-taking, impact and compassion are essential not only for us to continue to evolve but to fundamentally survive as a species. The Dalai Lama, spiritual leader of Tibet and global emissary of compassion, has said "*Compassion* is not religious business, it is human business, it *is not a luxury*. It is essential for human survival."

Stephen Porges—as we recall from previous sections, is a pioneering brain-body researcher, professor and institute director—gave a talk on Compassion at *Stanford University* and emphasized that he wants people to not focus solely on psychological processes, but on the underlying physiology—in this case not just talking about compassion conceptually but as an embodied experience.[16]   He reminds us, like much of Frans de Waal's research with animals mentioned at the beginning of this section, that the nervous system circuits and the basis for compassion is also shared by other mammals. In Porges' polyvagal theory, he emphasizes how important feeling safe and relaxed is for us humans and how it especially shows up in our nervous system and muscle tension activation in the face, chest and belly because our biology has evolved from earlier reptilian and mammalian nervous system circuitry. Using the science of psychophysiology, Porges explains how when we feel threatened either physically or socially/emotionally, our defense systems in the chest and belly inhibit "compassion" and "positive social behavior". In common terms, if you are feeling fear or anger, it inhibits you from feeling relaxed open-hearted compassion. There really is a physiological basis to "open-hearted" compassion because his research again demonstrates the body-based requirements for the muscles of the chest to be relaxed, which is incompatible with our defensive or even judgmental system activations.

Because compassion is literally a body and brain-based capacity, like a muscle, we need to practice and strengthen our capacity for feeling compassion. Scientists studying compassion have discovered that the average person—not the Dalai Lama who meditates for hours and does compassion practices daily—has a limit to how much intensity and duration that his or her body can feel compassion. The consensus so far seems to be that for the average person, it is easier to feel compassion for a single individual compared to large groups. Also, just like we learned in the *Attunement section*, we have to be able to regulate our own emotional states and stay resourced in order to be available to attune to others needs; so too, staying in compassionate connection requires our capacity for emotional presence and regulation. You have to be okay with feeling some degree of distress while keeping your compassionate heart open, as opposed to being overwhelmed in turning away or becoming numb. There is a term called **Compassion Fatigue** which Charles Figley, PhD, Distinguished Chair Director or Traumatology at Tulane University defines as "a state experienced by those helping people or animals in distress; it is an extreme state of tension and preoccupation with the suffering of those being helped to the degree that it can create a secondary traumatic stress for the helper." Symptoms of this can include constant stress and anxiety, substance abuse, hopelessness, sleeplessness, nightmares, decreased pleasure, and an overall negative attitude. The technical name for this burnout is *Secondary Traumatic Stress*, which is a better name because newer research indicates that it is *not compassion*, but actually empathy which gets fatigued.[17]   First of all, it is essential for all caregivers, social workers, therapists, rescue workers, etc. to maintain good self-care practices and stay resourced so they do not burn-out. Secondly, remember that empathy is actually shared emotional resonance in which we feel the state others are feeling, and in the case of Secondary Traumatic Stress, sometimes if helpers lack healthy boundaries and high emotional presence to be able to feel and release feeling states, then they can sometimes over-empathetically take on the state of those in distress, which is the true source of the burnout. Interestingly, in experiments with empathy, research suggests that practicing compassion as a motivation to service rather than empathetically taking on other people's states could even prevent fatigue and burnout.[18]

From a brain correlate perspective, Dan Siegel, whom explained previously in this section the importance of maintaining Me-Maps as well as You-Maps and We-Maps, cites evidence that the middle pre-frontal region of the brain is required for compassion, noting that fMRI scanning shows heightened activity when a person imagines actions for the larger social good, and increased immoral behavior when that region is damaged.[19] A person's brain must be able to have integrated, Me-Map, You-Map and We-Maps to maintain resourced compassion; otherwise if they get lost in the You-Map, burnout weighs them down.

Many of us do not necessarily feel safe in the world, and have belief systems and associated nervous system defense patterns to help protect us and keep others and the world out of our hearts. At one time, perhaps this helped us survive or was useful for some period, but living with a closed guarded heart is like walking around with a tense closed fist all of the time in case you need to punch someone—our heart like our hand is designed to open, close and reach out and touch others. When we feel angrily reactive or fearfully immobilized, it is difficult to live with an open heart, developing a greater compassion for our larger humanity with a larger span of Awareness—a larger interconnected whole—beyond our own exclusive concern with our own impulses, survival fears or self-esteem needs.

Our body physiology filters and affects our perception of the world. If we are stressed, scared or threatened, it colors how we see and feel the world, as it does when we are feeling relaxed and open-hearted. Chances are the same person would respond very differently to the same circumstances based on fearful stress or relaxed openness. The benefit of doing compassion and other developmental practices is that they train our nervous system to activate these body-based circuits more easily, more often and progressively changes our baseline nervous system functionality. This not only makes us more compassionate human beings but we get to experience some of the higher virtues of human presence such as deeper love, passion, ecstasy, joy, and beauty.

The two most significant barriers to empathy, perspective-taking, compassion, and impact are self-absorption and group-us-vs.-them-thinking. Remember the research done on the conventional people in which they reacted when their "friend" was potentially being shocked as they did when they themselves face the shock, but not when the "stranger" was shocked; if you only identify with yourself, your family, your friends or your group versus feeling a sense of universal humanness, then you stay in more limited bubble of possibility. Dan Siegel reminds us that "ironically, being personally happy *requires* that we greatly expand our narrowly defined individual preoccupations. *We* are built to be a *"we"*—and enter a more a more fulfilling state, perhaps a more natural way of being, when we connect in meaningful ways…Science has shown well-being and true happiness comes from defining ourselves as our "selves" as part of an interconnected whole—

connecting with others in authentic ways that break down the boundaries of a separate self."[20] As we feel beyond our self-absorbed view with expanded Awareness we can feel a sense of being an essential part of a larger unified world and an interconnected network of living creatures, each of which is an inseparable part of this living Aliveness.

True compassion by contrast is not the taking on of others pain but living with an open, compassionate heart from a deeper, more resourced presence and asking how we can we most be of service to our world in alleviating suffering and aligning with the evolutionary impulse of life in co-creating a better world for us all. Let us honor the compassion that radiates out of a brave heart, for it is easier to turn away and bury our heads in our electronic devices than really look at the state of the world and cultivate our unique gifts to be of service. This my friends, is found with presence, the essence of compassion, "to love together with".

Ken Wilber in one of my favorite all-time interviews, answers the question *"How does one know they are evolving?"* in a segment titled *Hurts More Bothers You Less*,

> *"the more awake you become...the more you actually feel the world...the pain increases...and so do the positive emotions...the happiness is happier and so on but...you become so sensitive you can feel everything that's arising for everybody...we have to give ourselves plenty of room to both feel absolute perfection in everything that's arising and yet see one person starving and you will start crying so hard it will kill you...that's extraordinary thing about that. So of course you want to work to alleviate suffering...but in the Absolute side, the analogy is if you're in a dream at night and there are thousands of people starving there are two ways you can stop their hunger, one is in the dream you can try to feed them all, the second is you can wake up and...they're both right they're both true and so playing both of those is what's so extraordinary...to engage that suffering without ever turning away and then again it hurts more bothers you...and why should you get involved because you made a deep deep promised at the bottom of your soul to do that and you really can't turn away."* [21]

➢ **EPIC**
  Empathy: the capacity to emotionally resonate with & share the feelings of another
  Perspectives: the capacity to mentally imagine & take multiple points of view
  Impact: the capacity to preemptively or retroactively imagine or sense the effect of words & actions on others & the world
  Compassion: the capacity to feel a heartfelt awareness of others' struggles that inspires a desire to radiate loving kindness or take action & be of service to alleviate suffering

➢ Paul Ekman's cross-cultural research demonstrates the universal nature of human emotions across cultures from people in industrialized cities to people in indigenous tribes being able to read & name specific emotions through facial expressions in still photos without ever even meeting. He has also shown that humans born blind, express the same emotions through the same facial expressions.

➢ Mirror Neuron system in our brains is thought to be the basis of empathy, language learning, POV perspective taking, skill learning via imitation, and even the ability to sense underlying intentions.

➢ A lack of emotional literacy & empathy could stem from either a lack of development since childhood, a shutting down of the function at some point, a lack of emotional presence with certain emotions such that we could empathize with others, or damaging of associated brain functions as in the case of autism spectrum disorder.

➢ When our resonance circuits are not developed, when we have high levels of unmet needs running us or when we are hijacked by heightened emotional intensity, we can lose awareness & a felt sense of others as fellow human beings & instead relate to others as objects.

➢ In addition to emotionally resonant attunement of another's state in empathy, we can also take mental perspectives by make complex perceptual maps imagining another point of view, intentions, & meaning-making lenses, which Siegel calls Me-Maps, You-Maps & We-Maps.

➢ Ultimately, the highest expression of impact awareness honoring the collective values of universal justice & care were epitomized by great social change leaders like Martin Luther King, Jr., Rosa Parks, Gandhi, Nelson Mandela & others who leveraged in their revolutionary campaigns toward greater equality, inspired by a sense of universal ideals such as the Golden Rule, the equality of human rights, respect for the dignity of each human being beyond gender, race, culture, religion or creed, rather than on concrete rules.

➢ Compassion means "to love together with" is a positive emotional state somewhere on the spectrum including a mixture of love, concern & a twinge of sadness. It requires a shared humanity of connection, identifying the person as a fellow living being & being able to feel that we share the same desires & struggles, like me, this other being is part of this living world that is not always easy.

➢ Because compassion is literally a body & brain-based capacity, like a muscle, we need to practice & strengthen our capacity for feeling compassion. Scientists studying compassion have discovered that the average person has a limit to how much intensity & duration that his or her body can feel compassion. Also practicing compassion as a motivation to service rather than empathetically taking on other people's states could even prevent fatigue & burnout.

➢ Let us honor the compassion that radiates out of a brave heart, for it is easier to turn away & bury our heads in our electronic devices than really look at the state of our world. True compassion is not the taking on of others pain but living with an open, compassionate heart from a deeper, more resourced presence while asking how we can we most be of service to our world in cultivating our greater human potential, alleviating suffering & aligning with the evolutionary impulse of life in co-creating a better world for us all.

BEHAVIORAL FLEXIBILITY & SHADOW

Did you know that when you negatively judge or positively idolize others, that it is a disowned shadow part of you?

Are you becoming more fixed in your identity as you age or becoming freer, more expressive & more functional?

How free are you in allowing a dynamic range of potential ways of being to be expressed without avoiding or overly identifying?

"The people in the world whom we hate, judge, or have strong negative reactions toward are direct representations of our disowned selves. Conversely, the people in the world whom we overvalue emotionally are also direct representations of our disowned selves."

- Hal & Sidra Stone -

WHAT IS **BEHAVIORAL FLEXIBILITY & SHADOW**
the capacity to accept & express a dynamic & even paradoxical range of ways of being without disowning or exclusively identifying

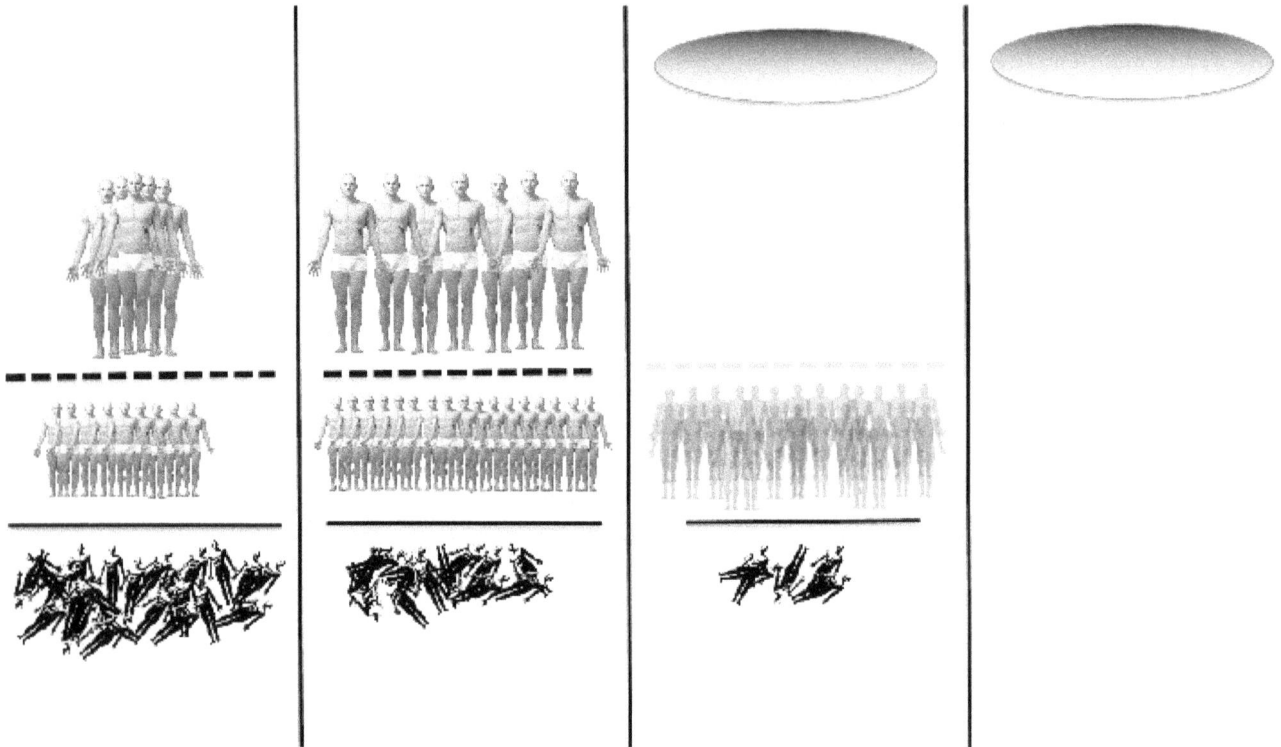

WHY DOES **BEHAVIORAL FLEXIBILITY & SHADOW** MATTER

Dynamic Range of Expression: allows freer more functional ways of being & expressing in work, relating & life

More Responsive & Skillful: less rigidity, compulsion & reactivity; more adaptable functional in the world

More Acceptance/ Less Critical: more acceptance & less criticism of self, others & life as more parts are allowed to be & express

Less Judgment of Others: all judgments are disowned parts that you project onto others or buried as unknown annoyances

Reclaiming Power: reintegrating disowned shadow aspects reclaims our own buried power & skills

Rapport & Intimacy: reclaiming irritations & annoyances; deeper connection thru embracing a greater range of ourselves & others

Freedom of expression: greater range of potential expression that feels more

Service: less motived by needs & greater capacity to be utilized as an instrument of service & contribution in the world

Paradox: more available life force comes with a greater ability to include the paradoxical spectrum of life

Immediacy & Emergence: less conditioned from the past, more free for something novel to emerge & be expressed

BARRIERS TO **BEHAVIORAL FLEXIBILITY & SHADOW**

Fearing & Judging the world: the parts within we cannot touch are projected out onto others & the world

Dissociation: limited range of expression due to not feeling & inhabiting your body due to trauma, defense or hyper-mental

Hyper-Mental: limited range of expression due to overly theoretical, living in fantasy, lost in the past or future,

Image Positioning: hiding something or trying to say something to be seen in a certain way or meet expectation

Hesitation or Withholding: guarded, hiding, fear of being judged or criticized, fear of saying the wrong thing

Fear of being Seen: hiding or blocking real expression to avoid criticism, disapproval or rejection

Shame: unreleased shame related to past experiences of feeling flawed, not good enough, rejected, judged, or not belonging

Fear of Rejection or Punishment: lie or morph your real expression to avoid disapproval & loss of connection

Stoic / Rigid: if certain qualities are buried & not allowed then we become fixed & rigid in relating

Emotion & Trauma: dead zones, suppressed emotions or body-stored trauma that keeps attention stuck in physical or dissociation

Limiting Beliefs / Disowned Shadows: assimilated experiences, beliefs & traumas that limited acceptable range of ways of being

Family or Cultural Norms: assimilated beliefs about which ways of being are acceptable in exchange for belonging

Lack of Experiential Opportunities: limited life experiences to express a more dynamic range of parts

Spiritual Bypassing: using spiritual practices & beliefs to avoid your emotions, body, life & participation in the world

BEHAVIORAL FLEXIBILITY & SHADOW DEVELOPMENT SUCCESS STORY

Like most adolescent minds, I had my preferences & prejudices, likes & dislikes, qualities I proudly identified as me & those that I judged in others & the world. Moving up to Berkeley in Northern California during my young 20s was like unexpectedly being thrown into a behavioral flexibility training simulation. San Francisco Bay area is perhaps one of the most progressive & technologically innovative as well as eccentric, hippy & new-agey place on the planet. The first few weeks my inner shadow judgment alarm system was going off almost continuously. Well, I didn't know any psychological techniques or 321 shadow processes at the time, so instinctually I tried to embrace alternative ways of being in the world as best as possible by opening my heart & mind while being more curious. Sometime later I took a workshop called voice dialogue where I learned more about the primary parts each of us identifies as a personal sense of self & that it is our own shadow parts we reject in ourselves & in so doing, judge externally in others. Fascinating & humbling at the same time, I started exposing myself to other ways of being, those that I had previously been unaware of, uninterested in, or judged in the world: watching documentaries, reading alternative articles, going to museums, racial/cultural/gender-orientation diverse events, etc. traveling to other countries experiencing other cultures' foods, tradition & ways of being was probably the most fun. I traveled through Europe exploring nine different countries in six weeks, which in a concentrated amount of time showed me what incredible range of behavior of flexibility we humans have. Then I started dancing & attending different experiential workshops to really increasingly embody a greater freedom in the range of ways of being. Eventually, I learned the 321 Shadow Process & started to integrate projected judgment charges & idolizations at the end of the day in reflection. As this noticing & Awareness increased, the reclamation process increasingly happened in real time. Eventually as the personal sense of self becomes increasingly transparent, fading in & out, increasing relaxing open as Awareness itself, the degree of freedom spontaneity & skillfulness in living & relating from immediacy increases dramatically. The shadow practice continues, with deeper & darker disowned parts being discovered, along with preferences & judgments ever more subtle; as the container expands to include more & more of the collective there is more Awareness spanning the range of light & dark.

"The more I meet you from the original presence of this moment I'm not anymore bound to my behavioral patterns. As long as I'm bound to the behavioral patterns, I cannot meet you out of spontaneous presence, from a more awake state because I will try to connect to you through my behavior. This means I need my behavior in order to compensate for something else. All of that is okay, and there is a possibility to awaken from it so it makes life more alive and less entangled. If I meet you from the deeper presence, my own clarity is not clouded from my own behavior that needs something in that moment, which means I can see you more clearly. Presence is a high clarity because it's original. It's fresh. The screen is empty. The screen is clear."

- Thomas Hubl -

HOW BEHAVIORAL FLEXIBILITY & SHADOW DEVELOPS

There is probably substantial disagreement about how behavior develops so we are not going to spend as much time going into that in this section. Perhaps we can agree that some combination of genetic nature and environmental nurture contribute to our developing human behavior, some of these many later (environmental nurture/conditioning) factors may include pregnancy, birthing experience and nursing, parent attachment style, sibling order, parenting, meeting developmental needs, trauma, education, culture, etc. On the genetic influence of behavior, numerous research studies have studied personality factors in identical twins separated at birth and raised apart; the most famous study of which has been following 100 sets of identical twins since 1979 confirms the genetic hypothesis of a significant portion of our personality, independent of environmental conditioning factors.

So rather than focusing on all those factors, let us instead start in the present moment and focus on the ways behavioral flexibility relates to presence—specifically to the self-actualization and self-transcendence processes discovered by Abraham Maslow, a leading pioneer of the human potential movement. In this section we will be exploring behavioral flexibility toward these two themes of self-actualization and self-transcendence, specifically related to understanding personality structures, including our primary ways of being, reclaiming buried shadow parts, becoming more integrated and functional in the world, and ultimately—after including more parts of our self—increasingly relaxing fixed behavioral structures into the vulnerable open-heartedness of love and profound freedom of deeper presence.

As we increasingly liberate ourselves from more rigid patterns of self-contracting limitations of personality temperament tendencies, dysfunctional personality, family and cultural beliefs based on unmet needs, survival strategies, getting attention, securing validation and maintaining connection, we get greater access to our human potential for greater responsive functionality in the world, more complex ways of being, more dynamic freedom of expression, more spacious Awareness and Presence.

> *Have we ever noticed that the inner dialogue within our mind often has conflicting viewpoints and at times can feel like an inner tug-a-war or debate?*
> *Have you ever noticed that we feel very different when you are working, versus studying for an exam, relaxing on vacation, playing sports, or making love?*
> *Have you noticed that the way you relate to your lover is different than your children, friends, boss, or strangers?*
> *Have you ever noticed the qualities we judge in others, we either do not like in ourselves or pretend it does not even exist in us?*

If we conceptualize our mind as being a single ego structure, as many traditional psychologists have done, then it does seem congruent with our experience. However, if we allow, as progressive psychologists Hal Stone PhD and Sidra Stone PhD say in their *Voice Dialogue*[3] that our sense of self is not as narrowly defined nor as fixed as some may think, but instead comprised of a multitude of different structural parts, then it is able to account for these seemingly conflicting motivations and ways of being. Note that this is distinct from multiple personality disorder (DID) where the person often has had a severe traumatic childhood experience and no longer has a continuity of awareness between one split personality and another. In other words, when they are in one distinct personality they do not have awareness of the others or remember what they did in another personality. It is like there is no CEO and the employees have no idea of what the others are doing. By contrast, according to *Voice Dialogue*, this multitude of parts also referred to as voices, sub-personalities, or potential behavior patterns—which are like pre-loaded human behavior programs built into the human psyche, existing in us all and that collectively comprise a constellation of our personality.

The word "**personality**" originates from the Latin word "**persona**", which literally means "*mask*". According to this theory, what we experience as our *personality* is essentially a combination of masks worn by our *true Self* 1. to function in the world, and 2. to protect its vulnerability from social harm (judgment, criticism, loss of connection or loss of love). These masks are not good or bad; rather just seems to be how the *human game* is played. These parts are the potential ways of behaving that we use to express ourselves in interacting in the world and relating to other people. A good analogy is to that of a CD changer with more than a hundred CDs that each plays a separate genre of music. Common potential ways of behaving include the following: *Gatekeeper/Protector, Controller, Critic, Perfectionist, Slob, Pusher, Relaxer, Pleaser, Selfish, Health, Sporty, Playful, Victim, Seeker, Power, Sexuality, Skeptic, Rationality, Warrior,* etc.

PARTS: POTENTIAL WAYS OF BEHAVING

Let us assume that our sense of self is trying to help us survive physically, emotionally and socially—which means relationally getting and maintaining praise, respect, freedom, and love, while generally trying to avoid criticism, rejection or un-love. As we are learning to orient to the world this translates as our operating system, (ego) paying attention to what to move and what to try to avoid. In an oversimplified way, this organizes certain parts to the forefront and attempts to bury other parts.

For example, if we expressed anger and were severely punished as a child, or if a parent had uncontrollable anger and hurt a family member in the midst of rage, then our mind might decide it is not safe or praiseworthy to express anger. In this example, the part of anger is disowned or becomes a shadow, which might manifest as us asserting that *"I don't get angry"* and then we are judging people that get angry. This might come out in our dreams as an angry character, or thinking others in our life have anger problems but not us, or having an underlying subtle feeling of anger, or even worse coming out as unconscious outburst at inopportune times. This burying of our potential ways of behaving, or disowning shadow aspects is equivalent to locking a child in the closet after it acts inappropriately a couple times and then trying to permanently deny its existence. Wanting to be honored as the other kids, it tries to get our attention by feeling irritated by certain qualities in others or wildly breaking out in inopportune scenarios.

SHADOW

The famous Swiss psychiatrist Carl Jung originally brought forth the concept of the shadow, which he considered to be aspects of the unconscious mind that were repressed, anything that lies outside the light of Conscious Awareness.[4] Ken Wilber offers a practical life application test to this describing a shadow as *"any part of consciousness that we cannot acknowledge in the first person as 'I'*".[5]   When an aspect of our sense of self poses a physical or social survival threat, our inner *Gatekeeper* can decide it is unacceptable and might be safer to try to bury it out of Awareness, and in rejecting it, it essentially says *"this quality is not me, it is in someone else"* (negative charge or positive idolization). In this case, a quality that threatens its social acceptance, the primary sense of the self system projects onto the 2nd person or buries it deep into the unconscious. When we project it, we transfer the quality from a 1st person "*I*" to a 2nd person "*you*". Why out of all the hundreds of human qualities someone possesses does that one particular quality bother us? The answer is because that judgment of an "*other*" reflects some quality within ourselves that is disowned or not acknowledged. If we totally reject the quality completely out of the light of conscious Awareness after hiding it away, it becomes a deeply buried 3rd person "*it,*" in which case a shadow arises as a sense of irritation, aversion, (or in the light side attractive idolization awkward wording) so unconscious we usually do not even know *why* we feel this way. Again, Ken Wilber and his colleagues at Integral Institute, especially Diane Hamilton[6], have designed a the 3-2-1 Shadow Process designed to help us reclaim these buried parts of ourselves, using shifts in perspectives as a way of re-identifying and re-integrating disowned shadow material—which we go into in greater depth in the Presence Academy online course.

Jung noted that *"everyone carries a shadow and the less it is embodied in the individual's conscious life, the blacker and denser it is."*[7]   Many of these disowned selves are often those deemed socially inappropriate such as **Selfishness**, **Aggression**, **Loud** & **Bold**, etc. However, others can be remarkably creative and powerful, but were perhaps discouraged along the way and were subsequently disowned such as: **Power, Aggression, Spontaneity, Sexuality, Relaxation, Spirituality**, etc. Similarly, certain other subpersonality parts are disowned relative to our cultural norms of behavior: **Pride, Brutal Honesty, Anger, Extravagance, Laziness, Irrationality, Humor, Self-Confidence**, etc.

Although our basic tendency is to be repelled by our disowned shadow parts, they can sometimes hold a fascination and magnetism to a disowned part in another and we can be attracted to relationships with people who embody disowned parts within ourselves as our psyche's goal is to be more integrated and realize the whole world is potentially inside. So, while we may be initially fascinated by that quality in our new lover during the honeymoon phase, it may change flavors to irritation or repulsion the more we have to face that quality in the other person that we have disowned in ourselves. We can assume the world is beckoning us to be as integrated and whole as possible, which might mean we attract in relationships with friends, teachers or a romantic partner the very qualities we have tried to bury in the basement of our own mind. The range of behavior and potential of the whole world lives inside and until we acknowledge these parts in ourselves, we will seek to complete ourselves in relationship and judge/idolize them in others.

DISOWNED POSITIVE SHADOWS

Just as we bury dark shadow aspects of ourselves, Carl Jung realized that we can also disown light aspects. These buried parts are not only those we negatively judge, but can also be those we wish we had. At the other end of the spectrum is the positive shadow or qualities we overly admire in others but are unable to recognize in ourselves. These qualities can be recognized when we feel an excessively positive admiration or attraction to a certain quality embodied in another person. Statements like *"she's so beautiful...I could never be that beautiful"* reflects less of an objective physical view of characteristics because research shows cultural perceptions of physical features are relative to culture and time period, but rather an inner radiance or way she carries herself. This does not involve technical skills like being a concert pianist, but rather subjective feeling states and qualities of behavior. Others include: *"Wow! He is so caring", "Wow she is so wise", "Wow! She is so funny"*, etc. Notice that the wow indicates a positive emotional charge or idolization, not a compliment of mutual recognition. Remember the whole realm of potential human ways of being lies inside of us. The whole point is rather than using the 5-7 subpersonalities of our primary self-system 95% of the time, we can loosen our exclusive identification with just a few and expand our potential to include a greater range of possibility and freedom of expression. This process of evolving from an unconscious, limited *Primary Self System* to an Aware Ego Witnessing Puppeteer, to Awakening Presence creates a much *more free, functional, and dynamic life*. Through the *Voice Dialogue* process, a person can embrace both sides of the spectrum to thus more freely and consciously choose the appropriate part to use in the appropriate situation. So pay attention to our judgments and idolizations; be curious about what is underneath them.

ALL JUDGMENT IS A REFLECTION OF OUR DISOWNED SHADOW PARTS

For clarity, simplicity and ease of language, let us refer to the critic as being more internally oriented, and judgment as being external. Nobody likes to feel judged and yet we all judge others to varying degrees. It started in childhood, as our parents, relatives, and teachers tried to mold us to conform to their personal and cultural belief systems. Whether we changed our behavior to conform or rebelled, we likely subtly assimilated their judgments. Perhaps our own inner critic added their judgments to its internal lists of *"should and should not engage"* into maintain social esteem and criticized us if we violated those rules to protect ourselves from further judgments and loss of love.

As we grow, this process continues whether people judge us silently or through words. The adage *"it's not what you say but how you say it that counts"* is quite true. In this case, as we can feel an air of judgment from people. Along with past shame, fear of judgment is one of the most significant blocks to true vulnerability, (see the *Vulnerability section*) which is required for deeper connection from an open heart.

Whomever or whatever we judge in another person is ultimately an indication of a disowned shadow part of within ourselves. Underneath our judgment of the "*other*" is an intense negative repulsive charge (or positive alluring charge when we idolize our own shadow in others), which is the defining factor of a disowned part within us. Remember that most people have a constellation of a few parts that collectively comprise their sense of personal self which Hal and Sidra Stone refer to as the *Primary Self System* and those few parts have their *own agendas, values, and motivations*. If for example, a person's *Primary Self System* included **the Perfectionist, the Inner Critic, the Pusher, the Responsible**, and **the Organizer**, this "*Super Mom*" might be strongly oriented to keeping her house spotlessly clean, organized, and efficient. Imagine then that on the spectrum of neat-freak—organized—slob, she was pushing the farthest boundary for *Mrs.* Clean and had disowned the *Slob*; assume that messiness is one of the things that bothers her most. Now, because her primary self-system's directive is for her to realize wholeness and that all human potentials lie inside her, she might attract a partner, son, friend, employee, etc. who represents that disowned part of herself and she would likely have significant negative internal emotion charge and external projected judgment about this quality. The same would be true if in the opposite direction it would be imbalanced and possibly dysfunctional, if someone only was identified with the *Slob* and didn't know how to engage any degree of cleanliness or organization when necessary; if she was so identified with the

Perfectionist and the *Organizer* that she spent excessive time cleaning and organizing to the sacrifice of other important areas of her life including open-hearted connection. We do not have to regularly use our disowned selves, in this case, the Slob, but rather to allow that these extremes are both human potentials and without strong emotional charge and over-identification to one side to be able to more consciously choose when to engage cleanliness and organization and when it is more functional to relax and not worry as much about those things. Also recognize that it is from the perspectives and values of the Primary Self-System (in this example *the Perfectionist, the Inner Critic, the Pusher, the Responsible, and the Organizer*) from which the judgment comes. The *Aware Ego*, or *Puppeteer*, who embraces all and holds all the strings of the subpersonality parts does not judge; it is the other primary parts that judge our other teammates.

THE QUALITIES WE JUDGE POSSESS POWER & SKILLS FOR US TO RECLAIM

The objects, ideas, or people that we judge the most intensely can be our greatest teachers helping us to integrated split off parts of our integrated self. Our judgments can illuminate the hidden shadows of our mind and once integrated lead to greater wholeness, spontaneity, enjoyment, as well as functionality, skill, and success in the world. Our modern world is full of prejudice and judgment. The judgments are by primary parts projected out at others via inordinate emotional reaction the buried shadow parts within ourselves. We project judgments onto loved ones, friends, coworkers, political figures, actors, athletes, performers, etc. Judgment is so rampant and frequent that we usually don't even realize that we are engaging in frequent judgments. We all do this to varying degrees. However, the least judgmental people are the most integrated, because those parts they accept within themselves they also accept externally in others and the world. Just as we want to embrace all potential ways of being, if we try to disown *judgment* and get rid of it all together (*"I'm a non-judgmental person"*) then we also bury it's virtuous upper half *discernment*—the wise heart-open Awareness and being a good *"judge"* of character. If we disown judgment then we will lose access to the whole spectrum of these virtues. There is a difference between *judgment* with a closed heart, emotionally negative charge and a repulsion to the judged quality versus a spacious, wise, open-hearted *discernment* that allows and sees with clarity as it is for its virtue and darker impacts, that quality in one's own personality systems and the world. So, instead of saying *"don't judge,"* instead invite ourselves or others to own their own judgments and use them to reclaim buried parts of themselves that possess locked up power and skill. It also wastes a lot of our potential energy to suppress parts of ourselves. Reclaiming shadows not only makes us freer to express a wider range of potential behaviors making us more functional, responsive and skillful in work and life, but it really increases our compassion and improves the closeness of our relationships when we are maintaining distance due to being repulsed by our own projected shadows.

EACH PART HAS A DUAL NATURE WITH LIGHT/DARK FEATURES

As we just illustrated with *discernment/judgment*, each part has its light (functional strengths and virtues) in addition to its darker (harmful and destructive) side. The Rebel part, for example, is commonly thought of in its darker, more destructive form or but its upside can be a powerful force leading to an unprecedented social change in the midst of illegitimate authority (historical examples include: slavery abolitionists, Rosa Parks, Gandhi, and Martin Luther King, Jr). So, we ideally want to embrace all parts with greater Awareness so that we get access to the polarity of each quality, especially its virtues.

DEEP ACCEPTANCE FOR REINTEGRATING

From the perspective that *the ego* is not a single entity but rather a **collection of parts** each with specific motivations and rules of engagement—each is just doing its job and the fallacy is to get mad at a single part for carrying out orders when the real problem is unconscious identification with just a few parts, poor integration and an attempted burying of other parts. Integration doesn't sound that sexy and desirable, but when we get the freedom and skillfulness its importance becomes apparent. Just like a sports player that can only run straight as opposed to the flexible functionality of being able to agilely move in multiple directions, so too someone with greater behavioral flexibility is able to express himself or herself in the world with greater responsiveness, flexibility, spontaneity, creativity, humor, depth, freedom, and effectiveness. The less behavioral flexibility and the more unintegrated shadows, the more rigid, stuck, dull, boring, and inflexibly habitual or chaotic, reactive, and unconscious our behavior is likely to be.

LEADING THE INNER TEAM WITH THE AWARE EGO

As we begin the process of becoming more aware of these primary parts, secondary parts, and buried parts, we can cultivate the freedom to drive our own chariot or lead our inner team as a conductor rather than unconsciously being dragged through life by our collection of primary parts (operating ego). Hal & Sidra Stone, creators of *Voice Dialogue Theory*[8], acknowledge that this is an evolving process of being unconsciously being run by our *Operating Ego of Primary Selves* to leading our inner team as the *Aware Ego*. As we become increasingly conscious of our inner parts and who is present each moment, we increasingly develop the Awareness and Freedom to choose which part to responsively engage in the appropriate situation.

Thus the *Aware Ego* can be compared to a Puppeteer, Symphony Conductor, or Charioteer. As the *Aware Ego* increasingly takes the reins, the primary parts continue to operate, but as awareness grows and we are able to consciously switch out of them without being unconsciously identified with/led by them. Thus the *Aware Ego* development is a process by which the primary parts lose power as exclusively identified drivers as they are increasingly seen as objects, as we develop greater behavioral flexibility or dexterity in our freedom of allowing secondary parts to increasingly express themselves and also reintegrate our disowned shadow parts. Rather than having our orchestra conductor tied up below and a few instruments (parts) playing their own tunes, an *Aware Ego* is a more conscious and skilled conductor standing above a much greater range of instruments to choose from depending on the situation. The *Aware Ego* is a coordinating mechanism that mediates between the parts, and the more we are able to embrace the multiplicity of parts within us without exclusively identifying with just a few, the more we are able to play in more dynamic and harmonious tune and functionally orchestrate our lives in greater smoothness and skill. Ultimately, one goal from many people is not to necessarily act out all ways of being, but instead to consciously embrace the whole world within ourselves and in doing so, actualize the power and freedom of being a highly functional integrated human being in the world.

FREEDOM FROM THE PAST

Thomas Hubl points us to possibility in articulating *"sometimes when you meet clearer people, like people who have transcended and included parts in themselves, they are not so easy to predetermine. It's not so easy to put them in a box because their field is freer from structures that provide hooks for other people to plug into...Sometimes a lot of fear can come up. Sometimes it's just a shot of refreshment so you need to open your eyes and look who is there and really meet presence with presence."*[9]

Of course, on one level, being nicer would make a positive impact on the world, yet Mystic Thomas Hubl describes a scenario in which playing nice can come with an underlying fear as well as the deeper presence beyond nice / not nice:

> *"The past means the wiring in me, in my behavior, in my expression that has already a preformed direction. So if I need to be nice to you because I'm afraid of you, if I need to be nice because I'm afraid of aggression, they already had a preformed offer into this moment. If my energy field is present, there is neither nice nor not nice. It's not about being not nice. It's about freedom. A loving meeting can happen, but it's not there to protect me from aggression. I'm not smiling at you that you will not hurt me. I'm here to meet you. If there is a danger, my intuition will tell me because I'm present enough. If there is no danger, I don't need to smile at you. You don't hurt me because it's my past that tells me this, that there is a danger, not the current moment. That's a big difference."* [10]

BEING INSTRUMENTS OF SERVICE

Sometimes people try to be of service to secure righteousness and rewards in their afterlife; other people want to be helpful to prove their worthiness or lovability, and still, others to try to make themselves feel better and make up for past wrong-doing

---

BEHAVIORAL FLEXIBILITY & SHADOW SUMMARY & KEY TAKEAWAYS

➤ Behavioral flexibility allows us greater self-actualization & self-transcendence: specifically more responsive & less reactive defensiveness, less rigidity, less habitual & exclusively identified, more integrated & functionality in the world & more dynamic freedom of expression.

➤ Voice Dialogue Psychologists Hal Stone PhD & Sidra Stone PhD conceptualize our sense of self not as a single fixed entity but as a constellation of parts each with specific motivations, rules of engagement & potential behavior patterns that are like pre-loaded human behavior programs built into our human psyche & existing in us all.

➤ Each subpersonality part has a dual light/dark nature with functional strengths & virtues as well as more dysfunctional & harmful sides.

➤ Shadow: Carl Jung originated the concept of the shadow, which he considered to be aspects of the unconscious mind that were repressed, anything that lies outside the light of Conscious Awareness, while Ken Wilber offers a practical life application test to this describing a shadow as "any part of consciousness that we cannot acknowledge in the first person as 'I'".

- Disowned shadows can have light positive or dark negative aspects.
- Negative Shadows: The people we judge are like mirrors that reflect own hidden shadow parts. The objects, ideas, or qualities in people that we judge with a negative emotional charge point us to the hidden disowned shadows of our mind that once integrated lead to greater wholeness, spontaneity, enjoyment, as well as functionality, skill & success in the world
- Light Shadows: disowned subpersonality parts are not only those we negatively judge, but can also be those positive qualities we wish we had, qualities that we admire in others but have not yet embodied or are unable to recognize in ourselves. These qualities can be recognized when we feel a positive charge or admiration or attraction to a certain quality embodied in others.
- Shadow in relationship: Although our common tendency is to be repelled by our disowned parts, they can sometimes hold a fascination & magnetism to a disowned self in another. We can be attracted into relationships with people who embody parts that we have disowned as our psyche's goal is to be more integrated a& realize the whole world is potentially inside. So, while we might initially be fascinated by a strange quality in a new partner, eventually that shadow quality might begin to irritate us, as again it is an unacknowledged part within ourselves.
- Disowned shadow parts are subpersonalities that have been partially or totally excluded from our conscious awareness & life. The judgment & intense emotions attached to disowned parts require tremendous energy to keep suppressed, contained & disowned. In an attempt to eradicate certain parts of our psyche that we don't like, we make them stronger by driving them into the unconscious where they tend to limit our range of expression & act out in unconscious ways. It is only when we face acknowledge & integrate the shadow's presence inside us can we neutralize its potential negative impact on us.
- It is possible to honor a subpersonality part & allow it to be integrated without having to live it. Just because we acknowledge the potential to act in a certain way does not mean that we will or have to.
- Rather than getting mad at a single part for carrying out orders, the real problem is more related to unconscious identification with just a few parts, poor integration & an attempted burying of other parts.
- To begin to notice & reclaim disowned parts, pay attention to the emotional negative charges you feel in your body or the admirations in relation to others.
- The 3-2-1 Shadow Process helps us reclaim these buried parts of ourselves, using shifts in perspectives as a way of re-identifying & re-integrating disowned shadow material from 3rd to 2nd to 1st person perspectives.

STAGES OF WORLDVIEW DEVELOPMENT

On a daily basis, how wide of a world are you aware of ?

- Me just my personal experience, desires, needs & survival

- Me & my family/friends

- Me & family/friends & tribe/community

- Me & family/friends & tribe & country

- Me & family/friends & tribe & country & global humanity

- Me & family/friends & tribe & country & humanity & cosmos

"The depth and capacity of what a person can notice can expand throughout life...
at each developmental stage, there are capacities available that weren't imaginable before"...

"as development unfolds, autonomy, freedom, tolerance for ambiguity, as well as flexibility, reflection, and skill
in interacting with the environment increase while defenses decrease."
–Susanne Cook-Greuter

WHAT ARE **STAGES OF WORLDVIEW DEVELOPMENT**
the developmental structure of the human ego in its progressive capacity to expand its span of identity, worldview & values

more
PRESENCE

less
PRESENCE

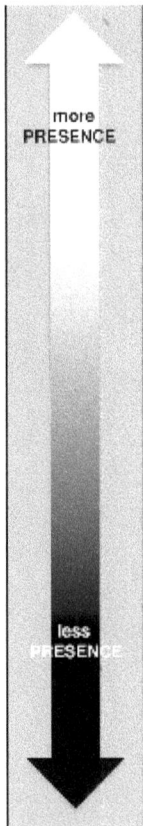

UNITIVE **Unified – Emergent Elegance (& beyond)**
TOURQUISE **Experiential - Construct Aware**
TEAL **Integral – Functional Self-Actualizing**
GREEN **Relative – Authentic Connective**
ORANGE **Rational – Achieving Individual**
AMBER **Mythic - Fundamentalist Member**
RED **Power Gangs – Impulsive Exploitive**
MAGENTA **Magic - Tribal Animistic**
INFRARED **Archaic – Survival Instinctive**

WHY **STAGES OF WORLDVIEW DEVELOPMENT** MATTERS

Self-Awareness: understanding your current values, worldview & sense of identity

Mapping your Journey: understanding your developmental history & next phase

Group-Awareness: understanding predominant value systems in a group, organization, industry, culture or nation

Compassion: for humanity in our uniqueness & diversity; each of us being on a similar developmental journey

Development Enhancing: as development increases so does span of Awareness, while exclusive identity with self-centeredness
    decreases

Acceptance: ability to receive & integrate feedback increases as does acceptance of self, others & the moment

Authentic Freedom: the freer & less conditioned the sense of self, the greater is the capacity for novel, spontaneous, transparent
undefended & authentic expression

STAGES OF WORLDVIEW DEVELOPMENT BARRIERS

Lack of Awareness: not being aware of this developmental map & research
Resistance: blocks to consideration
Disowning of Hierarchy: Green stage can tend to be anti-hierarchical
Cognitive Capacity: limits of understanding
Self-Absorption: overly focused on having your own needs met before being resourced enough to attend to someone else

STAGES OF WORLDVIEW DEVELOPMENT SUCCESS STORY

Connor was born out of the oceanic consciousness of his mother's womb and like every human baby was initially completely dependent on his caregivers for survival (INFRARED). As a toddler, he was animated by instincts & his five senses. As he continued to grow (MAGENTA), develop & explore the world, he followed the way of his parents for whom his survival, shelter, warmth & nourishment depended upon. Next (RED) as a growing child, his will began to develop & he exerted force to get what he wanted & satisfy his impulses & desires. Egocentric with limited time awareness in a world of magical forces in which he wanted to play, he wanted to do what he felt like when he wanted. The only thing that tempered his impulses was his desire to avoid punishment & maintain his parents' love. As a teenager growing up in a fundamentalist religious (AMBER) family, he sought to understand the rules, to live a more righteous life, to belong as a good socially acceptable young man & member of the church, converting others to the one right way of living so that he & they could be righteous enough to earn a future reward in heaven. Eventually, as he continued to develop (ORANGE) & more frontal activity came online in his brain, he became more self-reflective, rationally question previous assumptions about the previous worldview. He began to have his own individualistic achievement goals & increasingly saw how combined with intention, action & hard work, he could achieve his goals, be successful & earn personal freedom. He was ambitious & studious, excelling in the University & industriously working side jobs to earn money. Yet, at a certain point (GREEN) he began to realize there were more ingredients to happiness than merely his own personal success. He wanted to live his authentic life, help others & contribute to a more peaceful, sustainable world. His medium became international development working with indigenous peoples in Africa & South America. As he continued to evolve he realized merely helping or supplanting our Americanized ways onto these other cultures was not the most effective way to sustainable enhance their development. He started to see systems within systems (INTEGRAL), understanding the most empowering longer-term multi-factorial interventions were those that actually empowered leaders in their own cultural context from within, then training others to do the same all over the world & be functional actualizing participants in our evolving world. We began working together in a coaching capacity to include greater relaxation inside with greater attunement, empathy & connection with others while leveraging his system's thinking, functionality & effectiveness so that he could further actualize his unique purpose & gifts while contributing to the evolution of humanity.

> *"No problem can be solved from the same level of consciousness that created it."*
>
> - Albert Einstein -

UNITIVE **Unified – Emergent Elegance (& beyond)**
TOURQUISE **Experiential - Construct Aware**
TEAL **Integral – Functional Self-Actualizing**
GREEN **Relative – Authentic Connective**
ORANGE **Rational – Achieving Individual**
AMBER **Mythic - Fundamentalist Member**
RED **Power Gangs – Impulsive Exploitive**
MAGENTA **Magic - Tribal Animistic**
INFRARED **Archaic – Survival Instinctive**

Please note that this section is about worldview and identity so be careful NOT to identify too much with a stage. Your stage of development is like a lens; it is not "you". The totality of "YOU" is much greater. All systems and models are merely maps designed to help you navigate the terrain of being human. Be open-minded and curious, see what resonates and could be useful. As Bruce Lee once said, "Research your own experience, accept what is useful, reject what is not & express something uniquely your own."

HOW THE IDENTIFY, VALUES & WORLDVIEW OF EGO DEVELOPMENT DEVELOPS

It is visibly obvious that a child goes through specific stages of development from birth to infancy and into childhood nursing, crawling, walking, running, cooing, talking, etc. Although Childhood Development is a well-established field in psychology, some researchers began focusing on how adults continue to develop from an infant's self-centered worldview into mature adulthood. They were curious how some adults' behaviors and worldviews still resembled the impulsivity and egocentrism of teenager development, while other people seemed to continue on to develop greater maturity, wisdom, and effectiveness while engaging with increasing complexity in the world. Fascinatingly, just as in childhood development, they discovered that adult development also tends to grow in specific stages, which has been validated by research across cultures, regardless of gender, race or personally since the late 1960's. Developmental psychology researchers over the past four decades have clarified that adults can continue to mature and develop in terms of stages of ego development which includes a mix of identity, worldview and values. Indeed, there appear to be specific structure stages of adult ego development, each of which tends to evolve in complexity in the way that we view, interpret and relate to the world (worldview), terms of our value-systems (what is important) and self-identity (what "I" identify with). So humans tend to develop from birth through adulthood in a progressive sequence of stages, which we might imagine looks like an increasingly widening spiral—indeed one of the most popular Stage Development theory systems is named *Spiral*

Dynamics originally developed by Clare Graves. Although others including Ken Wilber[1], Suzanne Cook-Greuter[2], Jenny Wade[3], Don Beck and Chris Cowan[4], have researched and theorized their own versions of these stages of development, despite a few subtle nuanced distinctions, overall their models share astonishing consistency.

Stages of development are an important quality of developing presence because they illuminate what we value most (values) and can include in our span Awareness (worldview) without exclusively identifying with as an ego (identity). This Stage Development theory describes the evolution in individuals, groups, and cultures towards greater span of identity, worldview perspective-taking, and values—all of which impacts our effectiveness and ability to relate to greater complexity in life. Being aware of the trajectory of our developmental history which we share with all humanity, we can clarify our current orientation as well as what is next for us. Furthermore, it can help us understand the center of gravity (average baseline stage of developmental worldview) of the family, organization, community or nation we are a part of and help us relate to others with greater compassion and effectiveness. Understanding these stages and how they tend to develop can also offer an inspiring view of our collective human evolutionary trajectory and potential.

INFRARED Archaic – Survival Instinctive

WORLDVIEW:
Motto: survive my own way
Primary Motivation: survival & satisfying instinctive biological urges & drives
Theme: life is a struggle; I do what I have to do to stay alive
Thinkning: instinctual 5 senses
Time Concept: present simple

IDENTITY:
Identity: no distinct self-differentiated from others or the environment

VALUES:
Survival: staying alive, fed & warm
Instinctual: animated by natural instincts, 5 senses & survival impulses
Physiological Needs: water, food, shelter, warmth, sex
Safety Needs: protect myself & my stuff

EMERGENCE in HUMAN HISTORY: Semi-Stone Age 250,000 years ago
OCCURRENCE: infants; mentally ill homeless & institutionalized, late-stage Alzheimer's, dependent elderly

MAGENTA Magic - Tribal Animistic

WORLDVIEW:
Motto: follow & appease the way of the ancestors
Primary Motivation: staying safe, warm & fed as a tribe by honoring the way & rituals of the ancestors & staying in good favor with the spirits
Theme: honor, obey & appease the elders, parents, ancestors & spirits
Thinking: magical
Time Concept: present simple day to day with an honoring of the past which is alive in the present[5]

IDENTITY:
ego-centric with focus on safety & gratification of impulses & basic needs

VALUES:
Tribal Magic: interpreting magical signs & desires of spirit beings
Stay Safe & Secure: the world is dangerous & alive with mystery
Tradition: following the rituals & way of ancestors
Honor: honoring the ancestors, traditions as well as sacred objects, places, things
Tribe/Family Loyalty & Bonds: respecting, obeying & allegiance to chief, elders, ancestors, parents & the clan
Animistic: everything has a spirit (rocks, water, plants, animals, people, etc.),
Spirits Must be Appeased: good spirits make good things happen while bad spirits can curse
Tribal Rituals: rites of passage, cycles of nature, superstitions, luck charms & curses/vengeance

EMERGENCE in HUMAN HISTORY: 50,000 years ago
OCCURRENCE: very young children; some adults in gangs, indigenous tribes & less developed countries

RED Power Gangs – Impulsive Exploitive

WORLDVIEW:
Motto: I & my gang has to be the most powerful way
Primary Motivation: self-serving power-oriented focus on own needs, interests & protection
Theme: world is a wild jungle where the strong dominate while the weak serve
Thinking: concrete short-term
Time Concept: present simple day to day predominates with very short view of past & future, low impulse control & ability to foresee consequences of actions[6]

IDENTITY:
ego-centric with impulsive focus on the gratification of desires, power, self-protection & personal advantage

VALUES:
Power & Dominance: being powerful or aligning with those in power for protection & provision
Impulsive Action: do what I want & feel like, I react by the impulses I feel if I want something I want it now
Immediate Gratification & Sensory Pleasure: do what feels good & enjoy as much as I can while avoiding shame
No Guilt or Remorse: do what I want, no matter; my only inhibition is to avoid punishment
Reactive: strong fight/flight/freeze response, quick to fight or attack,
Belonging & Loyalty to my Gang: aligned subservience to those in power who will provide & keep me safe
Protection: need for self-protection to cover my sense of vulnerability
Self-Serving Exploitation: dominance & exploitation of others, slavery & exploitation of unskilled labor
Respect: proving myself using courage, cunning & aggression for respect & my belongingness to the gang

EMERGENCE in HUMAN HISTORY: 15,000 years ago
OCCURRENCE: young children terrible 2's thru teenagers, gangs, feudal kingdoms, wild rock stars

AMBER Mythic - Fundamentalist Member

WORLDVIEW:
Motto: be good & live the one right way with us
Primary Motivation: stability, belonging, righteousness & future reward
Theme: be a good person & member by following the rules of the one right way to gain future reward
because life is controlled by a Higher Power that punishes evil & rewards good deeds & righteousness
Thinking: mythic literal absolute (black & white)
Time Concept: past, present, future; past & future extend in imagination beyond personal experience but hypothetical futures bound by historical past[7]

IDENTITY:
group/nation-centric oriented to righteousness & group belonging through conformity & value adoption; self sense is defined by relation to the group (us vs. them), sacrificing self for a larger nationalistic or religious cause

VALUES:
Fundamentalist: there is literally one right way
Absolute Thinking: right/wrong, good/bad, white/black, us/them, speak from memory & generality
Us vs. Them: either you are a member of our group or against us, differing values are vilified or avoided
Belonging: desire to be accepted & patriotic membership to group or country
Righteous Living: morality, duty, faith, integrity, self-control, stability, order, family, righteousness
Missionary: attend to social welfare of our own group & convert others to the one right way
Conforming: maintain rules & stability of the group which defines righteous living & socially acceptable behavior
Obedience: to higher authority & rules, conformity & duty now to earn future reward
Controlling Impulsivity: enforce not following the rules through guilt

EMERGENCE in HUMAN HISTORY: 5,000 years ago
OCCURRENCE: can begin in teens, religious fundamentalists, totalitarianism, national patriotism

ORANGE Rational – Achieving Individual

WORLDVIEW:
Motto: the most successful way
Primary Motivation: self-reliance to achieve material progress, success & freedom
Theme: If I learn the rules of the game and strive to be my best, I can achieve my goals & be successful
Thinking: rational; more interested in reasons & causes, capable of self-reflection & longer-term planning
Time Concept: past, present, future; present is a composite of the past, but it may or may not determine the future; future orientation is for setting goals & working towards achieving them[8]

IDENTITY:
World-centric externally oriented toward self-esteem & autonomy: personal freedom, achievement, success, & material progress through the use of science & individual effort, yet with a more mature sense of responsibility

VALUES:
Achievement & Prosperity: striving, professional development, optimism, success, wealth
Self-Reliance: individualism, financial Independence & personal freedom
Consumption: use of the earth's resources for material progress, status, *"the good life"*
Goal-driven & Action-Oriented: effective use of time competitive & opportunistic to achieve results, improve & get ahead
Competition: strategy, improvement & growth
Practical: demonstrated results & efficiency,
Rational Objectivity: cause & effect, laws of science can explain life
Science & Technology: interested to understand reasons & causes to conquering nature & prosper

EMERGENCE in HUMAN HISTORY: Scientific Revolution 300 years ago
OCCURRENCE: Capitalism, Corporate America, materialism, fashion industry, sales, marketing, Scientific Revolution, genetic engineering

GREEN Relative – Authentic Connective

WORLDVIEW:
Motto: all ways are relative yet equal
Primary Motivation: be authentic & create peace, connection, community & sustainability the world
Theme: everything is relative but every one authentic expression deserves to be honored & together we can co-create a more connected, sustainable & harmonious world
Thinking: relative connective, inclusive, shift toward inner experience (*previous stages exterior focused*)
Time Concept: greater awareness of past, present, future; present is a composite of the past but it may or may not determine the future

IDENTITY:
world-centric-self seeking authentic expression & connection in holistic relation to others in a relative world

VALUES:
Peace, Love, & Harmony
Connection: inclusive, community, bonding, dialoguing, collaboration & sharing resources
Humanitarian: caring, helping & responding to human needs & equal distribution of resources
Relativism: everything is relative depending on perspective, multiple perspectives aware, pluralism
Authenticity: self-expression, vulnerability, emotional awareness, examines previous self-identities
Ecological Sustainability: sensitivity to the environment
Diversity Celebration: multicultural worldview, human rights, equality, tolerance, individual differences
Sensitivity: honoring everyone's feelings, perspective & voice; feeling heard & acknowledged
Consensus Decisions: we are all equal everyone so everyone's voice deserved to be included in decisions
Alternative: holistic health, questioning assumptions & conventions, anti-hierarchy, anti-capitalism
Spirituality: spiritual but not religious

EMERGENCE in HUMAN HISTORY: 1960's years ago
OCCURRENCE: universities & academia, sustainability, holistic health, yoga communities, hippies, environmental & diversity/human rights advocates, Authentic Relating

TEAL Integral – Functional Self-Actualizing

WORLDVIEW:
Motto: the best option for now with all things considered
Primary Motivation: to be integrated, living fully & functionally in the world, developing & actualizing our unique potentials as we increasingly participate in & create systems that contribute to the collective evolution
Theme: I & you & We & It are all evolving
Thinking: evolutionary integrative & systemic, functional interdependent & prioritizing
Time Concept: infinite past & future; present is a composite of the past & orientation to self-author desired future[9]

IDENTITY:
integrating multiple sub-personalities into a complex yet coherent enduring core sense of self-identity which is a culmination of all previous development[10]

VALUES:
Integration
Self-Actualization: life-long learner, seeks feedback for growth & meaning-making, greatest fear is unfulfilled potential,
Skillfulness & Competence: dynamic functional competence, best action for now with all things considered, excellence
Best Practices: hacking, recognizes underlying principles, prioritization, integrating theory/principles/application
Systemic Strategic Thinking: aware of dynamic systems interactions, systemic change agents,
Complexity: understanding systemic interconnectivity & processes, creative problem solving,
Autonomous: agency/self-authoring, appreciate need for autonomy amidst interdependent systems
Paradox Aware: aware of internal & systemic paradoxes, more effectively navigate complexity & multi-variables
Evolving Nested Hierarchy: acknowledge natural interdependent nested hierarchies within a system in any context
Evolutionary developmental view: able to see & appreciate that people & cultures span a continuum of development with each stationed at different levels of capacity (each with its virtues & shadows) & that each preceding level   has made important contributions to the structure & function of our world
Everything is True but Partial: integration of differences into interdependent prioritized tapestry: all perspectives are "true" but some more comprehensive & others more partial

EMERGENCE in HUMAN HISTORY: 50,000 years ago
OCCURRENCE: systems theories, Integral Institute, Peter Senge's organizations[11]; eco-industrial parks[12]

TOURQUISE Experiential - Construct Aware

WORLDVIEW:
Motto: the way of the Tao
Primary Motivation: devotion to living from immediacy, awakening & service
Theme: embracing inherent life paradoxes & awareness that language, meaning & even the self are constructed, transitory & limited
Thinking: unitive concepts perceived; cross-paradigmatic[13] ; being more aware of constructed nature of meaning making: all sensory sources of knowing including thoughts, emotions, body states, intuition,   dreams, etc. *"can become as important as rational deliberation for making sense of experience & for finding meaning in life"*[14]
Time Concept: time is constructed simultaneously infinite & historical[15], global-historical perspective beyond own lifetime[16]

IDENTITY:
ego-self is seen as transparent, a construction, a *"central processing unit' that actively creates a sense of identity"*, makes *meaning & tells a story with about itself & the world. In its increasingly felt transparency, this continuous "re-storying"* of "me" which is now realized to actually be an impetus to further development. The existential process is embracing the felt sense of self in both its uniqueness and as "a blended part of a larger, compassionate whole...while rarely feeling understood in their complexity by others."*[17]

VALUES:
Construct Aware: increasingly aware of constructed nature of mind, conceptualization, meaning, language & self
Ego-Transparency: awareness of self-construction, ego-dismantling process, Causal Vantage Awareness
Habits of Mind: desire to unlearn automatic, conditioned responses & habits based on memory & cultural reinforcement
Paradox & Polarity polar opposites arising as two irreconcilable sides of the same coin, mutually necessitating & defining each other
Accepting: more comfortable & accepting of existential realities, uncertainty & mystery
Spontaneous & Experiential Functioning: living more in immediacy with peak states / flow-states being common
Integrated & Experiential Knowing: continually attend to interaction of sensations, thought, emotions, speech, action, energetics, intuition, & perception (ordinary & extrasensory) internally & in relation to others, group, culture & time
Deep Evolutionary Perspective: tend to have developmental understanding; treat time & events as symbolic, analogical, metaphorical (not merely linear, digital, literal)[18]
Universal Order & Global Renewal recognition that everything connects to everything else in ecological alignments & dynamic living universal order; the possibility & actuality of a "grand unification"
Awakening & Service: inspired & devoted to awakening while being an instrument of service in support of others

EMERGENCE in HUMAN HISTORY: emerging now
OCCURRENCE: some modern mystics & spiritual teachers, Otto Scharmer's U-Theory, David Bohm's
    theories; Rupert Sheldrake's morphic fields; emergent holistic-systems thinking, Raina DeLear
& Annalisa Aldeberg's Luminous Awareness Institute, John Thompson's Circling Europe

---

UNITIVE Unified – Emergent Elegance (& beyond)
Insufficient research available

WORLDVIEW:
Motto: Wu-Wei action/non-action
Primary Motivation: none merely living as the Ground of all Being[19]
Time Concept: grounded in the timeless infinity of Eternal Now AND existing in historical time[20]

IDENTITY:
witness or Non-dual Awareness itself

VALUES:
Wu Wei: action/non-action without attachment to outcome
Compassion for evolution as well as the joy & suffering of individuation & existence[21]
Love:
Elegance[22] :

STAGES OF WORLDVIEW SUMMARY & KEY TAKEAWAYS

➢ Stages are like a set of lenses that filter our worldview & span of Awareness, guiding principles for how to live & what is important (values)[23] & organize our sense of self (identity)[24] the lens of each stage effects the way our view of the world is interpreted, what we can be aware of & influence, how decisions are made, & how we should behave

➢ The overall stages of development is likened to a dynamic spiral (Spiral Dynamics[25]) wave-like structure, not rigid stair steps,[26] as each stage evolves from lesser to greater complexity

➢ While we take various perspectives each day, the most complex worldview stage we have integrated & tend to most often spontaneously respond with is referred to as our "center of gravity"[27]

➢ While we don't skip stages, we can have regressive moments & phases.[28]

➢ Stages develop progressively like a set of Russian Nesting Dolls in which each stage is said to transcend AND include previous as all previous stages remain part of our potential way of viewing, interpreting & relating to the world, even as our center of gravity develops to a higher complexity

➢ Each stage has 3 phases: a Wobbly entrance, Solid center, Disintegrating exit; the later transition from one wavelike stage to the next can be unsettling process—a time of uncertainty, questioning, & doubt—as our life is destabilizing to relax ego structures & reveal previous worldview limitations as we are learning new ways of being in the world

➢ These stages are like structures of the human mind the same adult human developmental stages have evolved over human history & develop in the same consistent pattern across cultures regardless of gender, race or culture

➢ More complex stages are not better or higher, each stage provides important values & guiding principles for humanity to be integrated & hopefully utilized in healthy ways yet each stage has both healthy (virtues) & unhealthy (distortions) expressions

➢ Previous stages that we have not healthfully integrated become shadows that we judge in others; commonly we tend to judge the values of the previous stage we lived from which can be a natural process of disidentifying from the values we were previously subject to, but eventually, even those can be healthfully integrated

➢ Conditions of living (historical times, cultural norms, friends, community, geographical location, resources, & life circumstances) can be limiting or growth-stimulating factors that most influence developmental progression through stages[30]

➢ States vs. stages vs. vantage: although we can experience any state in any moment[31], our current center of stage gravity is like the structural lenses of identity & worldview while our current baseline vantage is like our span of felt Awareness. While spiritual states & our baseline Vantage can evolve, our worldview & ego mean-making system (stage) will always inherently be limiter of our perception & interpretation of state so integral development would include both state & stage development

➢ Spiral Wizards refer to people who are more consciously aware of the stages within themselves & able to meet & relate other people, situations,and cultures with compassion, rapport & skillfulness wherever they are. some researchers encourage that change agents be Spiral Wizards in the world who respect current stages of development & create organizational and political interventions that area a half stage ahead of those involved to avoid alienation & rebellion[32]

VANTAGE

This moment right now, can you feel:

Physical body, your skin & bones

Subtleties like emotion, energy, breath, orgasm or shared resonance

Spacious Openness like infinite empty mind,
infinite wide open loving heart & great compassion,
and/or infinite sea of bliss

Witness the ever-present observer of the objects of experience beyond space, time, identity & concept

Non-Dual seamlessness, subject & object dissolve into Awareness itself

---

"Spirit can be known, but not said; seen, but not spoken; pointed out, but not described; realized, but not reiterated. Conventional truths are known by science; absolute truth is known by satori. When we use finite words to try to represent ultimate Suchness, the most we get is poetic metaphor (or metaphoric statements), but the absolute is known only by a direct realization involving a transformation in consciousness (satori, sahaj, metanoia), and "what" is seen in satori cannot be stated in ordinary dualistic words, other than metaphors, poetry, and hints (if you want to know God, you must awaken, not merely theorize)."

- Ken Wilber -

WHAT IS **VANTAGE**

the capacity to inhabit an increasingly more comprehensive body/view of the present moment

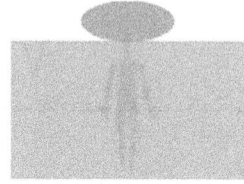

Physical   Subtle   Spacious Awareness   Witness Awareness   Non-dual Awareness

Physical
physical body,
dense matter,
skin & bones

Subtle
emotion, energy,
breath, orgasm,
sound vibration,
shared resonance
of empathy & rapport

Openness
felt sense of any 1 or
all of 3 centers including
mind, heart and/or belly
feeling vastly wide open

Witness
ever-present observer
of the objects of experience
beyond space, time,
identity & concept

Non-Dual
subject & object dissolve
into Awareness itself

WHY **VANTAGE** MATTERS

Map: having a map of vantages allows us to orient to the current body/view we experience the world through as well as clarify how to stabilize the next progressive vantage

Inclusion: some spiritual bypassers can tend to deny or avoid the body, emotions, relating with others or practicalities of life but all greater vantages transcend and include or contain all prior dimensions of experience

Inhabitation: some spiritual bypassers' baseline body-view is dissociated, which is very different from seamless unity or ever-present witness which would still be able to inhabit breath, body & emotions

Attuned Guidance: some teachers instruct students that the body, emotions & identity are not real, should be denied or gotten rid of, yet while easy to describe one's current vantage & naively think others have the same experience, masters attune to & sense into a student's unique next step

Practice: some teachers instruct students not to practice which is true once the conditions have been prepared & resting at the gate, but until effort & effortlessness dissolve, keep practicing while allowing lightning to strike

Pathologies: Dustin Diperna identifies 2 vantage point pathologies: non-dual reductionism & dissociation from shallower vantages[1]

BARRIERS TO **VANTAGE**

Dissociation: not feeling & inhabiting your body, being embodied, feeling unwelcomed, unsafe (fear/terror)

Hyper-Mental: excessive mental activity, overly theoretical, living in fantasy, lost in the past or future

Emotion & Trauma: dead zones, suppressed emotions or body-stored trauma (distressing) experience or ongoing experiences that keep attention stuck in physical or dissociation

Cultural Norms: some cultural belief systems are limited to & reinforce only the physical vantage

Bias: judging & dismissing subtleties like emotion & energetics which limits development of greater vantages

Fear of Unknown: some have had a peak state of experience beyond their current baseline vantage & without having a healthy context to interpret that state, might have either shut that possibility down or took a vow to block it

Hardware Limitation: because vantages tend to stabilize progressively, without practice some can stay at the same baseline for years

Confused Identity: exclusively identified with thought, body, sense of self, space, time, individual vantage, etc.

Spiritual Bypassing: using spiritual practices & beliefs to avoid your emotions, body, life & participation in the world

Fear / Terror: believing "the world is not safe", "it is not safe to be me", "it is not safe to be in my body"

VANTAGE DEVELOPMENT SUCCESS STORY

In his younger years, Paul was a self-proclaimed meat-head, high school football lineman & then a personal trainer. His view & experience of the world was through his physical body. In college, an injury limited his physicality & forced him to begin to develop a more comprehensive vantage or body-view of the world. In addition to relating to the physical world through will & force, he began to become more aware of the subtle body-view including subtleties like breath, emotion & rapport with others. Eventually, his profession of helping people train & transform their physical bodies evolved to include coaching people in multiple areas of their lives. What at first began as him wanting to better himself for himself, eventually transformed into a dedication to evolution, service & something greater than himself. This grew into him getting into mindfulness & flow states, yet because vantages develop progressively like a set of Russian Nesting Dolls he was "trying" to do mindfulness from a physical & subtle vantage of the world. As he progressively began to stabilize a more comprehensive vantage of the world, he realized the that "mindfulness" wasn't a thing but a door into greater peak states. Increasingly, he experienced peak states of deep relaxation & spaciousness while engaged in his daily activates with a spacious quiet mind & great heart openness. Progressively this openness vantage also began to become a more stabilized base view of the world. Currently, the Witness vantage is in the process of stabilizing, states which he previously got brief tastes or glimpses of but now are his baseline felt view of experience. Today, Paul still enjoys fitness & while each of the less comprehensive Vantage, like physical & subtle, get included, his movement & exercise happens from a greater body-view Vantage. Now he professionally teaches Mindfulness to peak performers, Navy Seals, athletes, working professionals, etc., helping them to develop a greater vantage & integrate mindlessness in the engagement of their life, work & sport.

> *"If the doors of perception were cleansed everything would appear to man as it is, Infinite.*
> *For man has closed himself up, till he sees all things thro' narrow chinks of his cavern."*
> - William Blake -

Many of the great wisdom traditions had similar interpretive maps of progressively developed states of consciousness. Much of this chapter builds on the work of Ken Wilber[2] (one of the greatest living synthesizing philosophers and mapmakers), Daniel P. Brown[3] (Psychologist and Professor of Psychology at Harvard) and Dustin Diperna[4] (author, meditation instructor and integral comparative religion expert).

Vantages

Buddhism Vajrayana	Hinduism Vedanta	Christianity Mysticism	Taoism Chinese	Islamic Sufism
Non-Dual Awareness	Turiyatita non-dual	Spirit	Tao unspeakable	Quiab primoridal nature
Witness	Turiya ever-present Witness			
Very Subtle	Causal transcendent bliss	Soul	Shen	Ruh
Subtle	Prana subtle life force	Psyche	Chi	Nafs
Gross Physical	Gross Physical	Body	5 Elements	Jinn

Adapted from "The Great Chain in Various Wisdom Traditions", compiled by Huston Smith

The above chart is adapted from a diagram compiled by Huston Smith titled "The Great Chain of Being in Various Wisdom Traditions."[5]   Smith was one of the greatest comparative religious scholars of the past century, professor of philosophy at MIT from 1958-1973 and professor of religion and philosophy at Syracuse University until he retired in 1983. This Great Chain is a nested hierarchy or holarchy—like a set of Russian

Nesting Dolls—in which each part is both a part of the larger container and a whole, in and of itself. In this case, each progressively greater Vantage transcends, yet also envelops to include the previous views. There are many ways to slice a pie, as in the above comparison chart some systems named four and others five Vantage distinctions, but what is more important is that there is a progressive process and some signposts to check for as Vantages of presence develop greater stabilized views. In Diperna's words, in addition to correcting for cultural biases and historical limitations adopting a 'faith neutral approach' to spirituality, these comparisons "also allow us to access underlying commonalities that hold true across cultures and traditions."[6] He goes on to clarify that even though different traditions had various ways and practices for pointing out shifts in Vantage, the deep structures of Vantage and the progressive nature in which they tend to be stabilized for most practitioners are constant across traditions. This model is a faith neutral—meaning non-religious—five stage progressive Vantages or body/views of the human experience.

According to the Hindu (Vedanta) & Buddhist (Vajrayana) systems, the body/views are standard potentials with the human hardware system. Even in infancy we all start with Physical and Subtle (Emotional) phases, although some people and more often men, can shut down the 2nd Subtle body/view such that they only experience the physical material world—an experience of life that David Deida likens to a clenched fist in the face of infinity. However, the greater body/views of 3rd Spacious Openness, 4th ever-present Witness and 5th Non-Duality, while fundamentally always available, are for most tasted through temporary state experiences and can eventually be stabilized as a permanent baseline Vantage. In other words, when the 2nd Subtle Vantage is stabilized, the subtleties of life can be consistently felt each moment, and likewise when 4th ever-present Witness is stabilized, it is accessible in the three basic human states of consciousness waking, dream, and deep sleep states. Ken Wilber explicates that "permanent realization and mastery demands development and evolution through the actual levels of stages (ego development) and Vantages, a developmental process that converts 'temporary states' to 'permanent traits.'"[7]

In addition to having a clear faith-neutral (non-religious) map of the inherent developmental structure states of Awareness, ensuring that we transcend AND include all vantages helps to avoid what Diperna calls vantage point pathologies.[8] The first non-dual reductionism occurs when someone denies or ignores anything dualistic, asserting that only the Absolute Truth of Non-duality is true and the relative side of the coin is not true or is an illusion. Which in Diperna's words often stems from a misunderstanding of how Non-Dual Awakened Awareness functions moment to moment due to a realization that is more conceptual than an authentic, direct Awareness. The second pathology, a dissociation from shallower vantages, as the name implies, occurs when lesser vantages are denied. Again in Diperna's words, as one participates in relative reality from a 5th Non-Dual vantage, lesser identities do not disappear once exclusive identification has been transcended. Practitioners who succumb to denying vantages or aspects of the relative are by definition creating unconscious shadows, which tends to lead to unhealthy dynamics for themselves and especially in their interpersonal relations. Furthermore, Diperna brilliantly illuminates that even if we have stabilized a greater vantage and even if we no longer exclusively identify with lesser vantages, we still relate in the relative interpersonal world through the unique prism of all vantages (physical body, subtleties & emotions, personality typology, etc.). Two final points before we dive into the five vantages in more specifics: there is a big experiential difference between talking about a state you read about, heard someone else talk about, or even once experienced in the past versus directly accessing and transmitting a vantage through every level of our being. Secondly, to be the most skillful instrument of service and change agent in the world, all involved would be benefited by us being the most integrated being on every level so that we have greater access to a fuller range of our potentials and so that we are more skillful in meeting each individual or group at their current vantage and capacities.

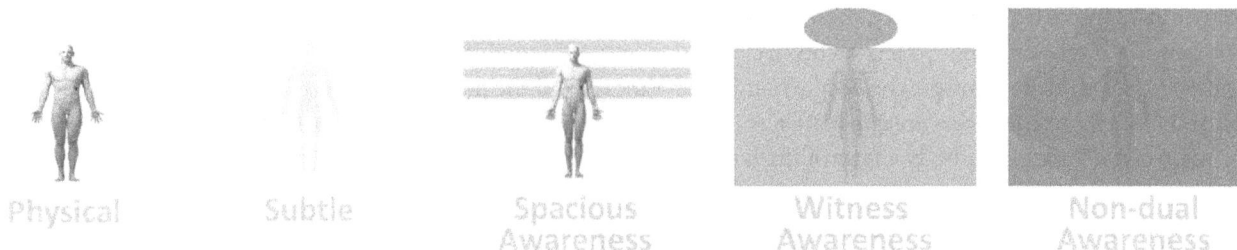

Physical   Subtle   Spacious Awareness   Witness Awareness   Non-dual Awareness

Physical: physical body, dense matter, skin & bones
Subtle: emotion, energy, breath, orgasm, sound vibration, shared resonance of empathy & rapport
Spaciousness: sense of any 1 or all of 3 centers including mind, heart and/or belly feeling vastly wide open
Witness: the ever-present observer of the objects of experience beyond space, time, identity & concept
Non-Dual: subject & object dissolve into seamless unified Awareness itself

PHYSICAL

We begin our human experience in the embryonic fluid of the womb, merged with our mother and experience the world initially from a vantage that feels like an undifferentiated ocean. Our developmental journey into adulthood offers the potential of ever-increasing Awareness, initially viewing and exclusively living from the physical vantage of skin, bones, rocks, tress and other dense matter with the 5 senses as a separate individual. For many of us, this vantage of gross physical sensorimotor Awareness will remain our baseline body or view of the world throughout our lives. Some of us who are still predominantly physically oriented to the five senses and are not as aware of subtleties of life and have not yet developed the human ability to feel the more nuanced aliveness, emotion and electricity of life.

STABLIZING PHYSCIAL: if you can't feel your body, come back to the physical vantage (use the Embodiment sections like *Breathing, Body Sensing & Grounding*, as therapeutic guides for where you might be taking detours)

TRANSITIONING into SUBTLE: when Physical is stabilized you can feel your physical body continuously & then Subtle phenomena like energy, emotion and rapport in connection will start to be not just in occasional peak states, but daily.

SUBTLE

Our bodies also have a subtle emotional and electrical aspects to them, in addition the above mentioned physical layer. When we can notice the Subtle Vantage of life, we can sense the subtle textures of experience including the subtleties of *emotion, energy, dreams, visions, the vibrations of sound* and *music, musical rapture, breath*, and *meditative absorption*. Attunement for example involves subtly tuning into and sensing our own state, emotions in others or the vibe in a room. Human connection is a huge playground for subtle phenomena including the shared resonance of empathy and the resonant rapport of an epic conversation or connection, as well as sexual ecstasy and orgasm.[9] Physically, the advanced bodily sensing awareness of martial artists, performers, athletes in the Zone and Flow states also contain sublte dimensions.[10] Just because certain interior felt experiences are not visually visible, does not mean that they do not exist. Some things can only be perceived from a certain viewpoint—in this case the Subtle Vantage. And if we can't feel it yet, we may want to practice and develop ourselves so that we can.

From basic anatomy and physiology, we know that our nervous system transmits electrical impulse to our brain and that every cell in our body has electrical potential. Do any of us remember, as a kid, shuffling our feet across the carpet and building up a charge to shock someone? The recipient couldn't see the person carrying the subtle electrical charge, but he or she could sure feel it when we shocked them! Medicine uses electrocardiograph (EKG), electroencephalograph (EEG), and Electromyograph (EMG), to measure electrical activity in the heart, brain, and muscles, respectively. Harold Saxton Burr, Yale University School of Medicine Professor of Anatomy and researcher into bio-electrics was one of the first great pioneers in the scientific study of subtle fields.[11] He is now most widely remembered for his 1932 formulation of "*An Electro-Dynamic Theory of Development*" in which he used a voltmeter to detect the electric potential of the body and proposed the term "L-Field" for the bio-electric fields of living systems. Subsequently, Burr's research has contributed to the electrical detection of cancer cells, neuroanatomy, and the regeneration/development of the nervous system, as well as his discoveries of the bio-electrics of menstruation and ovulation, which eventually led to the creation of fertility-indicating devices. Nearly 5,000 years ago Chinese Medicine discovered an intricate system of energy meridians that run throughout the body. Along with Stanford Professor of Material Sciences and Engineering and physicist William Tiller, the late Hiroshi Motoyama, scientist and founder of the California Institute of Human Science in my city of residence—whom I once had the privilege of hearing lecture and whose funeral I had the honor to attend—have been leading pioneers in research into scientific measurement in the subtle dimensions of human experience.

As with all of the higher vantages, we usually experience a glimpse in a peak state experience, which for the Subtle vantage might commonly occur as a moment of Grace, a Flow state, the Zone in athletics, or with the energetics of great connection in resonant rapport or making love. So, while we might initially only experience subtle textures in heightened states, if we want to stabilize this vantage so we can feel the subtle layer of Life at all times, we can either wait for grace to strike, allow it to happen very slowly over time or we can practice activities subtle state altering activities such as some martial arts, dance, music, yoga, breathwork, qi gong, energetic love-making, etc. that help to enhance our noticing of it and cultivation of more of it. Also some people organize their work intervals and lifestyle such that they can keep it circulating as well as cultivate it.

STABLIZING SUBTLE: many people have a mental block around subtle "energies", spanning the gamut from closed-minded materialist scientists, to dissociated hyper-mental naysayers, to numb macho jerks, to people who simply haven't yet developed themselves enough to be able to feel the subtle vantage of aliveness; some people can activate greater subtle energetic awareness but doing trauma healing to unfreeze previous emotional numbing or integrate dissociated parts. For others, doing regular subtle practices like yoga, breathing, dancing, qigong, taichi, etc. can activate greater subtle energetic awareness.

TRANSITIONING into CAUSAL SPACIOUSNESS: you can feel subtle energy in your body throughout the day and are attuned to when it is flowing versus stuck and use methods to make sure it stays vital and circulating then it is becoming stabilized as a baseline Vantage. Then you may start to experience Spaciousness of vast Openness in 1 of the 3 centers mind, heart or bliss.

SPACIOUSNESS AWARENESS

While the subtle dimension of Life adds felt texture, emotion, aliveness and electricity to our lives, the next body-view or Vantage is felt as a sense of spacious Openness extending infinitely in all directions, dramatically expanding our span of Awareness via one of three centers either from a vast empty Mind, a wide-open compassionate Heart, and/or a blissful Belly. While each of us have a personal heart and mind, these structures in the nested hierarchy of Vantages are the containers for Big Heart and Big Mind and as Zen teacher Dennis Merzel (Genpo Roshi) calls them.[12] David Deida poetically inspires us to feel outwards in all directions the ever-available Openness of Freedom and Love.[13] Adyashanti has discussed these three centers Openness in the Awakening process of the head, heart and gut—a process which he notes can vary from person to person in terms of having vast Openness admittance in one, two or three of these access points.[14]

As we may recall from the comparative chart of the great wisdom traditions at the beginning of this section, in relation to some Hindu Vedanta might call this the "causal" Vantage and in Vajrayana Buddhism it might be termed the "very subtle" Vantage. Others point out the infinite stillness of this Vantage. When the top center is spaciously Open as Big Mind it extends outward without boundaries as thoughts slow down or become relatively quiet and are automatically seen as empty upon arising. When the Big Heart center is vastly Open extending outward without boundaries, it can feel like immense joy, love or compassion for humanity or Life itself. When the Big Bliss center is infinitely Open, it can feel like a sense of great fullness or an infinite field of bliss that extends outwards without boundaries.

Some people have experienced a temporary extraordinary state of infinite spacious, while even fewer people, either through meditative practices, conditions of living and/or by grace, have stabilized this sense of infinite openness as a baseline body-view Vantage of the world. Some new agers like to say the phrase *we are all one* or *it's all love* which feels true at deeper levels of reality, however usually this is done as a mental reminder, as opposed to a direct transmission, by retrieving a memory and repeating a mental concept they have read or heard or once felt as a temporary state experience in the past. Anything not directly accessible in the immediacy of this present moment is but a mental concept or memory. At a certain stage of development, language, mental concepts, and even the sense of self become increasingly seen as constructed. It is somewhere between this Spacious Openness Vantage and the next, Witness Vantage, that the personal sense of self is increasingly seen as a more transient and less fixed identity that progressively begins to fade in and out as the exclusive central organizing point of Awareness Terry O'Fallon suggests that this Spacious vantage starts to become a baseline in association with Construct Awareness of Turquoise Stage[15] (see *Stages of Worldview section*). So, in order for this to be a vast openness embodied experience versus a mental concept or memory, it requires brief glimpses of access to this Vantage eventually become stabilize as the baseline body-view or Vantage.

STABLIZING SPACIOUSNESS: if you can't feel infinite Spaciousness throughout the day while walking, working & Talking, then it has not yet stabilized as the baseline Vantage.

TRANSITIONING into WITNESS: when the expansiveness of Spaciousness Awareness opens up, space is felt as empty & free, next the greater Vantage of Witness is like an ever-present camera that both contains & is beyond the felt sense of relative time and the transient sense of self

WITNESS

The next greater container in the nested hierarchy of Vantages is called Witness Awareness. It is an ever-present Observer of experience, like a unified camera neutrally noticing the totality of life. This ever-present witnessing quality of Awareness is thus beyond time, space and sense of self, as this Witnessing is observing the passage of states, forms, and experiences throughout an individual's daily Waking life, while in Rapid Eye Movement (REM) states of Dreaming and even possibly during deep dreamless sleep. Most of us spend our entire lives exclusively identified with our personal sense of self or "me" and its incessant thoughts, emotions, preferences and identifications, yet the ever-present camera neutrally Witnesses all that arises in Awareness—transcending and including. Witness Awareness is most commonly cultivated through mindfulness practice and meditation training, initially experienced in temporary glimpses when the exclusive identification with my sense of self temporarily relaxes. Some "spiritual bypassers" can tend to deny or avoid the body, emotions, relating with others or the grounded practicalities of life but all greater Vantages transcend AND include (contain) all prior dimensions of experience. Dissociation out of the body is not the same as ever-present Witness which would include body, breath and emotions—as even in a seamless state these could be highlighted and felt. While Witness is a profound view to experience even momentarily, let alone when stabilized, its ever-present unified camera-like observation still has an individual observer viewpoint. Yet, the neutral Witnessing capacity of this Vantage is able to increasingly see with clarity as Dustin Diperna elucidates in his book *Streams of Wisdom*[16] , the "confusions of Awareness" and progressive clarifications that come with greater Vantage: including confusion with thought, body, personality, space, time, in this Vantage even the individuality of the Witness and, ultimately as even the subject-object duality of the witness is absorbed in the next Vantage.

STABLIZING WITNESS: as just mentioned the ever-present camera of Witnessing Awareness observes & is free from exclusive identification with thought, body, personality (sense of self), space & time. So there are some fucntions to skillfully play with in the relative while being free from them having "you".

TRANSITIONING into NON-DUAL: A view from this Vantage, just before crossing over feels like an *almost* seamless, deeply contented and neutral, observing camera view. Then even the individuality of the camera is seen as empty, as the subjective Witnessing merges with the objects of Awareness into unified Seamlessness.

NON-DUAL

It is only when this subjective observer and the objects of observation—when the observer, observed and observation all merge and become seamless—that the Non-Dual nature of Awareness is known. Pure seamless immediacy, arising and falling away, transcending and including, none other than Awareness itself. Thoughts may still arise, words may still be spoken but their constructed nature is seen as artifacts arising in awareness, mere abstractions to the more direct fabric of Presence. We could use many poetic metaphors but they would merely be pointers. In the Tibetan Mahahudra Tradition of which Daniel P. Brown[17], a psychotherapist and professor of psychology at Harvard, is a lineage holder, there is a localized and non-localized version of this Vantage of Awareness—in the latter of which even the localization of the seamlessness is seen as empty, as Awareness opens to a non-localize, Non-Dual simultaneity—a universality of perspectives.

Sometimes it is best not to say too much, as some things can only be pointed to and to relax Open the gateless gate of Awareness that has been here all along, all words, concepts, images, memories or signifies of what it's like can be relaxed and released. Ken Wilber puts it best:

> *"Spirit can be known, but not said; seen, but not spoken; pointed out, but not described; realized, but not reiterated. Conventional truths are known by science; Absolute truth is known by satori. They simply are not the same thing. In short, there is Non-Dual or Absolute truth, and there is relative or conventional truth, and one simply cannot take an assertion of the latter and apply it to the former. When we use finite words to try to represent ultimate Suchness, the most we get is poetic metaphor (or metaphoric statements), but the Absolute is known only by a direct realization involving a transformation in consciousness (satori, sahaj, metanoia), and "what" is seen in satori cannot be stated in ordinary dualistic words, other than metaphors, poetry, and hints (if you want to know God, you must awaken, not merely theorize)."*[18]

VANTAGES SUMMARY & KEY TAKEAWAYS

➤ We are always in a state & every state consists of a view of the world & corresponding body of matter-energy; together this body-view is called a Vantage.

➤ Although anyone can experience any state, at any moment, at any stage of development, we each have a current baseline that determines the container-like body-view Vantage we experience throughout daily life.

➤ These Vantages tend to develop & stabilize in a progressive order from Physical > Subtle > Spacious Awareness > Witness Awareness > Non-Dual Awareness.
Physical: physical body, dense matter, skin & bones
Subtle: emotion, energy, breath, orgasm, sound vibration, shared resonance of empathy & rapport
Spacious: sense of any 1 or all of 3 centers including mind, heart and/or belly feeling vastly wide open
Witness: the ever-present observer of the objects of experience beyond space, time, identity & concept
Non-Dual: subject & object dissolve into seamless unified Awareness itself

➤ Each Vantage is, like a set of containers or Russian nesting dolls, of decreasing size placed inside one another, so that each greater vantage contains all previous Vantages within it.

➤ Having a map of Vantages allows us to orient to the current body-view we experience the world through, as well as clarify how to stabilize the next progressive Vantage.

➤ Dustin Diperna identifies 2 vantage point pathologies: non-dual reductionism & dissociation from shallower Vantages.

➤ Some "spiritual bypassers" can tend to deny or avoid the body, emotions, relating with others or practicalities of life but all greater Vantages transcend AND include (contain) all prior dimensions of experience. Even in a profoundly seamless state, these features could be highlighted & felt.

➤ Sometimes it is best not to say too much, as some things can only be pointed to; poetic metaphors can guide us to the steps of the palace gate, that which has essentially been here all along.

VANTAGE DEVELOPMENT MAP

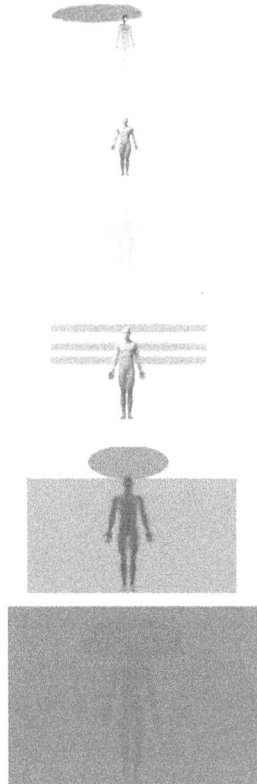

Dissociated – disconnected from body emotion & others; living from the mental view, Awareness confused with thought

Physical only – sensing & feeling abilities have been shut down, numbed, or disbelieved; Awareness confused with physical body, "I only believe what I can see & touch"

Physical + some Subtle – physical 5 senses is predominant with some subtle states

Subtle + Physical – subtle is stabilizing; Awareness confused with personality

Subtle + Physical + some Spaciousness – subtle + physical with some openness states

Witness + Spaciousness + Subtle + Physical – witness is stabilizing in waking states transparency of personal self fades in & out Awareness confused with individual view

Witness + Spaciousness + Subtle + Physical – ever-present witness is stabilizing experience is increasingly seamless camera can be aware while body is sleeping

Non-dual + Witness + Spaciousness + Subtle + Physical – non-dual localized Awareness

Non-dual + Witness + Spaciousness + Subtle + Physical – non-dual non-localized Awareness

IMMEDIACY & NOVEL EMERGENCE

Do you respond to questions with clichés, canned lines & pre-rehearsed statements?

Do you prefer to cling to the safety of habits, staying in your comfort zone & creating a carbon copy of already known past experiences?

Is your movement, speech & life arising out of the immediacy of the emergent evolutionary aliveness of the ever-present moment?

"The ability to shift from reacting against the past to leaning into and presencing an emerging future is probably the single most important leadership capacity today...

"Isn't there a way to break the patterns of the past and tune into our highest future possibility— and to begin to operate from that place?""

- C. Otto Scharmer -

WHAT IS **IMMEDIACY & NOVEL EMERGENCE**

the capacity to allow & navigate fresh ways of being, situations, communication, insight & innovation to arise from the immediacy of the moment

WHY **IMMEDIACY & NOVEL EMERGENCE** MATTERS

Evolutionary Improvement: allowing something to change, grow & evolve allows the possibility of something more functional, adaptive, efficient, etc.

Genetic Evolutionary Adaptation: underlies the evolution of a species

Cultural Evolution: allows new ways of being & living together socially for greater happiness, harmony, sustainability & yet unimagined possibility

Innovation: allows new ideas, methods, systems, process, products & technologies to be invented or improved

Creativity: an essential feature of the creative process; duplication is a copy from the past, while creation births something new from immediacy

Intimacy & Authentic Relating: allowing something fresh & emotionally vulnerable allows a real, living connection & closeness

Access to Presence: immediacy is a doorway to the present moment

BARRIERS TO **IMMEDIACY & NOVEL EMERGENCE** MATTERS

Dissociation: not feeling & inhabiting your body due to trauma, defense or hyper-mental

Hyper-Mental: excessive mental activity, overly theoretical, living in fantasy, lost in the past or future

Limiting Beliefs: assimilated experiences, beliefs & traumas that limited acceptable range of emergent ways of being

Image Positioning: hiding something or trying to say something to be seen in a certain way or to meet an expectation

Emotion & Trauma: dead zones, suppressed emotions or body-stored trauma that keeps attention stuck in the body or dissociated

Cultural Norms: assimilated family beliefs about what is possible or which ways of being are acceptable

Habits & Carbon Copies of the Past: habitually or unconsciously recreating what is known from the past

Adherence to Tradition, Rigid Policies or Procedures: limiting what is possible

Fear of the Unknown: clinging to the safety of habit & what has already been known

Need to Control: compulsion to control in order to try to ensure the desired outcome

Closed-Ended Conclusions: fixate attention on a previously known outcome before it has had a chance to arise freshly

Same Consciousness: Einstein's quote "you can't solve a problem from the same consciousness that created it"

IMMEDIACY & NOVEL EMERGENCE DEVELOPMENT SUCCESS STORY

Elon was a musician, educator, businessman, husband, father and passionate participant in the evolution of human consciousness. Originally he wanted to bring more presence to his wife, his young son & newly emerging work project. What began as a project writing a book, evolved into an online program & eventually became buying a school for progressive children's education. He focused previously sporadic meditation into a devoted practice each morning, helping him to tune his instrument, aligning with higher intentions, while simultaneously allowing this emergent process to express itself through him. Elon knew the true musician on the mastery path trains for those flow states of such immediate presence that the musician, the playing & the music become one—so as he increasingly loosened the grip on the exclusive identification with his personal sense of self he increasingly experienced flow states of becoming the instrument being played. He has also felt for some years that he symbolically "had a unique song to play"...that there was a unique purpose that wanted to be expressed through him via his work in the world. So devoted to his musical craft & to passionately educating students, now he more clearly sensed the emergent coalescing.

"Learn to notice the difference between wired thinking (our stories, patterns, structure) and original thinking (arising spontaneously from our core intelligence)... Be a "living update" of yourself – continuously expanding and integrating the new levels of being and development into all that you were yesterday. Novel creative intelligence brings excellence."

– Thomas Hubl –

"If we always do what we've done we will get what we've always got"

- Tony Robbins -

In this final section, we will discover why deeper presence as the doorway to immediacy and novel emergence, is so vital to humanity's future. For much of human history, our evolutionary process seems to have been slower. It's estimated that it took us a million years to make a tool and our Paleolithic ancestors spent 190,000 years as wondering hunting and gathering nomads before the Agrarian Age had us settling into farming communities between 10-12,000 years ago.[1] The more recent *Industrial Revolution*, *Scientific Revolution*, and *Digital Age* have evolved much more quickly comparatively.[2] We can certainly honor our ancestors, as well as the richness and diversity of cultures, the wisdom of ancient traditions, and the perennial philosophy threads that live through our essential humanity, but it is through the evolutionary creative impulse of Life Itself from which new ways emerge. While there is certainly a stability of sticking with tradition and what has been safely known, this also creates a stagnation that inhibits the evolutionary impulse of emergence from creating something even better.

While most of humanity is consumed with subsistence living and daily survival (almost half the world — over three billion people — live on less than $2.50 a day[3]) and most of the rest of us are distracted from deeper considerations by entertainment and social media, our world begs us to awaken to our greater human potential and more consciously participate in the evolutionary process. With less presence we are less compassionate, less ethical, less innovative, less able to take multiple perspectives beyond our own, less aware of our impact on our planet and future generations. While presence can grant us greater access to these skills and virtues, more importantly for the emergent process of human evolution, it allows the creative power of immediacy and novelty to come forth. And this planet could greatly benefit deeper presence that enables us to co-create a more functional, ethical, and sustainable world.

Yet, it is not through the ordinary thinking mind, pros and cons lists or perpetuating carbon copies of the past that solutions to humanities greatest challenges will emerge. In our finite relative human world, truly novel solutions emerge when presence opens to the immediacy of the ever-present moment—the gateway to inspiration, innovation and new possibilities. **Flow states** are the access-point to our greater creativity and innovation at work.[4] Otto Schamer from MIT and his team of organizational consultants are using their **U-Theory Process** in helping organizations to overcome inefficiencies, fears and habits of the past by accessing deeper presence at the *"bottom of the U"* to allow space for the emerging future to be realized and take form.[5] Diane Hamilton a master facilitator and mediator, author, and an authentic contemporary spiritual teacher who is devoted to exceptional human relations and committed to transforming conflict into creativity, trains facilitators and trainers (**Integral Facilitator**) to leverage emergence and presence in organizational group dynamics for collaboration, transparent communication, conflict resolution and innovation.[6] Andrew Hewitt, a Harvard MBA grad, is stewarding the evolution of business and has founded **Game-Changers 500** (http://gamechangers.co) which ranks the world's top for-benefit, purpose-driven evolutionary organizations who are using business as a force to create meaningful impact in our world, while maintaining a financially successful organization. Evolutionary Organizational & Design Consultants, Shiloh Boss and Davin infinity (**Designing the New World**) leverage the principle of emergence and design strategy to empower business leaders with solutions to not only optimize their own organization, but to be a more powerful positive force in shaping humanity's future. Buckminster Fuller, legendary systems theorist, designer and social architect said *"You never change things by fighting the existing reality. To change something, build a new model that makes the existing model obsolete."* In this vein, Daniel Schmachtenberger, an evolutionary philosopher, global solutions strategist and founder of Critical Path, Global a research and design institute, is devoted to fostering more conscious participation in our global evolution by developing integrated processes capable of organizing and supporting a redesigned world-system that potentiates and sustains the highest quality of life for all life, now and ongoing.

For some, consideration of humanity's evolution and the emergence of more sustainable global systems is beyond their span of Awareness, but emergence is not just for systems and organizations. Our interpersonal relations are also an important area where the immediacy of presence can profoundly enhance our lives. We tend to relate in familiarized ways that reinforce our limited identities, prevent the deeper authentic connection of emotional vulnerability and embodied presence. We often repeat the same stories, regurgitate the same clichés, and meet each other with the same repeated greetings from the habits of our minds: *"How are you?"..."Good. How are you?"..."Good".* The best conversations with the most epic rapport happen when the deeper presence of the listener and/or the speaker, allows genuine curiosity to arise out of the immediacy of the moment in asking a question and when the speaker courageously shares something fresh, unmemorized, unprepared, or unrehearsed. Extemporaneous public speaking and comedy improvisation actually come from the same emergent energy of speaking from immediacy—just on a group level. Yet, our conventional habits of relating commonly inhibit the aliveness and depth of intimate connection made available through with the immediacy of presence. **Transparent Communication** (Thomas Hubl), **Circling** or **Authentic Relating** (Decker Cunov, John Thompson and others) and **Getting Real** (Susan Campbell)[7], offer processes to help people learn to relate from deeper presence and connection. Current body sensations, emotions and thoughts internally or curious noticing externally are all profound doorways into immediacy from which greater transparency connection and closeness can emerge. Spouses commonly greet each other with the staleness or dismissiveness of a thousand times prior, instead of meeting fresh each moment, attuning to the novel aliveness of our own inner world and the interior of our partner in our individual and shared landscapes full of fresh sensations, emotions, thoughts, needs, desires and energies that are as ever-changing as the weather. In romantic partnership, along with *Sexual Polarity*, authentic relating from immediacy are two keys to ongoing relational freshness, epic passion attraction, and ever-deepening connection. Our partner can be a hindrance to our bright and shiny object syndrome or a doorway into the immediacy of infinite Presence, through whose face we can see all the faces.

At a certain stage, our own personal development requires living from greater immediacy, as well. We humans can sometimes be creatures of comfort and cling to our habits, but this inhibits spontaneity, behavioral flexibility, and the creativity of the aliveness of new possibilities. Presence is also the doorway to new insight, inspiration, and intuition— none of which come from the past memory or habit. Rob MacNamara, author, professor, high-performance coach in applied developmental psychology, elegantly describes the traps of habituation in his brilliant book *The Elegant Self*.[8] Dustin DiPerna illustrates how the freedom from exclusive identification with thought, freedom from exclusive identification personal sense of self and freedom from exclusive identification with time are essential shifts that allows us access to the wider field of immediacy from which novel aliveness can emerge.[9] Our mission then, should we choose to accept it, is to realize the liberated aliveness of this unconditioned immediacy in the world, wide awake, while fully engaging in the "*marketplace of life*," as Thomas Hubl calls it. The continual relaxation of the seemingly solid, conditioned personal identity, allows a deep and spacious aliveness as the natural emergence of the present moment referred to in Taoism as **Wu Wei**, which might be translated as action/non-action or effortless/effort or a **relaxed elegant engagement in the immediacy of the moment**. The less we are inhibited by our past trauma, the less enculturated we are by mythology, the less conditioned we are by habituation, and the less defended we are by our egos, the more we are able to awaken greater human potential as individuals and as a collective humanity.

Indeed, our physical bodies are not only made of the raw materials of this planet, which are themselves **billions of year old stardust** from this vast Universe we are all a part. Although some might forget otherwise, humans are not the center of the universe, and our individual and collective consciousness are part of and participants in this great evolutionary process of Life, which we are experiencing here on Planet Earth. While it is perhaps an honor beyond what our human mind can comprehend to be alive and participants during this critical time in our evolutionary process, the privilege also comes with profound responsibility. Life here on our Planet is evolving at an ever-quickening pace, yet we are on a Critical Path not without major global challenges that need wisdom, ethics, discerning consideration including social justice issues, global economics, politics and governance, education and school systems, health-care and wellness, sustainability of our food-system, genetics, technological innovations, artificial intelligence, robotics, virtual reality, and energy resources and sustainability. Will we use our presence for the evolutionary good of all and allow creative solutions to emerge or will we continue to fight against each other? We need your novel creativity, your unique gifts, your ethical care, your full engagement and your loving awake presence to help shape the positive evolution of our world.

How do you feel inspired to contribute to the evolution and betterment of our world?

What were you born to do and how can something new emerge and be lived through you?

What else is possible we haven't even considered?

IMMEDIACY SUMMARY & KEY TAKEAWAYS

➢ Immediacy is the doorway to deeper presence & novel emergence which is vital for humanity's future.

➢ While there is certainly a stability of what we have habitually done & what has been safely known, this also creates a stagnation that inhibits the evolutionary impulse of emergence, the creative impulse of Life Itself, from creating something even better.

➢ With less presence we are less compassionate, less ethical, less innovative, less able to take multiple perspectives beyond our own, less aware of our impact on our planet and future generations.

➢ While most of humanity is consumed with the daily survival of subsistence living & most of the rest of us are distracted from deeper considerations by entertainment and social media, our world beckons us to awaken to our greater human potential & more consciously participate in the evolutionary process for the benefit of our world.

➢ It is not through the ordinary thinking mind, pros & cons lists or perpetuating carbon copies of the past that solutions to humanities greatest challenges will emerge. in our finite relative human world, truly novel solutions emerge when presence opens to the immediacy of the ever-present moment—the gateway to inspiration, innovation & new possibilities.

➢ Interpersonally, we tend to relate in familiarized, habitual ways often repeat the same stories, regurgitate the same clichés, & meet each other with the same repeated greetings from the habits of our minds which reinforce our limited identities, prevent the deeper authentic connection of emotional vulnerability & embodied presence.

➢ The best conversations with the most epic rapport happen when the deeper presence of the listener and/or the speaker, allows genuine curiosity to arise out of the immediacy of the moment in asking a question and when the speaker courageously shares something fresh, unmemorized, unprepared, or unrehearsed.

➢ Freedom from exclusive identification with thought, personal sense of self & time are essential shifts that allows us access to the wider field of immediacy from which the novel aliveness & relaxed elegant engagement of presence can emerge.

PART 5　EMERGENCE & CHALLENGE

Your work, loved ones and the totality of Life Itself,
yearn for your deeper presence

"We convince by our presence."

— Walt Whitman —

American poet, journalist & mystic
(1819-1892)

We can read all the great books, listen to all the top podcasts,
wear special clothes, travel to exotic lands,
rattle off all the fancy lingo until our lips turn blue,
but ultimately what we embody and transmit
through our embodied presence is what is felt,
impacts others and matters most.

Hopefully this guidebook,
this map of embodied presence,
will be of service to you
whether for yourself,
your loved ones or
those whom you help.

Some of the skills may already be strengths for you,
other skills you might be actively developing,
while a few may have been blind spots
you were previously unaware of.

Either way, may the benefits, barriers, success stories
and description of how the skills tend to develop
offer you inspiration and greater clarity about
your current limitations or next steps
to further develop each skill.

MOTIVATION TO PRACTICE

A greater clarity of Awareness and a deeper motivation can help us stay animated by the flame that fuels our inspiration to practice. When our motivation comes from trying to look good, be enough, to be perceived as smart or desire for fame, it rarely has a strong enough energy to sustain us.

Initially, some people begin their personal development quest to overcome struggle, heal pain, or feel a sense of belonging & connection. These are common and reasonable impetuses to begin. Other common motivations toward development include being more valuable in one's career, skill enhancement, being more functional in life, the pursuit of excellence, life-long learning or greater understanding.

Eventually, and here enters the samurai's dedication to development to be of service, some people practice and train to actualize greater potential, so that they can live their purpose in the world, be of service to others and contribute something greater the world beyond themselves as an active participant in the evolution of humanity.

Even fewer people, paradoxically, begin to transcend (and include) the very personal self seeking all of the previous development, offering their lives to the awakening of greater freedom, love, wisdom and compassion in service.

Whatever our motivation to practice, greater clarity can help inspire & guide our developmental becoming and it is important that we connect with it before, during and after practicing.

WHY NOT JUST LET IT HAPPEN?

We can and most people do. In the metaphor of the river as the evolutionary impulse to grow that flows through us all, some prefer to stay in their comfort zone or float along very slowly. Of course some people can even resist the growth oriented current or get stuck in undertow that keeps them looping in the same cyclical pattern. All of these are possible ways to navigate the river of life and we all seem to have some degree of freedom to choose. However, we can also practice which is like paddling with the developmental current—the evolutionary impulse to awaken greater potential, to live aligned with our unique purpose, to enhance our capacity to love and to live with greater presence, free in the midst of It all. We can not only focus our attention to enhance the process, but we can allow the intention of our practicing to be inspired by these deeper motivations as we increasingly align our lives with the awakening process. As this increasingly happens, the efforting to grow relaxes and is overtaken by the inspired flowing of the evolutionary impulse of Life itself.

As we stand on the shoulders of giants in this coming age,
may we bow in humility and stand empowered with sacred pride, honoring all
those who have gone before us, often in solitude or secret,
wearing groves of human potential for a time in the future
When more of humanity would safely and openly
be able to actualize and integrate presence
into our daily lives.

May we become deeply embodied,
skillful loving human beings
while relaxing Open,
unified as the source of It All.

PRESENCE

Presence in Work

Presence in Love

Presence in Life

www.ingramcontent.com/pod-product-compliance
Lightning Source LLC
Chambersburg PA
CBHW061955090426
42811CB00006B/936

9 780578 524030